THE EU &
TURKEY
a glittering prize or
a millstone?

7

edited by Michael Lake

This book is published by the Federal Trust whose aim is to enlighten public debate on issues arising from the interaction of national, European and global levels of government. It does this in the light of its statutes which state that it shall promote 'studies in the principles of international relations, international justice and supranational government.'

Up-to-date information about the Federal Trust can be found on the internet at www.fedtrust.co.uk

© Federal Trust for Education and Research 2005

ISBN 1 903403 61 8 (Paperback); 1 903403 75 8 (Hardback)

The Federal Trust is a Registered Charity No. 272241

7 Graphite Square, Vauxhall Walk,

London SE11 5EE

Company Limited by Guarantee No.1269848

Front Cover: Yves Herman/Reuters/Corbis

Printed in the European Union

Contents

IV: Society

V: Security

VI: Selected International Views

VI: A Very Special Case

VII: The Last Word

Contributors

Hakan Altinay is Executive Director, The Open Society Institute Assistance Foundation-Turkey, Istanbul. He was previously Regional Director for the Asian and Near-East at Pathfinder International and Black Sea Coordinator at the International Research and Exchanges Board.

David Barchard is a writer and consultant on Turkish and Eastern Mediterranean politics, economics and society. He reported for The Guardian from Ankara under the two military governments of 1971-73 and 1980-82, specialising in human rights issues. He is the author of three studies of Turkish-European Union relations, and is currently writing a book on the end of Ottoman rule in Crete and the inter-play between Christian-Muslim ethnic conflicts and European public opinion in the 19th century.

Pat Cox was President of the European Parliament from 2002 until 2004.

Ahmet O. Evin, founding dean of the Faculty of Arts and Social Sciences, Sabanci Univerity, is also on the board of Istanbul Policy Center affiliated with the same University. He has previously taught at Harvard, University of Pennsylvania (where he was director of the Middle East Center), New York University, Bilkent University, the University of Hamburg, and Northwestern University. He served as director of Education of the Aga Khan Trust for Culture (Geneva). He is currently in Athens as an Alexander Onassis fellow.

Professor Nihat Bülent Gültekin, The Wharton School, University of Pennsylvania, former Governor of the Central Bank of Turkey.

Lord Hannay CH GCMG, formerly British Ambassador to the European Communities and to the United Nations and former special adviser to the British Government on Cyprus.

Michael Lake was EU Ambassador in Turkey (1991-98) and Hungary (1998-2001), European Commission official 1973-2001. He is a former Journalist 1953-73 (The Scotsman, The Daily Herald/Sun, The Guardian, weekly commentator on BBC World Service).

Dr Andrew Mango, former Head of South European and French Language Services, BBC World Service; Member of London Middle East Institute and editorial boards of academic reviews in London, Paris, Ankara and Israel. Author of *Atatürk*, (John Murray, 1999), The Turks Today (John Murray, August, 2004) and other studies of modern Turkey.

John T. McCarthy, Managing Director, ING Bank NV, Turkey: Mr McCarthy has lived in Turkey for 20 years, speaks fluent Turkish and is married to a Turk. He is convenor of the EU Business Group, Istanbul.

Yiannis Papanicolaou, lately Director General of the International Centre for Black Sea Studies, former member of cabinet of Prime Minister Andreas Papandreou, formerly lecturer at the London School of Economics.

William (Bill) H. Park is Senior Lecturer in Defence Studies, King's College, London.

Mark R. Parris was US Ambassador to Turkey from late 1997 to 2000. Ambassador Parris held senior positions during the Clinton administration at the National Security Council and State Department. Ambassador Parris retired from the US Foreign Service in 2001, and has since remained active in US - Turkish affairs.

Nicole Pope, Swiss-born long-term Correspondent of *Le Monde* in Turkey, co-author of *Turkey Unveiled: a History of Modern Turkey* who is currently writing a book on Honour Killings.

David Shankland, Senior Lecturer in social anthropology at the University of Bristol. Formerly the Assistant and Acting Director of the British Institute of Archeology, Ankara, and author of many scholarly articles and the monographs *Islam and Society in Turkey* (1999) and *The Alevis in Turkey: the Emergence of a Secular Islamic Tradition* (2003).

Professor Norman Stone is Professor of International Relations at Bilkent University, Ankara, and Director of the Russian Centre. Previously Professor of Modern History at Oxford, his principal publications are The Eastern Front 1914-1917 and Europe Transformed 1878-1919; he will shortly publish The Atlantic Revival 1960-1990 with Random House.

Foreword

It is a personal pleasure for me to preface a publication which represents an impressive achievement as a multi-faceted approach, in clear language, to one of the major challenges facing the European Union today – the nature of its future relationship with Turkey.

This timely publication comes at a time of unprecedented transformation in Europe, itself progressing to a continent-wide Union of peace, justice and prosperity, and embracing a newly-designed institutional and legal architecture for more than 400 million citizens. At the same time, Turkey is making unprecedented progress in internal and constitutional reform, modernisation and engagement. The strategic question is whether the renewed and reconciled Union will embrace Turkey as a potential member or instead seek a form of 'privileged partnership'. Is Turkey ready for the European Union, and is the EU ready for Turkey?

This book is an honest and multi-disciplinary attempt to illuminate the dimensions of the challenge from different perspectives. I admire its breadth, depth and relevance and believe it will be a useful reference, not only for policy-makers and practitioners but for any citizen who reads it.

Pat Cox
President of the European Parliament
(2002 - 2004)

Introduction

One sunny morning in March, 1991, I went to the Turkish Ministry of Foreign Affairs in Ankara to present a copy of my credentials to the then Minister, Mr Kurtcebe Alptemocin. This was customary before a new Head of Mission presented his or her credentials to the Head of State. Mr Alptemocin greeted me warmly: '*Hosgeldiniz,*' he said. 'Welcome.' Then he sat me down and stated severely: 'Our relationship is frozen.' So it was.

It was the year that communism fell. Two years earlier the European Commission had reported that Turkey was not ready to join the European Community. In the new era of freedom and justice in Europe, Turkey felt unloved.

The first Gulf War had ended two days after my arrival. The end of the Cold War and its disciplines in the south-eastern border areas alongside the Soviet Union, together with subsequent United Nations sanctions against Iraq, had contributed to a continuing economic and political vacuum in the Kurdish areas of south-eastern Turkey and northern Iraq. This vacuum provided fertile ground for the Kurdish separatist, initially Marxist-Leninist terrorist group, the PKK, to undermine Turkey's domestic and external stability. A 'dirty war' of state defence and retaliation followed, which lost Turkey two key European constituencies: the media and the European Parliament. This provoked a stream of constant criticism from Europeans, sometimes justified, sometimes misguided. It was a heavy burden on the relationship.

When I arrived, Turkey was in denial. There was no Kurdish problem; there were no human rights problems; the Cyprus problem had been solved by the Turkish army's intervention in 1974.

Europe was also in denial. Greece blocked all EU funds earmarked for Turkey for 20 years. The European Parliament, often urged on by Greek MEPs, passed one anti-Turkish resolution after another. Only after six years of often bitter criticism in support of the Kurds did a Flemish lady from the Green Group, a member of the often fractious European-Turkish Joint Parliamentary Committee admit to me: 'We now realise that there is not a single Kurdish organisation in Europe that is not infiltrated by the PKK.'

Nevertheless, EU governments recognised Turkey's importance and relations began to unfreeze. When 450,000 Iraqi Kurds fled to Turkey on the day I presented my credentials to President Özal, the EU provided, over the next three months, by far the most substantial international aid to get the refugees out of Turkey and back to northern Iraq. Turkish diplomats lost no opportunity to remind the EU that when Turkey and the European Economic Community had signed an Association Agreement in 1963, it clearly stated that Turkey was a European country, and foresaw both a preliminary Customs Union and eventual membership.

So in 1993, negotiations began for a Customs Union between the new European Union (Maastricht, 1992) and Turkey, which no one in the European Commission, nor the European Parliament, nor the Council of Ministers, really believed Turkey could manage. In the event, negotiations were completed properly and efficiently in two years flat.

The Customs Union was not conditional on Turkey meeting new political criteria, but the European Union maintained steady pressure over that period on Turkey over its human rights record. I never made a speech – of which I made scores during my seven years' posting – without referring to human rights. Along with the process of familiarity brought about by negotiations on the Customs Union, Turkey's state of denial was changing.

Early in 1995 the European Parliament had passed a resolution opposing the Customs Union by three to one. The most severe opposition came from the largest group, the socialists. But whereas socialist MEPs usually made up their own minds how to vote, in this case the party leaders of the biggest socialist parties in the group, Tony Blair, then leader of the Opposition in the UK, and Felipe Gonzalez, Prime Minister of Spain, took the view that the Customs Union with Turkey was a strategic necessity and instructed their party group leaders in Strasbourg to vote for it. Moreover, the leader of the Chamber of Commerce of Diyabakir, representing 12,000 Kurdish businessmen, wrote me a letter in support of the Customs Union. How could the European Parliament, nursing its grievances, refuse? They voted in favour, by two to one, many through gritted teeth.

Modernisation and sophistication, already emerging fast in a Turkey beginning to face up to reality, were perhaps the factors least recognised at that time in the European Union, periodically infected with historic prejudice. Long-outdated perceptions persisted of poor, ill-educated Turkish migrants arriving to do jobs the Germans and Belgians didn't want to do, the men in their baggy pants and the women in their shapeless long skirts and headscarves. European politicians, flying in and out of Ankara but without crossing a street in modern Turkey, returned more impressed with the local politicians than they expected, but still shaking their heads and unaware of the changes taking place in a rapidly urbanising country.

By 1997, the Customs Union was two years old. The year before, the enterprising Turks had created 60,000 new enterprises, while more than 80,000 raised new capital for expansion. Only 829 businesses had failed. Many Turkish cities, deep in the interior of the country, had an annual growth rate of above five per cent. They became known as Anatolian Tigers, sporting satellite dishes, their citizens plugged into the Internet and disco music thumping from their cars as they drove past. The city of Gaziantep, close to both the Iraqi and Syrian borders, had a constant annual growth rate of 10 per cent, year after year.

But the severity of the 1982 Constitution remained an ever more conspicuous anomaly in the modernising Turkish democracy. It was the worst in Turkey's modern history, a military imposition after the breakdown of democracy in 1979, imposing unheard of restrictions on human rights and freedom of expression and remorselessly implemented by the State Security Court.

By far the most severe and important critics of the situation in Turkey were not the armchair critics of the European political parties but the Turks themselves. By now Turkey was seeing the beginnings of a civic society, an explosion of NGOs covering everything from birth control to human rights, from the arts to improving local government.

In 1997 the Turkish Businessmen's and Industrialists' Association, TUSIAD, published a charter for reform which is today recognised as a noble, even heroic benchmark for the historic reforms which the new Turkish AK Government has now passed into law. The TUSIAD report called for reforms at all levels of Turkey's domestic politics, including the economy, human rights, freedom of expression, the Kurdish problem and the electoral system. There were no taboos, no gaps. Unrecognised for what it was in 1997, in fact a blueprint for a modern Turkish society able to join the European Union, it lay on the table ripening rudely like a cheese. Meanwhile, successive coalitions of traditional parties failed to take note of it and come to terms with their own pro-European ambitions. Civic society was seething, but it did not yet have the strength to have a direct impact on the politicians. That, too, was to change, as successive Turkish governments turned their attention more and more towards full accession to the European Union.

In February, 1997, a 'contact group' of EU foreign ministers, arising from the Bosnian conflict and known as 'the Quint', met in Rome with the then Turkish Prime Minister, Mrs Tansu Ç-iller, and solemnly reaffirmed Turkey's eligibility to join the EU. This decision was confirmed by an EU Ministerial meeting at Apeldoorn where member states agreed that Turkey should be treated according to the same objective standards and criteria as all other candidates (by now the countries of central and eastern Europe were banging on the door) and this understanding was approved by the EU-Turkey Association Council meeting of 29 April, 1997, thus becoming part of the legally binding *acquis communautaire*. A leading supporter of Turkey at the time was the French Prime Minister, Alain Juppé, now a leading opponent of negotiations with Turkey. He is not the only European politician apparently to have forgotten formal decisions that had collectively been taken confirming Turkey's eligibility for full membership of the European Union.

This solemn decision of 1997 was reinforced yet again at the European Council meeting in Helsinki, in 1999, where Turkey was officially recognised as a candidate. There was no argument here about Turkey's culture, its religion, its size or any of the other obstacles which certain European political parties are now presenting as insuperable obstacles. These issues were simply noted and the decision approved.

By this time Turkish civic society was having a serious impact on Turkish politicians. Thousands of citizens were giving their time and money. The media and the airwaves, some giving free advertising space and airtime, were full of EU fever.

At Copenhagen in December 2002, Turkey was told that if, in two years' time, it met the 1992 Copenhagen Criteria of democracy, the rule of law, human rights, care and protection of minorities and a full market economy, negotiations with the EU would begin 'without delay.' The EU made a solemn promise. It has kept all its other commitments to the 10 new member states on time, and we European citizens should now expect it to keep its promised obligations to Turkey. The EU has enough problems without breaking its word on matters of principle.

Under the incentive of meeting the Copenhagen Criteria, Turkey has carried out a root and branch reform of its legislation and the Constitution to remove the restrictive anomalies imposed by the military in 1980, to remove the majority of the military itself from the National Security Council and to subject the military budget to civil transparency and control for the first time ever. It is fair to say that the previous coalition government of old, traditional parties had already started down this road with a commendable package of reforms in August 2002. The new Muslim-oriented AKP government of Recep Tayyip Erdogan has completed seven packages of deep, sweeping reforms, including reforms to clean up and modernise the whole banking system, plus a large package of Constitutional reforms. Implementation of these is, after a false start, steadily moving forward.

The death penalty has been abolished for anything and everything. Broadcasting in Kurdish – once not even a dream – has started on State television, along with Kurdish films and theatre. The Kurdish nationalists Leyla Zana and her companions have been released from prison; journalists and others (including Prime Minister Erdogan himself) are no longer imprisoned for their utterances; human rights abuses have not yet completely ended but are now conspicuous instead of being the norm; protection for women has improved and by mid-2004 the European Commission was speaking of a critical mass of Copenhagen reforms having been achieved.

Although long awaited by the Turkish public, these reforms have been European-driven. They are irreversible. They are not irreversible because the Prime Minister wishes them to be so, but because civic society, inspired by the charter for reform laid down by TUSIAD in 1997 and supported by a large proportion of the population, is firmly behind them. The financial and banking reforms of the early millennium; the huge and continuing fall in the rate of Turkish inflation; the sustained growth of the Turkish economy praised by the IMF; the abolition of security restrictions on freedom of expression and human rights; growing respect and rights for minorities; Turkey's growing role as a host for major international events from the Eurovision Song Contest to the Nato Summit – all these welcome developments make clear that we are now looking at a country which has undergone a significant social transformation, an enlightenment.

Since the Customs Union, Turkey has generally followed EU Common Foreign and Security Policy where there has been one to follow. It has been particularly active and helpful in the Balkans. Long a strategic partner of the United States and Israel's only partner in the Mediterranean, it has delicately distanced itself from American policy in Iraq and made clear its deep concern about Ariel Sharon's hardline policies, both moves corresponding with general sentiment in the EU.

It will take time for some Europeans' prejudices and perceptions to catch up with modern Turkey. But when one looks at the appalling record of some of the existing member states during the 20th century (two World Wars, the Spanish Civil War and 40 years of communism scarcely compare well with Turkey's recent record of almost century of peace) Turkey, too, should be treated and rehabilitated in people's minds. Turkey has been a staunch member of Nato for 50 years, it has obeyed all UN sanctions against Iraq to its own immense cost, it has achieved reconciliation with Greece and supported a deal over Cyprus, heavily backed by the Turkish Cypriots. It stands as a strategic asset of the first quality free from war, invasion or revolution in a neighbourhood of traditional turbulence. By the time negotiations finish, perceptions and reality will have merged, and Turkey's contribution to the European Union's own security and prosperity will be properly recognised, as a prize asset.

In spite of the apparently hesitant, even grudging decision by the European Council on 17 December 2004 to open accession negotiations with Turkey, the political weight behind the decision should not be ignored by either Turks or Europeans. Much of the hesitancy in the EU leaders' decision was for domestic consumption. But they knew what they were doing. There is a deep commitment behind the decision based on self-interest which the EU will reverse at its peril.

The barrage of essentially negative background reporting in some sections of the media, concentrating almost exclusively on the difficulties lying ahead, has obscured a solid range of positive aspects to the debate about which public opinion, a key factor in the future of this exercise, deserves to be better informed. Even at the height of French public opposition to starting negotiations, opinion polls showed, paradoxically, that a majority in France would support Turkish membership of the EU if, after the negotiations, it fulfilled all the conditions for accession. Like every other candidate country, it will of course be required to do so.

Barely reported at all in the Western European media is the obvious truth that the decision to open negotiations for Turkish membership of the EU was not made as a favour to Turkey: this is not how the EU operates. The accession of Turkey, on the contrary, is regarded as essentially in the interests of the European Union – it will enhance stability strategically, politically, socially and economically

– and it will *also* be of great benefit to Turkey, which is at the same time in the interest of the EU.

Most important for the European Union, starting negotiations with Turkey will bring an immediate advantage of more predictability, reliability and commitment to shared values, not by imposition, but by common consent. This is not a phenomenon much in evidence elsewhere in the region neighbouring Turkey.

I believe that this book, written with admirable clarity by specialists, is a unique tool enabling the interested, non-specialised professional to understand modern Turkey. I have found it fascinating to edit the volume. I heartily commend it to readers.

Michael Lake
European Commission Representative
in Turkey from 1991-98,
and in Hungary, 1998-2001.

2 March 2005

The Modern History of a Solid Country

Andrew Mango

Nazım Hikmet, the romantic Communist who is Turkey's best known and best loved poet, likened his country's territory to a horse with its body in Asia and its head in Europe towards which it is galloping. Turkish horsemen first broke into Asia Minor in 1071 on their westward migration. By the end of the twelfth century they had settled in such numbers that the whole peninsula became known in Europe as Turkey – a name first attested in the Italian spelling, Turchia. It was in the north-western corner of Turkey that the Turkish warlord Osman declared his independence in 1299, laying the foundations of the Ottoman dynasty. In 1347 Ottoman Turks crossed into Europe as allies of the Byzantine emperor, and Turchia became Turkey-in-Asia. Istanbul, the hinge between Turkey-in-Asia and Turkey-in-Europe, fell to the Turks in 1453, enhancing the role of the new Ottoman Empire as a player in European politics. It became an ally of France against the Habsburgs, of England against Spain, of Genoa against Venice. The Treaty of Karlowitz, concluded in 1699 after the failure of the second Turkish siege of Vienna, marks the end of Ottoman expansion in Europe. In the two centuries of decline that followed, the Sick Man of Europe, as Tsar Nicholas I called the Ottoman state, was not, as is often thought, the passive object of European rivalries, but continued to lend its strength to different rivals in succession, most notably to Britain against France and then against Russia At the same time, Ottoman statesmen tried to arrest, and succeeded in delaying, the decline of their state by remodelling it on European lines.

Wars notwithstanding, there was always a lively exchange of goods and ideas between the Ottoman Empire and Christian Europe. In the years of Ottoman expansion, cash-strapped European monarchs admired the Ottoman standing army and meritocratic administration, while the Ottomans imported European military technology. Fashions were exchanged: Europe took to turquerie in interior decoration; the Ottomans built mosques in baroque style. The nineteenth-century reforms, known collectively as Tanzimat (the reordering), brought Europe to Turkey in a more substantial and permanent way. Although the Ottoman state, as a dynastic multinational empire, shared problems with Austria-Hungary and

Russia, it was republican France which exerted the strongest cultural influence and was the main source of inspiration. While Britain became the main trading partner of the Ottomans, investment capital was largely French. The reforms speeded up when the Ottoman Empire joined Britain, France and Sardinia (the precursor of united Italy) against Russia in the Crimean War. With the treaty of Paris, which ended the war in 1856, the Ottoman Empire became a member of the concert of Europe. When local administration was reorganised in 1864, a *conseil général* was set up in every province, as in France. The capital, Istanbul, was divided into *arrondissements*, like Paris. The reform process culminated in the introduction of the first Ottoman Constitution in 1876 and the election of the first parliament. Sultan Abülhamid II dismissed it in 1878, but his absolutist rule did not stop the spread of European practices.

The Ottoman Empire did not die of maladministration. In many instances, it provided better administration than some of its successor states, at least initially. Like Austria-Hungary, it was killed by the spread of the ideology of nationalism. The Tanzimat reforms, which proclaimed the equality of the sultan's subjects before the law, gave rise to economically dominant minorities – in the main Christians who were the first to adopt the new knowledge developed in the West. In the division of labour on ethnic lines, which had developed in the Ottoman state, non-Muslims acquired a near-monopoly in trade, the crafts and the professions. They became the main beneficiaries of the reforms, and they sought to crown their rising prosperity with political independence. The Young Turks believed that by reintroducing the Constitution in 1908 they would persuade their Christian fellow-citizens to give up their separatist ambitions. Events proved them wrong. The ideology of nationalism spread from Ottoman Christians to Muslim Albanians and then to the Arabs. Having lost most of Turkey-in-Europe in the Balkan Wars of 1912/3, the Young Turks compounded their mistake by trying to repair their fortunes through the German alliance in the First World War. In 1918 the Ottoman Empire went down in defeat together with its allies, Germany and Austria-Hungary. The Great War destroyed what was left of a multinational empire which had enjoyed an orderly administration modelled on European lines. The events that followed completed the disintegration of the Ottoman multinational society.

The contraction of the Ottoman Empire since the end of the seventeenth century and the expansion of Tsarist Russia had set off wave upon wave of Muslim refugees who sought shelter in the remaining Ottoman dominions. Millions of Muslims of diverse ethnic origins fled from the Balkans, millions more from the Caucasus, Crimea and elsewhere in the Russian Empire. There was little movement of Christians in the other direction until 1913. In fact, Ottoman prosperity after the Tanzimat had attracted immigrants from the independent but poor Greek state which had emerged in 1830. The advance which Ottoman Christians had gained on their Muslim neighbours in the late Ottoman Empire led them, and also their European protectors, to undervalue Muslim Turks on racist lines and to deem them incapable of progress and, contrary to all the evidence, even of self-rule. This delusion prompted the victorious Allies to attempt the final partition not just of the Ottoman Empire, but of its Turkish core, which they themselves had called Turkey for more than seven centuries. But it was to be partition by proxy. The Allies were war-weary in 1918; they could not wait to demobilise their large armies. The final partition was to be effected by Greeks in the west, Armenians in the east, and Arabs, championed by the French, in the south. What was left of Turkey was to be divided into spheres of influence. The Allies squabbled over their respective shares and it was not until August 1920 that they finalised their plans and imposed them on the Ottoman government in occupied Istanbul in the shape of the treaty of Sèvres. It was a dead letter from the start and was never ratified.

In May 1919, just as Greek troops began the occupation of western Anatolia, Mustafa Kemal, a young Turkish general who had won his spurs in the successful defence of the Turkish Straits in Gallipoli, and then on the eastern front against the Russians, landed in the Turkish Black Sea port of Samsun, ostensibly to disarm, but actually to reorganise the Ottoman troops in Anatolia. Mustafa Kemal was a realist of genius. He set precise limits to his military targets and his political objectives. He thwarted Allied designs in Turkey, but did not threaten the European empires. By a combination of force on the ground and of bilateral diplomacy, he induced first Italy, then France and finally Britain to abandon the Sèvres treaty. He used the Bolsheviks against the Allies, but did not allow them a foothold in his country. He isolated first the Armenians, whom he defeated in 1920 and threw back behind the 1877 Russian frontier, and then the Greeks whom he drove out of Anatolia in August 1922. He persuaded the Allies to evacuate Istanbul, the Straits and Turkish eastern Thrace without a fight, and after arduous negotiations he secured the international recognition of a fully independent Turkish state within the borders still held by the Ottoman troops when the First World War ended in November 1918. The last war of the Ottoman Empire, which had started in effect when Italy invaded Ottoman Libya in 1911, and had lasted for twelve years with only short pauses, ended finally with the conclusion of the treaty of Lausanne in July 1923. On October 29 of the same year, the Grand National Assembly, which Mustafa Kemal had summoned in Ankara on 23 April 23 1920 as the supreme organ of the Turkish resistance movement, proclaimed the Republic of Turkey.

The Republic started its existence as a proud, but desperately poor country. Outside Istanbul, the country was in ruins. Its population was overwhelmingly rural and almost totally illiterate. More than half had moved hither and thither in the war. The Muslim population of Anatolia, which had numbered 14 million in 1912, had fallen to 11.6 million by 1922. Women outnumbered men. There was an acute shortage of skilled labour as Christian tradesmen and craftsmen were replaced by Muslim peasant refugees. The first phase of republican history was one not just of nation-building but of building a coherent, economically functional society.

Mustafa Kemal, the first president and founding father of the Republic, was a rationalist. He could not set up a functioning democracy, although he created its institutions, but he could and did institute rational government which husbanded the country's resources for development. Having witnessed the tragic results of the gamble of the Young Turk leaders, Mustafa Kemal set his face firmly against any foreign adventures. He was lucky in one respect: Turkey was a Third World country with a First World elite of administrators inherited from the Ottoman Empire. They had received a modern secular education and were keen to push forward the process of modernisation which had started in the nineteenth century. The reforms which Mustafa Kemal implemented in the 1920s and 1930s had all been discussed earlier: secular government untrammelled by religious dogma, the emancipation of women, the introduction of the Latin alphabet, the adoption of the common era with its calendar and universally accepted days of rest, and the use of everyday Turkish instead of the mandarin Ottoman language. The ban on the fez and the discouragement of the veiling of women confirmed the habits of the Ottoman elite. A few years ago, when a Muslim revivalist student reproached a Turkish women professor for wearing 'alien clothes', she replied truthfully: 'What do you mean alien? These are the clothes my mother wore, and my grandmother before her.' What Mustafa Kemal did was to cut short the discussion of reforms, and say 'The time is now!' Educated opinion agreed. When he made surnames compulsory – and chose for himself the surname of Atatürk – it was seen as a matter of administrative necessity in a country which was in pressing need of rational government.

Atatürk's reforms were built on a premise which was widely shared in his day – that there was only one universal civilisation which represented 'the material and moral progress of humanity' (as a classic French definition put it). Atatürk wanted all his people – and not just a small educated elite – to join the mainstream of this single civilisation and contribute to it. He described the civilisation which he wanted his people to share as 'contemporary' or 'modern', rather than European or Western, but he knew where it was centred. 'Is there any people which in its quest for civilisation has not turned to the West?' he asked rhetorically.

Atatürk's motto 'Peace at home, peace in the world' had two components. At home, the orderly implementation of the reforms was paramount. Abroad, a few simple principles had to be observed for the sake of peaceful order: non-aggression, non-interference, and collective action in defence of the international order established by treaty. He was a nationalist and a champion of Turkish independence, without being either an isolationist or a neutralist. He entered into alliances with neighbours and supported sanctions against aggressors. Atatürk's successors have continued to apply his principles to this day. There is today a large and growing literature on Turkish foreign policy. But the proliferation of detail and controversies over tactics should not obscure the remarkable achievement of the political rulers and diplomats of the Turkish Republic. By building on Atatürk's legacy, they made sure that Turkey could develop in peace and use its resources to raise the standard of life of its people. The Ottoman Empire had been at war through most of its existence; the Turkish Republic is enjoying an almost unbroken century of peace. This achievement survived the Second World War thanks to the skilful diplomacy of Atatürk's chief lieutenant and successor, Ismet Inönü.

Atatürk's domestic political arrangements drew on the experience of the French Revolution. The Grand National Assembly which he had summoned in Ankara in 1920 was a Jacobin body which exercised both legislative and executive power. Not only did it pass laws, it also selected and could dismiss individual ministers, whom it called commissioners. It was also the highest judicial body, and until the death penalty was finally abolished in 2002, all death sentences had to confirmed by a vote in parliament. The first assembly which sat until the end of the War of Independence was a free and fractious body which did not hesitate to question and sometimes to challenge Mustafa Kemal's leadership. When it named Mustafa Kemal commander-in-chief, it imposed conditions and set a term to his powers. In order to provide effective government, Mustafa Kemal organised his own party – the People's Party, which later became the Republican People's Party. He controlled the assembly through this party and strengthened the executive by acquiring the right to name a prime minister, subject to parliamentary approval. Opposition to Mustafa Kemal was carried forward to the second assembly which proclaimed the republic. But when Mustafa Kemal began implementing his reforms (which amounted to a cultural revolution), the opposition was suppressed, although in principle the assembly retained supreme power. In the absence of a political opposition, there was little effective resistance to the reforms, and far fewer victims than had been the case in any comparable upheaval elsewhere. Then in 1930, when Turkey was buffeted by the world depression, Mustafa Kemal experimented briefly with a legal opposition in order to channel popular discontent, in contrast with many European countries where the depression had led to the overthrow of democratic government. When the opposition threatened to become a vehicle not of criticism of the government's performance but of reaction to the reforms, it was dissolved and the republic reverted to single-party government.

Atatürk's successor, the second president Ismet Inönü, conciliated some of the personal opponents of the republic's founder, but political progress was arrested by the outbreak of the Second World War. Inönü shared Atatürk's concern that the reforms should be safeguarded and pushed forward. But his priority was to ward off the threat which the World War and then the Cold War posed to his country's independence and territorial integrity, and laboriously achieved economic progress. For two years after the end of the Second World War, Turkey was uncertain of Western support as it resisted Soviet encroachment. Then in 1947 the Truman doctrine gave it an assurance of American aid. This allowed President Inönü to attend simultaneously to his country's security, economic wellbeing and political liberalisation.

In the Republic's first free elections in May 1950, the Republican People's Party was replaced in power by the newly formed Democrat Party. Celal Bayar and Adnan Menderes, founders of the victorious party, became president and prime minister, respectively, while Inönü became leader of the opposition in parliament. The smooth changeover was hailed as proof of Turkey's maturity and of the solidity of the institutions bequeathed by Atatürk. But one weakness of these institutions was at first unnoticed: by concentrating all power in the Assembly, and in the absence of any checks and balances, the country's first Jacobin-inspired constitution left the way wide open to dictatorship by the parliamentary majority. Moreover this majority was enhanced, as under the electoral system inherited from the Ottoman Empire the party first past the post captured all the seats in a given province. Events were to show that in these conditions there was only one force that could restrain a ruling party determined to stay in power by combining populism with political repression. Only the armed forces could call demagogues to order. Argentina was ruined by a military dictator who debauched the economy in order to gain popular acclaim. In Turkey, it was the generals who opposed the fiscal irresponsibility of power-hungry elected politicians.

Population growth had been held back by the mobilisation of a large army during the Second World War. Demobilisation coupled with advances in public health opened the way to a demographic explosion. This large and rapidly growing population clamoured for an immediate alleviation of the poverty to which Atatürk and Inönü's balanced budgets had condemned them. The Democrats responded to the clamour, relying on American support which became institutionalised when Turkey joined Nato in 1952. But while the United States was the guarantor of last resort, it would not meet all the demands the Turkish government made on it. Menderes ran out of money in four years. To secure re-election he restricted the rights of the opposition. More dangerously, the less he could satisfy the material aspirations of the electors, the more he appealed to their religious sentiments. It was a recipe for disaster. Educated opinion, which had at first supported the Democrats, turned against them as salaries were eroded by inflation and prepared to fight the government under the banner of Kemalist reforms, which, in fact, the Democrats' demagogic utterances had left largely untouched. In 1958 Menderes was forced to apply to the IMF for help and to introduce a stabilisation programme – the first of many which were applied and then abandoned in the forty years that followed. As discontent grew, he tried to hamstring the opposition in parliament and silence the press. On 27 May 1960 he was overthrown by a military coup which was supported by the majority of educated opinion. Put on trial on the advice of academic jurists, he was sentenced to death and hanged together with two of his ministers.

Surprisingly, this first military coup gave birth to the most liberal constitution Turkey had ever had. Its purpose was to keep in check the majority party, by setting up a second chamber, a constitutional court, autonomous institutions, economic planning, guaranteed political and social rights, and proportional representation. The unintended consequence was a succession of weak coalition governments, severely restricted in their ability to act as they became subject to the same social and political pressures that had brought low the Democrats. At the same time, the conduct of foreign policy which had been comparatively simple in the 1950s, became more difficult as it became clear that Nato did not cover all the national interests of the member states. In France, the refusal of the Americans to support the occupation of the Suez Canal created a climate of mistrust among Nato allies which led a decade later to the withdrawal of France from the military structure of the alliance. In Turkey, first the need for more economic aid than the Americans and their allies were willing to provide, and then the failure of the United States and of Britain to support the settlement under which the island of Cyprus became independent in 1960, prompted the search for a more independent foreign policy. But unlike France, Turkey could not provide for its own defence outside Nato, and remained a committed member of the alliance. It was in the relatively free and optimistic atmosphere created by the return to civilian rule in 1961 that Turkey signed an association agreement with the European Economic Community. 'Turkey is part of Europe today,' declared Professor Walter Hallstein, president of the Commission, when he signed the association agreement in Ankara in September 1963.

Since the nineteenth century, Turkish politics have been strongly influenced by opinion prevailing in the West in general and in Europe in particular. Parliamentary democracy, the principle of the separation of powers and of checks and balances on the executive, economic planning, even the example of combining membership of alliances with the pursuit of the national interest outside them – all these came from the West. In 1968 another Western phenomenon – student radicalism – spread to Turkey where it found fertile ground in the discontents of a rapidly changing society. Young people started killing each other as they argued whether capitalism or socialism would deliver development. As advocates of military socialism threatened the cohesion of the armed forces, the high command intervened again in 1971 and forced a national government on parliament. The constitution was made more restrictive, banning any activity likely to endanger national unity. The National Security Council, which had been established in 1961 on American lines in order to channel military advice to the government, became more powerful. Individual rights and the autonomy of public institutions were restricted for the sake of national unity.

Having restored law and order under a harsh regime of martial law, the military gave political power back to elected politicians. It soon became apparent that military intervention had not brought a cure. An amnesty designed to reintegrate the militants into the community let loose ideological fanatics, many of whom were helped and abetted by the Soviet Union, acting through proxies. Disorder on the campuses and in the streets was mirrored in the administration and in public institutions which filled with political appointees. In the economy, inflation soared in response to overspending by populist politicians. As unstable coalitions and minority governments succeeded each other, the number of victims of political violence climbed to 5,000, the country came to the brink of civil war, and the economy was brought to its knees. In the midst of this turmoil, the government acted decisively on two occasions. In July 1974, the prime minister, Bülent Ecevit, dispatched Turkish troops to Cyprus. The Cypriot president, Archbishop Makarios (who had himself violated the constitution ten years earlier in order to exclude the Turks from power) was then overthrown in a plot organised by the military junta in Athens.

In January 1980, when Süleyman Demirel was prime minister, his chief economic adviser Turgut Özal reached an agreement with foreign creditors, and introduced free market policies. Step by step, import tariffs were reduced, exports encouraged, capital was allowed to move freely in and out of the country, and the national currency became convertible. As usual, the stabilisation programme began by lowering the standard of living of the mass of the people. A government responsive to pressure groups would have had difficulty in persisting with it, but in September 1980 Demirel was overthrown by the high command of the armed forces which had become alarmed by the country's drift to civil war. The coup enjoyed overwhelming support by a public tired of disorder.

The 1980 coup was the harshest of all military interventions, and the generals stayed in power longer than on previous occasions. But by 1983 they had achieved most of their immediate objectives. Law and order had been restored, and the economy had recovered. All existing political parties were dissolved, and their leaders banned from politics for ten years. A third constitution (or fourth, if one counts the provisional constitution drawn up during the War of Independence), the most restrictive to date, sought to depoliticise not just the administration, but society. But one objective eluded the generals. They had sponsored two polite parties – a centre-right one led by a retired general and a centre-left one under a retired senior civil servant – and they hoped that these would succeed each other in power. But, as an afterthought, they authorised Turgut Özal to form a third party – the Motherland Party – although they advised people to vote against it. Turgut Özal won the elections held in 1983 under the new constitution, and cohabited happily with the new president, General Kenan Evren, who had been head of state under the military regime.

All went well until 1987. Exports soared, economic progress allowed a modernisation of the infrastructure, and relations with European democratic institutions were resumed. But dangerous tensions were developing below the surface. The pressure for higher wages and subsidies was increasing. More dangerously, terrorism, which had been suppressed by the military, assumed a more dangerous form in 1984, when a violent Kurdish separatist organisation of Marxist-Leninist inspiration – calling itself the Kurdistan Workers Party or PKK – launched an insurgency in south-eastern Turkey from its headquarters in Syria. In April 1987 Özal applied for full membership of the European Community, undeterred by the thought that the application had few chances of success. But the immediate challenge was internal.

With elections looming, Özal gave way to union pressure for higher wages. He had to defend himself against the old politicians who had re-entered the lists when the ban on them was lifted by popular referendum and who had re-formed their parties under new names. Özal won the elections, but at the cost of stoking inflation and endangering the success of his own stabilisation programme. In 1989 he moved up to the presidency of the republic, leaving to his successors the difficult task of dealing with the economic and social consequences of his surrender to populist politics. As president of the republic, Özal took charge of foreign policy, trying to establish Turkey as the most reliable ally of the West in the vast area of instability which had opened up as a result of the collapse of the Warsaw Pact and then of the Soviet Union. In 1989 he raised his international profile by hastening to support the US-led coalition which ejected the Iraqi dictator Saddam Hussein from Kuwait. But Özal was trying to punch above his weight: domestic order was again in trouble.

By the end of the 1980s it seemed that the ten-year curse continued to hold sway, and that the military who had re-established order in 1960, 1971 and 1980, might have to do so again. But the generals did not want to intervene again, and populism, now partnered by crony capitalism, ran on unchecked. In 1991, Özal's successor Mesut Yılmaz, was defeated in parliamentary elections and replaced in government by a coalition led by Süleyman Demirel. The coalition played to the gallery. As a result, inflation rose and the PKK insurgency worsened.

In 1993 Özal died suddenly, and Demirel seized the chance to move to the presidential palace. He was succeeded by Turkey's first woman prime minister, Tansu Çiller, an academic economist whose mistakes caused a major economic crisis, and yet another appeal for help from the IMF in 1994. No sooner had the IMF programme begun to bear fruit than it was abandoned, and government overspending resumed. Nevertheless, Çiller succeeded in persuading US president Bill Clinton, the European Commission and the European Parliament that she was capable of implementing a wide-ranging programme of political and economic reforms. On the basis of her assurances, a Customs Union with the European Union came into effect on 1 January 1996 – the first time this had been agreed with a non-member.

Çiller's charm worked better abroad than at home. In the middle of the 1994 economic crisis, the Welfare Party, led by the veteran Islamist politician Necmettin Erbakan, captured control of the town halls of Istanbul, Ankara and a host of other cities. At the end of 1995, Welfare emerged as the strongest single party in parliamentary elections. Çiller had positioned herself as a champion of the secular state against political Islam. But after a series of complex political manoeuvres, centred on bargains by which politicians sought to escape investigation into corruption charges, she agreed to serve under Erbakan. The coalition took office in 1996 and in less than a year incurred the hostility of the armed forces, educated opinion, the business community and the trade unions. At a meeting of the National Security Council on 28 February 1997, the commanders demanded that the government should take measures against political Islam.

As Erbakan procrastinated, some of Tansu Çiller's party colleagues broke away, forcing the coalition to resign. Erbakan and Çiller had agreed earlier that they would succeed each other in the premiership until fresh elections were held. But President Demirel had other ideas. When Erbakan resigned, he called on the Motherland Party leader, Mesut Yılmaz, to form the new government. Yılmaz managed to cobble together a parliamentary majority and became prime minister once again. This time he initiated the long process of reform. But his coalition fell apart before he had made much progress.

Tansu Çiller had given the military a free hand in dealing with the PKK insurgency. Now they took the bit between their teeth and forced the Syrian dictator Hafez al-Asad to expel from Damascus the PKK leader Abdullah Öcalan.

In January 1999, just after Bülent Ecevit had taken over at the head of a minority administration in the run-up to the elections, a Turkish commando team, alerted by friendly intelligence services, snatched Öcalan from Nairobi and brought him back to face trial in Turkey. A wave of patriotic feeling worked to the benefit of Ecevit and of the leader of the right-wing Nationalist Action Party, Devlet Bahçeli. They formed a coalition government with Mesut Yılmaz as the third partner. With reform firmly on the agenda, the government persuaded the European Council at its meeting in Helsinki in December 1999 to grant Turkey candidate status, and to extend to it the accession strategy applied to other candidates. The European Council took a step further in December 2002, when it promised that, if by December 2004, Turkey had satisfied the criteria for membership, accession negotiations would begin without delay. Democratic and economic reform were tackled simultaneously, as Turkey concluded a new stand-by agreement with the IMF and began implementing yet another stabilisation programme.

Shortcomings in governance were cruelly exposed in August 1999 when the authorities were slow to bring relief to the victims of an earthquake disaster which struck the country's industrial heartland on the eastern approaches to Istanbul. At the same time the scale and professionalism of foreign aid showed that the country had good friends abroad, and helped to bring it out of its isolation. In particular the generous Greek response, which Turkey reciprocated when Athens was struck by a less severe earthquake, created good will which had been sadly lacking in relations between the two countries since the outbreak of the Cyprus conflict in the mid-1950s. → 42 -

Ecevit's coalition made a good start with urgent structural reforms, but like all coalition governments, it had to advance at the speed of its slowest partner – in this case the Nationalist Action Party. In addition, the government was hampered by disagreements which developed with the new president, the former head of the constitutional court, Ahmet Necdet Sezer, who found fault with many government decrees. In November 2000, a loss of confidence in the government led to a flight of capital. The IMF increased its support. Then in February 2001, a public altercation between Ecevit and President Sezer, who accused the government of covering up corruption scandals, shook the markets. The government was forced to float the Turkish Lira, which immediately halved in value. A vice-president of the World Bank, Kemal Dervis, was put in charge of the economy.

Dervis renegotiated the agreement with the IMF, and the stabilisation programme was made tougher in exchange for yet more credits. Just as implementation started in earnest, Ecevit fell ill. His government was left rudderless as it grappled with the problems which had accumulated over decades of weak populist rule. The Nationalist Action Party objected to the privatisation of strategic utilities, demanded by the IMF, and to the recognition of cultural rights for linguistic minorities – the Kurds in first place – required as part of the criteria for EU membership. With the help of the opposition, the reforms secured parliamentary approval against the votes of the Nationalists in the government.

The markets once again lost confidence in the ability of the coalition to govern; Ecevit's key ministers, including Kemal Dervis and the long-serving foreign minister Ismail Cem (an architect of the rapprochement with Greece), resigned, and Ecevit was forced to agree to early elections. They were held in November 2002 and proved a disaster for all the coalition parties, none of which could secure the minimum 10 per cent of the national poll necessary for representation in parliament.

Ecevit had foreseen the result, realising that the IMF programme, with its insistence on a primary surplus of 6.5 per cent of the Gross National Product (a proportion higher than that demanded of Brazil and Argentina in similar circumstances), had caused widespread unemployment and a sharp drop in the standard of living. Yet, hampered as it was by internal disagreement, Ecevit's coalition had done much to clear the Augean stables it had inherited. One of its last achievements – securing parliamentary approval for the abolition of the death penalty – was emblematic of the more liberal and more self-confident atmosphere which it had created in the country. History will probably be kinder than the electorate in its verdict on Ecevit's last government.

The elections were won by a new party. It was called the Justice and Development Party (AKP) and had been formed by a group of modernisers within the Islamic camp, whose Virtue Party had been dissolved by the constitutional court. The modernisers were led by Recep Tayyip Erdogan, the young mayor of Istanbul who had forfeited his post and had served a brief sentence in prison for an offence against the secularist order – reciting in public a well-known poem summoning the faithful to battle. Only one other party, the oldest in the country – the Republican People's Party – was represented in the new parliament. As Erdogan was still banned from politics, the new government was led by his deputy, Abdullah Gül. The ban was lifted by a constitutional amendment in December, and Erdogan was elected to parliament in March 2003, when he took over the reins of government from Gül. On 1 March, before the changeover was complete, a government motion to allow US troops access to Turkish territory in order to attack Saddam Hussein from the north failed in parliament. Obloquy was heaped on Turkey in the United States. However, relations were repaired when, after the end of the war, parliament authorised the government to dispatch Turkish peacekeepers to Iraq. But as the Provisional Governing Council set up by the Coalition in Baghdad objected to their presence, the move was abandoned, and Turkey emerged from the crisis relatively cost-free.

Seldom had a newly elected government had to deal with so many pressing problems. In addition to the Iraq crisis where Turkey's alliance with the United States had to be safeguarded while avoiding an unpopular involvement in the conflict, Erdogan had to resist popular pressure to ease the austerity imposed by the IMF programme. He also had to reassess Turkish policy on Cyprus in the knowledge that the island was due to enter the EU in May 2004. Immediately after the elections, Erdogan decided that his priority was to ensure that the next European Council in Copenhagen should set a date for the accession negotiations. Amendments to the constitution and to many laws followed each other in quick succession, and by the end of 2003 the government declared that, as far as legislation was concerned, Turkey had met the criteria for EU membership. The military were subordinated to the civil power; instruction, publication and broadcasting in all the languages spoken in the country were allowed and legal provisions restricting human rights were removed. The ease with which the government made these changes owed much to its popularity, not least among the best educated, whom the military had championed. Implementation could not be completed overnight, but the government made sure that the reforms would not remain on paper and that they would be broadly put into practice by December 2004.

The settlement of the Cyprus problem was not part of the Copenhagen criteria. But the EU urged Turkey repeatedly to do all in its power to help reunite the island, since the accession to the EU of a divided Cyprus, represented by its internationally recognised government made up solely of Greek Cypriots, would obviously be an obstacle to the realisation of Turkey's membership aspirations. Erdogan responded by giving his support to the reunification plan drawn up by the UN Secretary General, Kofi Annan, with the strong backing both of the EU and the United States. It was a risky decision, since the Turkish Cypriot leader Rauf Denktash, who enjoyed wide popularity in Turkey, was strongly opposed to the plan. Erdogan's stance encouraged Turkish Cypriots who favoured a settlement. Elections held in Northern Cyprus in December 2003 brought to power a government determined to negotiate on the basis of the Annan plan, which the Turkish Cypriots approved by a majority of two-thirds in a referendum on 24 April 2004. But in a referendum held simultaneously on the Greek side of the island, the plan was rejected by an even larger majority. Erdogan's support for the settlement was warmly commended by the EU which promised to help the beleaguered Turkish Cypriots.

The scope of the domestic reforms, which the Justice and Development government pushed forward energetically, mirrored the extent of Turkey's transformation. It was a backward, under-populated, rural, isolated country when the republic was established. Today, two-thirds of its 70 million people live in towns; 98 per cent of men and 80 per cent of women are literate; 92 per cent of boys and 87 per cent of girls attend eight-year primary schools; there are one and a half million students receiving higher education and all villages can be reached by motor transport and have access to basic services – electricity, water and telephone. In 2003, Turkey recorded 14 million visits by foreigners and another six million by Turks living abroad. In the same year, Turkish exports amounted to 47 billion dollars and imports 69 billion. Calculated on the basis of the purchasing power of the currency, Turkey had the 20th largest economy in the world.

These figures are eloquent proof of the extent of Turkey's modernisation. Turkey's recent history has witnessed political and economic crises and military coups. But civil and external war has been avoided. The Turkish armed forces can claim a large part of the credit for this: they have intervened when disorder threatened to get of hand, returning to their barracks when the danger was passed and they have been averse to external adventure. But it is the spirit of solidarity and social cohesion of the people that has been the main factor in the country's (by and large) peaceful progress over the last half-century. Atatürk has taught his people that salvation was in their hands and that they should not seek foreign scapegoats for their ills. His advice, 'Turk be self-confident, hard-working and proud' was echoed recently by Prime Minister Erdogan. Asked what was the alternative to membership of the European Union, he replied 'The alternative is ourselves'.

The experience of the last decade has discredited populism as a nostrum for Turkey's ills. It has also discredited ideological extremism. Justice and Development, which has its roots in political Islam, has positioned itself as a centre-right party in the tradition of Menderes, Demirel and Özal. But it promises to take better account than they had of economic and political reality. In spite of recent disputes about the scope which should be allowed for religious education (disputes not unknown in many EU countries), the degree of support achieved by Erdogan among all classes of the population suggests that the old conflict between secularists and Islamists is waning, and may gradually become part of history, like the conflict between clericalists and anti-clericalists in Europe. The nationwide revulsion at the terrorist outrages in Istanbul in November 2003 has shown that religious fanatics are a marginal group which can be contained through the normal process of law.

The problem posed by the spread of Kurdish nationalism remains, and is more serious for the fact that nationalism is not always amenable to rational considerations of self-interest. But one should note that while the PKK insurgency was being fought, millions of Turks and Kurds continued to live peacefully side by side, to intermarry and to work together throughout the country. The loss of support suffered by Kurdish nationalists in the local government elections in March 2004, when Justice and Development increased its share of the poll, suggests that Turkish citizens of Kurdish origin do not wish to be treated as a separate minority, but see their future in a united multicultural society. The problem of Kurdish nationalism cannot be solved quickly, but it can be managed – and European practice can be helpful in this regard.

Survey after survey shows that for the vast majority of the Republic's citizens the most pressing problem is not Kurdish nationalism or religious extremism, but unemployment, particularly among the educated young. In the circumstances, it is remarkable that the hardships caused by the present economic stabilisation programme have not led to large-scale social unrest. There have been few strikes, and no bread riots, such as have occurred in many developing countries. Although economic recovery has speeded up during the year and a half that Justice and Development has been in power, unemployment has not been dented. The fact that the government's popularity has nevertheless increased suggests that the Turkish people have learned patience. They will need it not only at home, but also in their relationship with the European Union.

On 17 December 2004, the European Council accepted the advice of the Commission that Turkey had satisfied the criteria required of candidates to an extent sufficient for the commencement of accession negotiations. The Council decided that these negotiations should begin on 3 October 2005, but it warned that they could not be concluded until 2014 at the earliest, given that new rules were to be introduced in 2013 to govern the EU budget. In any case, surveys showed that in many EU countries public opinion was disturbed at the prospect of Turkey's accession. It will clearly take time to turn this public opinion around. One can therefore say with certainty that accession negotiations will be long. They are also likely to be difficult. Success will require all sides to show perseverance and patience. But the prize of Turkish membership is well worth striving for.

History demonstrates that Turkey is a solid country. A British diplomat, appointed to Ankara after years of service in the Middle East, once commented 'I've left shifting sands and touched firm ground'. The ground in Turkey is today more diverse and more developed than it was a generation ago, but it is still firm.

From Özal to the Present Day

Ahmet O. Evin

When Turgut Özal, eighth president of the Republic, suddenly passed away on 17 April 1993, there was a substantial twist of irony in the fact that his obvious (and unchallenged) successor was the then prime minister Süleyman Demirel. The paths of the two men had for many years been intertwined. Faced with serious foreign exchange shortages and threat of a total collapse of the economy when he formed a minority government in 1979, it was Demirel himself who had chosen Özal as his economic major domo to formulate a way out of the crisis. This appointment gave the first, decisive impetus to Özal's political career.

Özal's response to the crisis of 1979 was to prepare, with Demirel's full backing, a sweeping economic restructuring programme that aimed to 'transform the inward-oriented political economy into an export-oriented one'.[1] Demirel then pressed his cabinet, allowing no time even for a debate, to adopt what came to be known as the 24 January 1980 stabilisation measures. The measures, adopted after Özal's consultation with and the backing of the military high command, aimed to restore the confidence of the markets and pull the economy out of the impasse that had been exacerbated by the 1979 oil price hikes. The Demirel government, however, was unable to overcome the impasse in the political arena. With a deadlocked parliament unable to elect a president for months, while spreading anarchy claimed an increasing number of lives, the military stepped in on 12 September 1980.

Although the government was removed from office and the parliament closed, Özal was asked by the military to stay on and implement the economic stabilisation programme. He, in turn, demanded additional powers from the military government to carry out the task. Surprisingly, the military responded by appointing him deputy prime minister in charge of the economy, despite the fact that he had been associated earlier with Necmettin Erbakan's (Islamist) National Salvation Party (MSP). After two years of uncontested rule over the economy,

Özal was forced to resign in the wake of a scandalous collapse of an unregulated deposit-taking house in July 1982.

A few months after his resignation Özal began preparations for forming a new party to run in the upcoming elections following the adoption in a public referendum of the 1982 Constitution. The referendum also served to elect General Evren, commander-in-chief, as the seventh president of the Republic. The military leadership, however, was keen not to allow the kind of political fragmentation that had precipitated the 1980 intervention in the first place; to that end it sought to clone two parties (one slightly to the right and one to the left of the centre) and allow only those two parties to compete in the 1983 elections. It also took steps to exclude from the elections all political cadres it had removed from office whom it held responsible for the country's destabilisation in the 1970s.[2]

The veteran politicians, for their part, were conspiring behind the scenes to form new parties, thinly veiled replicas of their former ones. They would ask loyal friends from among those not banned from politics to be caretaker leaders until such time as they might be allowed to return to politics. For different reasons neither Evren nor Demirel were pleased with Özal's initiative to establish a new party. Demirel would have liked to see Özal join the Grand Turkey Party (BTP), which he had devised behind the scenes as a sequel to his own Justice Party (AP) that was closed, in July 1981, along with Bülent Ecevit's Republican Peoples Party (CHP). Özal, however, decided to part ways with the old guard and form a new political party that would appeal to a broader spectrum of voters.

'Everyone is still fighting the old battles,' Özal complained, concerned by the old guard's exclusive focus on criticising the military. 'We want nothing to do with these struggles. If the military stepped in, they did so with the best intentions. We saw it. We went along with them. Whether they knew what was best in the circumstances is altogether another question.'[3] Özal's accommodating style, and the fact that he had come to be personally known by the generals, saved him from the sanctions that disallowed all other political competitors to the two parties fashioned by the military. Meanwhile, the US government had also presented the generals with some persuasive arguments (notably in respect to the credibility of the transition and confidence of the markets) as to why they should let Özal run. As the November 1983 elections approached, Evren publicly voiced his opposition to Özal's Motherland Party as if he had begun personally to campaign against it. What appeared to be Evren's loss of nerve actually worked in Özal's favour: in 1980 the public was glad to see the military step in and put an end to anarchy; three years later the same public had had enough of the atmosphere of Spartan authoritarianism that smothered civic life. In the elections of 6 November 1983, the Motherland Party (ANAP) won 211 seats in the 400-seat assembly with 45 per cent of the votes.

With an absolute majority in parliament, Özal still continued his accommodating style towards President Evren. Although under the 1982 Constitution the executive powers of the presidency had been increased, there was no hint of serious friction between the president and prime minister. Rather than an uneasy cohabitation, the relationship between Evren and Özal resembled one that was based on a consensual division of labour. Özal deferred to the president in matters of national security (internal and external), while he himself assumed full command of the economy. During the process of 'civilianisation' over the next four years, the National Security Council, chaired by the president, provided politically stabilising ballast as well as a safety valve against further direct military involvement in politics.[4]

The 1982 Constitution had been conceived in reaction to the political fragmentation and polarisation of the 1970s. As such, it contained many restrictive provisions that were at odds with the basic precepts of liberal democracy. The ANAP government did not make any serious attempt to amend the constitution to seek enhanced democratisation in tandem with the transition to civilian, competitive politics, although it did adopt a law on 18 May 1987 which made it easier to amend the constitution in future. The same law also amended Provisional Article 4 of the constitution by repealing the 'ban on political activities of former party leaders'.[5]

Although the procedures did not require this repeal to be put to a referendum, Özal insisted that it should be and proceeded to oppose the repeal in the referendum campaign. The repeal was supported by a very small majority of 50.1 per cent in the referendum held on 6 September 1987. As a result, Demirel was able to return to the parliament after the 29 November 1987 elections as leader of the True Path Party (DYP), which replaced the BTP and brought into its fold former AP politicians whose bans had been lifted. Four years later, after the 20 November 1991 elections, the remaining three leaders of the old guard, Bülent Ecevit, Necmettin Erbakan and Alpaslan Türkes, also returned to the parliament as respective leaders of their own renamed parties: The Democratic Left Party (DSP), Welfare Party (RP), and the Nationalist Labour Party (MCP). It was thus only eleven years after the coup that all four of the political leaders whom the military blamed for leading the country into chaos, and whom it took great pains to exclude from the political arena, were able to take the centre stage once again.

During the extensive debates among top commanders that had begun nearly two years prior to their decision to stage the 1980 coup, some of them had strongly argued against staging a coup, citing previous interventions that had ended up with the same political actors, ousted by the earlier military regimes, making a comeback in a very short time after return to civilian rule. The past efforts of the military to improve the quality and efficiency of the political sphere, they claimed, had come to nothing. As a consequence, they feared, the integrity and prestige of the military institution had suffered. The results of the 1991 elections seemed retrospectively to confirm these apprehensions. Once having made the decision in 1980 to step in, the military, highly distrustful of the Turkish political cadres, had remained in power for a number of years and undertaken a major programme to restructure not only the political system but also the key institutions of the state. The fact that Demirel became prime minister of a coalition government after his DYP won a plurality of votes cast in 1991, and the fact that Özal, president since 1989, had to face a parliament dominated by the old guard and their familiar harangues, provided two strikingly ironic comments on what was supposed to be a reconstituted political sphere in Turkey.

Indeed the ambition of the military regime from 1980 to 1983 to reorganise the Turkish political arena led to a number of unintended consequences. One is the fact that, beginning with ANAP, Turkish political parties in power did not attempt to reverse the system of favouring the winning parties in the distribution of parliamentary seats, but instead attempted to take advantage of it. In the 1983 elections, for example, ANAP secured 53 per cent of the seats with 45.1 per cent of the votes. (The Appendix provide data on parliamentary election results and distribution of seats.) In 1986 and 1987 the Özal government proceeded to make constitutional amendments and changes in the election law to increase even further the favourable distribution of seats to the leading parties. As a result, in the 1987 parliamentary elections, ANAP came to occupy 64.9 per cent of the seats, having received only 36.3 per cent of the votes. Anticipating further loss of electoral support, Özal used ANAP's comfortable parliamentary majority in his bid for the presidency after Evren's term of office expired in 1989. The tide had turned and, with Demirel back at the helm of the DYP, the latter party captured 178 seats with 27 per cent of the votes in the 1991 elections, while ANAP got only 115 seats with 20 per cent of the votes.

The irony of unintended consequences sharpened in the wake of the 1995 elections, held on Christmas Eve, in which Mr Erbakan's Islamist Welfare Party (RP) garnered a plurality of 21.4 per cent of the votes and won 158 seats (28.7 per cent) in the parliament, the membership of which had been increased from 450 to 550. ANAP and DYP, having won 19.6 and 19.2 per cent of the votes, respectively, together controlled less than half of the seats. A government with RP in coalition with either ANAP or DYP would ensure a comfortable majority in the parliament, but such a coalition would be at odds with the secularist establishment, with Turkey's Western orientation (the Customs Union with the EU was due to take effect on 1 January 1996, a week after the elections) and, in short, with the very principles on which the Republic was established. A coalition without RP, however, would require three parties in order to obtain a parliamentary majority. That alternative would in effect bring together the two rival centre-right parties (whose leaders, Mr Mesut Yılmaz and Mrs Tansu Çiller had no love lost for each other) with one of the two left-of-centre parties in a coalition that would be plagued with disagreements. The result, predictably, was a series of unstable coalitions among incompatible partners.

The RP's share of seats would have been larger had it not been for a Constitutional Court decision, taken prior to the 1995 elections, to curb the excessive favouring of the leading party in parliamentary representation. In the 1991 elections Mr Ecevit's DSP had barely crossed the threshold with 10.8 per cent of the vote but had been assigned only seven seats, representing 1.6 per cent of he 450-member assembly. DSP brought a case to the Constitutional Court and successfully argued for reintroducing proportional representation among the parties represented in the parliament.

Its inability to prevent weak and unstable coalitions was another, second unintended consequence of the post-1983 election system. The 1999 elections, like those of 1995, produced yet again an unexpected twist in Turkish politics. Because the two major right-of-centre parties (ANAP and DYP) had alienated voters because of their ineptitude as well as corruption, and because RP had been closed by the Constitutional Court for advocating an Islamic regime to replace the secular Republic, the electorate turned to new alternatives. Mr Ecevit, who had been the caretaker prime minister of a minority government to prepare for the 1999 elections, won 136 seats with 22.2 per cent of the vote; MHP (the ultra-nationalist party under the new leadership of Mr Devlet Bahçeli) came in second with 18 per cent. The result, it could be argued, also reflected a growing sign of the electorate's wish to see in government leaders who had not been tainted with the rampant corruption of the previous decade. ANAP and DYP, in turn, captured only 25.2 per cent of the vote between themselves, down from the 38.8 in 1995. In yet another surprising development, CHP, the Republic's very first political institution, failed to cross the 10 per cent threshold and was excluded from the parliament.

The distribution of the seats required a three-way coalition to obtain a parliamentary majority. In the event, DSP, MHP, ANAP formed a government with Mr Ecevit as prime minister and Mr Bahçeli and Mr Yılmaz as deputy prime ministers. This coalition was delicately balanced with its leaders representing irreconcilable political views that embraced dirigiste étatism, ultra-nationalism, and right-of-centre economic liberalism at one and the same time. With tact and deference stemming from an instinct for survival, members of this coalition demonstrated a semblance of harmony and accommodation until the 2001 economic crisis.

The third salient point with respect to Turkish politics after 1983 is the fact that the 10 per cent threshold failed to discourage the proliferation of small parties and prevent them from crowding the political stage. Seven parties entered the race in 1987; among the six parties that competed in 1991, one of them, RP, included under its umbrella two other right-wing parties. The number of parties running in 1995 reached twelve, and an all-time record of 20 in the 1999 elections. The exclusion from the parliament of all but four parties in the 1999 elections hardly discouraged fragmentation in the political sphere; no fewer than 13 parties competed in the 2002 elections.

Out of these 13, however, only two parties won seats in the assembly. With the 34.4 per cent of the votes, AKP got 365 seats, while CHP made a comeback, winning 177 seats with 19.4 per cent of the votes. All other parties where excluded from the parliament, although one of the deputies, elected as an independent, later took over the leadership of DYP. Most of the old guard from the losing parties declared that they would retire from politics (and some of them actually did.) The crushing victory of AKP (a party founded by a dissident group that parted ways with Mr Erbakan and his associates) ushered once again, after 19 years, a large, new cast of actors into the political arena. Did the 2002 elections succeed in revamping the Turkish political arena and thereby accomplished what the military coup and the 1982 Constitution were unable to accomplish?

Before addressing the latter question regarding prospects for further reforms, it would be appropriate to consider whether the Özal period really left an indelible mark on Turkey's political culture and, if so, the ways in which that period might have affected the future course of Turkish politics. Özal is remembered variously as a great reformer who helped prepare Turkey for integration into global markets and as a glib politician who would cut corners and flouted the law when it suited him. These diametrically opposite assessments that evoke a Janus-like image of Özal also point to one of the key paradoxes that characterise Turkish politics: while the public respects strong leaders with a vision, it also expects political leaders to be capable of delivering patronage. Equally paradoxical was the fact that Özal, (the able technocrat who served under the military regime) came to be the capable civilian leader who steered a smooth transition to a civilian rule. Furthermore, and ironically, after he succeeded General Evren as president in 1989, Özal took full advantage of the executive powers of the presidency as defined in the 1982 Constitution. [6]

The most significant aspect of Özal's legacy is the transformation of Turkey's economic culture. Étatism was not merely a principle adopted by Attar's Republican Peoples Party (CHP) in the wake of the 1929 Great Crash. Its roots lay in the centuries-old Ottoman state tradition[7] which put the administration of the state before the management of its economy, in other words, the distribution before the creation of resources in society. The social structure that placed a premium on service to the state, and therefore assigned the highest status to those employed by the state, had necessarily impeded the development of a bourgeoisie. The middle classes were perceived merely as middle-income groups, among which those employed by the state were accorded a higher status than, for example, merchants. The Ottoman system not only rendered the state the biggest consumer (with the right to regulate prices thereby to distort the market) but, as a result, also perpetuated among the empire's subjects a culture of dependency on the state.[8] Dependency on the state continued to be distinctive feature of Turkey's economic culture after the founding of the Republic, not least because of a dearth of private capital. The state's predominant role in harnessing, directing, and redistributing resources provided a strong basis for clientelism after the transition to a multi-party system in 1950. Import Substitution Industrialisation meant, above all, protecting the domestic market from foreign competition. As for promoting inward-oriented economic policies, there was little difference between the étatist parties in Turkey and their so-called liberal rivals. Unlike the fundamental ideological differences that separated the socialist or communist parties in Western Europe from their liberal adversaries, the étatist and populist parties both utilised public funds in a redistributive fashion to promote their own centrally planned development policies, with a near-total disregard of the long-term sustainability of these projects. The main difference between what is called the left-of-centre and right-of-centre parties in Turkey was that the former (statist ones, notably CHP) preferred to direct resources to the State Economic

Enterprises, while the latter (Democrat Party and its successors) chose to extend patronage to clients outside the public sector. The result was the creation of non-competitive industries and continued dependency on international financial markets to make up for ever growing account deficits.

The 1980s marked the break in three significant ways from Turkey's economic culture inherited from the Ottoman tradition. One was the shift away from étatism as a collectively valued principle that was perceived to reflect the responsibility of the state toward its citizens. This shift also embraced the goal of allowing greater autonomy to the sphere of economic activity by diminishing the dirigiste-type of state intervention in the markets. The irony of it all lies in the fact that the austerity measures required for the 1980 Economic Stabilisation Programme to succeed were made possible by the military government then in power (instead of an elected liberal-democratic government) and the liberalisation of the economy was successfully implemented under what may be described as a bureaucratic-authoritarian type of government with a technocrat in charge of the economy.

The second break with tradition was the increasing emphasis placed by Özal, especially after he became prime minister, on the importance of entrepreneurial middle classes, which he called ortadirek (mainmast) The shift of focus from status groups to entrepreneurial ones marked a reversal of hierarchies in received economic culture. Largely because it had not experienced anything that even remotely resembled the Industrial Revolution, Turkish society had not undergone a process of embourgeoisement, and hence, had retained a traditional deference towards status. Status, in turn, was associated with education, professional distinction, or an official position of influence (recognition by the centre) or with being a local notable (recognition in the periphery)[9] Leadership was associated not with entrepreneurial but with recognised status groups and the latter were expected to regulate, assist, and enable the former to perform their economic functions properly.

The third break was the overriding emphasis placed by Özal on economic activity itself, paralleling the shift of focus to entrepreneurial groups and their contribution to society. Trade and commerce, he believed, were valuable in and of themselves; not only did they lead to economic growth but also constituted the most effective remedy against conflict and polarisation in society. His engagement with dynamic forms of economic exchange, almost like a fascination with toys, also set the tone of his political statements. He emphasised economic issues in his public statements and was reasonable and convincing while projecting numbers on the TV screen from his computer. By focusing public attention on facts and figures he succeeded in depolarising and depoliticising the political community, which had been used to hearing, for centuries, normative moral messages from the leaders. The adoption of a laissez-faire approach led to Turkey's economic recovery in the short term. But, in the medium term, his relentless advocacy of laissez-faire had the effect of making a new generation of Turks put opportunity before values. The motto of 'to each his own' in a fast expanding economy impeded the development of a proper regulatory environment and the establishment of the rule of law, leading to unfair gains and corruption.

In one sense, the Özal years represented a significant departure from the established norms of Turkey's political culture, particularly in terms of inculcating a feeling of economic empowerment to the individual: that is, creating a *homo economicus* out of the passive 'subject'. Concomitantly, there appeared a heightened public awareness of certain deeply rooted features of Turkish political culture. It was Özal himself who contributed to the broad popular understanding first of the notion of civil society (in the beginning confused with 'civilian' versus 'military' society, since the Turkish word is the same for 'civil' and 'civilian') and then of pluralism (a concept that was for a long time mistakenly perceived as being at odds with the nation building priorities of the unitary, modern Turkish state).[10]

The decade of the 1990s was also a period of missed opportunities for achieving development as well as the consolidation of democracy. Populist politics of successive governments resulted in two serious crises, in 1994 and 2001, leading to major devaluations. Record-braking inflation rates, another corollary of reckless populism, became one of the globally recognised characteristics of Turkey's economy. The discipline of the 1980 Economic Stability Measures was cast aside by Özal himself as early as the mid-1980s in the run up to the 1987 general elections. Under successive coalition governments after 1991, public spending, therefore budget deficits and sovereign debt, kept on increasing at a rapid pace, keeping the inflation rate, on average, around 60 per cent.

Yet Özal's concerted efforts to change Turkey's economic culture did not have a lasting effect on the country's political culture. The rise of entrepreneurial classes, for example, cannot be said to have given rise to individualism nor to have diminished the culture of dependency because of the continuing influence of clientelism in politics. A strong tendency toward 'in group-out group' orientation and a lack of tolerance for political opposition, two deeply rooted characteristics of Turkish political culture, continued unaffected throughout the 1980s and resulted in the fragmentation, during the 1990s, of the party system, mentioned above, as well as obstructing the development of democratic governance within the political parties themselves. Pluralism and associability, hardly consistent with the received values of Turkey's political culture, were further constrained by the 1982 constitution.

Apart from attempting to address the causes of immobilism in party politics, the 1982 Constitution aimed, above all, to achieve political stability and prevent Turkey from sliding back into polarisation and chaos that had precipitated the 1980 coup in the first place. To that end, it sought to restore the authority of the state by means of increasing the executive powers of the president, assigning priority to the National Security Council decisions in respect of policy, creating the High Board of Education to provide oversight to universities and ensure their compliance with constitutional principles (the military blamed the universities for harbouring radicals and thus contributing to the anarchy and destabilisation of the country in the late 1970s), and placing restrictions on associations and foundations. 'Governability', that is maintenance of law and order, took precedence over freedoms associated with liberal democracy. (Ironically, it was Mr Demirel as prime minister who bitterly complained to the generals in 1970s that he could not govern the country with the liberal 1961 constitution unchanged.)

The distinctions between the state and the realm of politics, and the rivalry between these two spheres, have been a unique feature of the Turkish polity ever since the 1950 transition to multi-party politics. The state historically represented the Ottoman high culture and produced the elites, and embraced its institutions; modernisation was introduced by the state elites. The political sphere, on the other hand, was the arena where, among others, the demands of traditional communities were voiced. While the latter saw in politics a space for freedom to exercise opposition to those in power, it was the former, which has had an abiding commitment to Turkey's European vocation.

Two significant issues that have influenced the relationship between the state and the political sphere merit brief attention in this context: nationalism and religion. The first one relates to the Kurdish issue and the destructive conflict it has engendered. The PKK guerilla organisation was formed in 1978 by Abdullah Öcalan, a strong-willed young man from a poor village in south-eastern Turkey who became involved in radical left politics as a scholarship student at Ankara University's elite Faculty of Political Science. When the PKK staged its first attack in two towns in eastern and southern Turkey on 14-15 August 1984, it came as a surprise to the state security apparatus. After all, the 1980-1983 military regime had adopted as its key mission the establishment of law order and had, to that end, taken draconian measures, such as arresting radicals and holding mass trials in martial law courts. Thousands of pro-Kurdish activists were in detention. The PKK's ability to strike and then engage in prolonged guerilla warfare removed from Turkey's political agenda any further regime liberalisation as well as the possibility of seeking a political solution to the conflict. For slightly over a decade after that, while Turkish security forces fought PKK terrorists, the conflict spread throughout south-eastern Turkey and to some of the neighbouring provinces. By the early 1990s a large part of the country was engulfed in what increasingly resembled a civil war; the more violently the terrorists struck, the harder the security forces clamped down. For the political cadres as well as the security forces, the military high command, judiciary and civil bureaucracy alike, there was only one way of dealing with PKK terrorism: defeating the enemy. Over the next decade and a half, the war in the South East claimed around 30,000 lives; more than 2,000 villages were razed to the ground and their inhabitants forced to relocate.

The severity of the Turkish authorities' response not only towards the PKK terrorists, but alongside them also toward civil activists who were merely calling for Kurdish linguistic and recognition, stemmed from a deeply felt and widely shared animosity in Turkey toward separatism. Modern Turkey had been established on the territory reclaimed and defended after the collapse of the Ottoman Empire. A deep apprehension of dismemberment had weighed heavily on the Turkish soul ever since the rapid disintegration of the Ottoman Empire at the end of the nineteenth century, followed by the partitioning and occupation of its territories after the First World War.

To his credit Özal was the first political leader to seek ways to begin solving the bloody conflict. He would publicly call attention, for instance, to his own partial Kurdish ancestry in order to emphasise how inseparable Kurds and Turks had become throughout history and as citizens of the Turkish Republic. The Turkish liberal view was that the conflict in the South East was largely the result of underdevelopment due to the neglect of the region. Peace could be achieved by means of economic development, which itself depended on stability and investment. The ambitious GAP (South East Anatolia) project involving 22 dams to harness and manage the waters of the Tigris and Euphrates had been initiated in the 1970s to generate electricity as well as provide irrigation to practically the entire region. This was the only project whose funding was not suspended as part of the 1980-1983 austerity measures. For the liberals, the GAP project was the locomotive that would attract investment and bring prosperity to the whole region. Hardliners, on the other hand, saw Turkey's investment in the region as yet another justification for claiming 'Turkishness' of the area and denying cultural pluralism there.

The Kurdish issue became of the key areas of tension between Turkey and the European Union. The EU's demand for the improvement of human rights and the recognition of cultural rights seemed, at the time, to be at odds with the reality of guerilla warfare on the ground. Also, the pro-Kurdish sympathies of many groups in Western Europe raised suspicions in Turkey of European designs to partition Turkey in support of separatists. Despite the strong tactics used in the repression of the PKK insurgence as well as of the political rights of activists, the majority of the Kurds, who actually live in the western part of Turkey outside the conflict zone, had not been subject to harsh discrimination in society. Today, faster progress is being made toward resolving this issue, because the EU is perceived to have become an honest broker by promoting Turkey's EU candidacy.

Like Özal, the AKP cadres, particularly local politicians in the war-torn South East, have been active in promoting peace and stability by means of encouraging participation and human rights reform. There are two significant ways in which AKP bears similarities to Özal's ANAP at its inception and one significant way in which the leadership and style of governance of the two parties differ from one another. One similarity is that AKP, like ANAP, is an original construct conceived by a small group of like-minded persons who took a chance and parted ways with an established political party. More importantly, the second is that both ANAP and AKP have constituted coalitions in themselves, bringing together, in the case of AKP, disappointed and disgruntled members of other parties from the right as well as the left and a mélange of conservative business persons, successful politicians from the local governments, new recruits into politics from many walks of life, including those from underdeveloped regions and from among the urban poor. The AKP embraces a broader range of political actors than Özal's ANAP, which focused on attracting recruits from among urban businessmen, nationalists, Muslim conservatives, and erstwhile leftists. This common feature of the two parties points to both their strengths and weaknesses in that their broad constituency would serve to attract a large number of votes from differing types of communities and individuals, but that a weak performance at the helm would bring the threat of the party's disintegration. In the light of the foregoing consideration, Mr Erdogan's commitment to pursue Turkey's European vocation would appear to be sincere, since he has bet his political future as well as that of his party on the successful progress towards Turkey's EU membership.

Sceptics, however, still doubt Mr Erdogan's and his close associates' real motive in pushing reforms to fulfil the Copenhagen political criteria. They question whether the reforms were primarily driven with the objective of subordinating the state elite, particularly the military, to the political leadership, and then revert to AKP's hidden anti-secularist agenda. After all, it was Mr Erdogan who had described democracy in 1993 as 'a vehicle which you ride as far as you want to go and then get off'. It was also he, later as mayor of Istanbul who forbade alcohol in municipal facilities (even in commercial ones) and to make such radical declarations as 'We support Sharia law'.[11] His zealous Islamic radicalism, still fresh in the memory, had resulted in his conviction for inciting religious hatred; in 1999 he was sentenced to ten months in prison and banned from politics for life. Could he have changed so radically, as he has claimed he had, since this release in 1999 from the prison?

Özal, too, had come from the conservative background and had described himself as a pious Muslim. He had also entered politics in Erbakan's MSP (one of RP's predecessors) but having failed to secure a seat in the parliament before the 1980 elections, he had been spared the ban on political activity. But, unlike Erdogan, Özal was a confirmed liberal from the very beginning. His piety was quintessentially Turkish in that he would participate in Friday prayers but would sip good French cognac while working with colleagues and bureaucrats late into the night. His laissez-faire approach extended beyond the economic sphere into that of religion and society. He would walk hand-in-hand with his socialite wife who had no claim to piety (in contrast to Mrs Erdogan clad in a headscarf), and hardly demonstrated even a remote compatibility with a Turkish conservative lifestyle. On the other hand, one of his brothers as well as a number of the political cadres he recruited to ANAP were conservative Muslims, if not Islamists.

The even more important distinction between the founders of AKP and ANAP was that the latter had an elite higher education, high-level professional experience of international institutions and global corporations, and had served at the highest levels of the Turkish civil service. Özal was familiar with the state: when he entered politics he was not an adversary of the state but could claim membership of the state elite. Having served the military government, he knew how to operate in Ankara better than most veteran politicians.

The issue of religion that has come to the forefront after the resounding victory of AKP in national and local elections has been one of the key political issues in modern Turkish history. Since the National Security Council decision of 28

February 1997, which resulted in Erbakan's resignation and then the closure of RP, there has been a renewed interest in the way in which secularism is defined and defended in Turkey. Also debated in this context is whether the secularist principles of the republic are too rigidly enforced so as to leave little room for the freedom of religious expression. Since September 11, Islam itself has become a focus of attention globally, with debates resulting in complex and often contradictory interpretations about the role of Islam in the Turkish polity and society. Some observers, both Turkish and foreign, have been arguing that a secular Turkey, as a strong member of the Western alliance, would be bulwark against the spread of fundamentalism and terrorist activities associated with it. Others saw the military as the sole guardians of what they perceived to be a radical form of secularism and, because they associated the military with Turkey's secular principles, they concluded that these principles were enforced in a repressive fashion. Some key facts were eclipsed by the ensuing controversial debates about religion in Turkey.

More recently the debates about Islam in Turkey have been generating greater controversy in the Western capitals than in Turkey itself. On one hand Turkey is hailed as a striking example of a democratic Muslim country whose membership of the EU would serve to absolve the European entity from accusations of being a Christian club. A democratic country with a 99 per cent Muslim population at the same time, it is further argued, particularly in Washington and London, it provides an example to show how the rest of the Muslim world could modernise itself. Devoid of any understanding of Turkey's history (and its relations with the Arab Middle East), this argument is not a convincing one either to most Turks or to Turkish specialists, who nevertheless do not virulently challenge it because it reinforces arguments in support of Turkey's EU membership.

On the other hand, a significant proportion of EU leaders and citizens (a majority in some countries) do not believe either Muslims in general, or Turks in particular, could be ever be secular in the post-enlightenment European sense of the word and they believe that EU membership of Turkey would expose European society to an even greater danger of radical Islam. In the face of visible Islam (Muslim women and men dressed in strange-looking garments who keep close to their own communities and who show no interest in making any effort to integrate into society in their host country's society), public opinion in many Western European countries finds it hard to imagine the prototypical Turk participating in the process of 'ever closer integration of the European peoples'. However, the optic through which Turkey is viewed (whether it is the historic image of the terrible Turk or the current one of the Muslim alien who resists European socialisation), has continued to obstruct familiarity, even among informed circles in Europe, with Turkish politics and society.

As a result, the question of religion tends to lead to zero-sum type of arguments in that secularism forced by the state would not be consistent with the Copenhagen political criteria, while continued adherence to the normative codes of Islamic society would be inconsistent with individual freedoms, the cornerstone of liberal democracy on which the very political criteria of Copenhagen were based in the first place. In Europe and the United States, there are, moreover, diametrically opposite views concerning the extent of interference in religious expression in Turkey. In pious America, the Turkish ban on women's headscarves in public offices and universities is considered to be a limitation of freedom of expression and continues to be cited as such in the State Department's annual human rights reports. In secular Europe, on the other hand, Islamic headgear on women is increasingly coming to be considered as a separatist-ideological symbol that reflects and reinforces a centrifugal pull from the mainstream, lately a more popular assessment that is closer to the constitutional interpretation of the issue in Turkey. And, in line with Turkish courts those in France and Germany have introduced bans on headscarves in schools. Arguments in favour of women's rights to dress in the way they choose to would seem to pale in the light of evidence from all parts of the Muslim world where the so-called Islamic norms of female attire, once introduced, would result in terminating women's rights to wear anything other than what is sanctioned by the tribe, community, or Islamist political leadership. While the overriding concern, at least in continental Europe, is with Muslim Turkey's capacity to integrate into the EU, the Turkish modernisers overriding concern was the domestication of religion so as to ensure a polity that was compatible with the requirements of contemporary civilisation. The overlap between these concerns, however, is obscured by the received prejudice concerning Turkey's 'otherness'.

In Turkey itself, there have been several paradoxes that characterise each and every one of the significant issues relating to Turkish modernisation, including particularly the role of religion. To begin with, what is called secularism in Turkey is actually a means for the state to control religious education and practice. The Directorate of Religious Affairs that was established following the abolition of the Caliphate in 1924 was made accountable to the prime minister so as to prevent the formation of autonomous religious organisations, which could potentially question or oppose the principles of the modern Republic. Closer in spirit and practice to the anti-clerical laicism of the post-enlightenment France, the Turkish Republic's model of secularism aimed to place the management of religious affairs under state control rather than separating religion from the state. Taken as one of the striking characteristics of the so-called Kemalist political order, the Republican version of secularism came to be viewed as the extension of étatism into the religious life of the nation in the same way as it extended into the arena of exchange in the form of economic dirigisme. Placing religion under the authority of the state was part of the modernist project while excluding all heterodox forms of Islam (such as the Alevi faith) from the purview of the Directorate and closing the religious orders was part of the nation-building project that aimed to establish a uniform definition of the new Turkish citizen.

On closer examination, the two parts of this effort point to diametrically opposite directions. While the nation-building effort strove to make a clean break with the past (the modern Turkish citizen ought to be secularised along with the agency that would look after its religious needs) the control of religious cadres had its roots, ironically, in the very principle on which the Ottoman government was based.[12] In the Ottoman system, the Grand Mufti (Seyh-ül-Islam) was excluded from the Imperial Council (Divan-i Hümayun), the highest executive body under the Sultan presided by the Grand Vizir. The two top judicial officials (Kadiaskers), however, were members of the Imperial Council and were required to take an oath of allegiance to the Sultan who was the source of secular law.

The Ottomans were the only Muslim Empire, which would place the Islamic judiciary under the Council of State, presided over by the Grand Vizir, so as ensure their loyalty to the dynasty rather than to the grand mufti. Also paradoxical, therefore, was the decision of the leaders of the 1980 coup to introduce mandatory religious education to secondary schools. It was possibly without fully realising the import of their decision that the military leaders of 1980 attempted to use religious values as a means of supporting nationalism against separatism and communism, which they viewed as being part of the same threat against the integrity of the state. It was the next generation of military leaders who effectively reversed, on 28 February 1997, what may be called the process of Islamisation that had been inadvertently set in motion by the 1980 coup.

To conclude, Turkish politics from the Özal years to the present witnessed a dynamic tension between continuity and change. In many cases what originally appeared to be a radical departure from the status quo turned out to be merely a difference in the style, not the substance, of politics. Populism and clientelism, for instance, continued to govern the political sphere throughout the 1980s and 1990s. More recently, however, the Turkish political sphere has been showing unmistakable signs of a slow and deliberate, but far-reaching, process of transformation. Four key factors can be said to have set in motion and help reinforce this transformation.

One was Turkey's self-confidence reaffirmed after the arrest of the PKK leader Ocalan. The chain of events that ended up with Ocalan's imprisonment began with Turkey's success in pressuring a reluctant Syria to expel him thereby demonstrating its effectiveness as a regional power. Several European governments were embarrassed for sheltering or giving him safe conduct in the course of his subsequent flight from one city to another seeking political asylum. The fact that he was eventually apprehended in the Greek ambassador's residence in Kenya, however, led to the positive development of the beginning of rapprochement with Greece, which, as a result, changed its policy of blocking Turkey's bid to join the EU, thus opening the way to the Helsinki decision of December 1999, giving Turkey a candidate status. Ocalan's arrest also marked a significant victory in Turkey's war against terrorism (a rare example of a successful campaign by national armed forces in guerilla warfare) which prepared the ground for a gradual softening of official views concerning Kurdish cultural rights.

The second was the total collapse of the economy in 2001, which set in motion the far reaching reforms that were essential for Turkey's progress toward EU membership. The previous collapse of the economy, after the 1994 crisis, had also helped to demonstrate graphically the consequences of populism and corruption.

Third, demographic changes can be said to account for significant corresponding changes in the country's political culture. Of the total population at the turn of the century, more than half had been born after the 1983 transition to democracy; of those eligible to vote in the 2002 elections significantly less than half had been adults to witness the 1980 coup. The new generation of Turks has not been familiar with the kind of violence that had been associated with polarisation along party lines. As a result, political competition, and therefore, a growing culture of debate came to replace the tradition of confrontation. Moreover, the pace of internal migration increased during the war with the PKK leading to a massive population movement not only from east to west but also from the rural areas in the South East into provincial towns. The expansion of urban areas cannot be said to have led, in a short time, to urbane cosmopolitanism in the rapidly growing cities. It did, however, lead to a heightened consciousness of urban services delivery, therefore of the effectiveness and quality of the local government. AKP's resounding victory at the polls, winning even a greater percentage of votes in the 2004 local elections as compared to the preceding national ones, was due to the success of its mayors (most of them, like Erdogan, formerly RP members) in providing far better services and making significant improvements in municipal areas. The newly obtained focus on judging local government on the basis of its performance was a significant step towards the empowerment of the citizen (the tax payer) to demand accountability, hence towards a democratic rather than ideological form of participation.

The fourth, and the central one, is the prospect of membership of the European Union, which helps to reinforce and consolidate political reforms. The effectiveness of the EU's soft power in spreading democratisation, in contradistinction to the way in which the United States chooses power projection to achieve regime change, is a much discussed topic today. In this context a sophisticated observer of Turkish politics has recently posed the question of whether the Turkish accession to the EU will turn out to be a European success story. However, the far reaching reforms in Turkey as well as the realistic consideration, for both sides, of Turkey's EU membership were made possible by the developments described earlier in these concluding paragraphs. Ultimately, it is engagement in a project (a challenging one like the modernising one of establishing the Republic) that accounts for the fundamental changes and points to the staying power of the reforms. It might not be far fetched to imagine the current Europeanisation project, like that of Atatürk, to result in bringing together the political leadership with the statist elites.

Endnotes

1 Henri Barkey, *The State and the Industrialization Crisis in Turkey* (Boulder, CO: Westview Press, 1990), p. 174.

2 Ahmet Evin, 'Demilitarisation and Civilianisation of the Regime,' in Metin Heper and Ahmet Evin, eds., *Politics in the Third Turkish Republic* (Boulder, CO: Westview Press, 1994), pp. 23-40.

3 Nicole and Hugh Pope, *Turkey Unveiled: A History of Modern Turkey* (Woodstock and New York: The Overlook Press, 1998), p. 161.

4 Metin Heper and Aylin Güney, 'The Military and Democracy in the Third Turkish Republic, *Armed Forces and Society* 22 (no. 4: 1996), pp. 619-642.

5 Ergun Özbudun, *Contemporary Turkish Politics* (Boulder, CO: Lynne Rienner, 2000), p. 62.

6 See, for example, Ahmet Evin, 'Demilitarisation and Civilianisation of the Regime,' and Ergun Özbudun, 'Democratization of the Constitutional and Legal Framedwork,' both in Metin Heper and Ahmet Evin, eds., *Politics in the Third Turkish Republic* (Boulder, CO: Westview Press, 1994), pp. 23-48; Metin Heper, 'The Executive in the Third Turkish Republic, *Governance* 3 (1990), pp. 299-319; Ergun Özbudun, 'The Status of the President of the Republic under the Turkish Constitution of 1982,' in Metin Heper and Ahmet Evin, eds., *State, Democracy and the Military: Turkey in the 1980s* (Berlin and New York: Walter de Gruyter, 1988).

7 Metin Heper, *The State Tradition in Turkey* (Walkinton. UK :The Eothen Press, 1985).

8 Serif Mardin, 'Power, Civil Society and Culture in the Ottoman Empire', *Comparative Studies in Society and History* 11 (June 1969), pp. 258-281.

9 The use of the terms 'centre' and 'periphery' are after the definitions put forth by Edward Shils, *Center and Periphery: Essays in Macrosociology* (Chicago: University of Chicago Press, 1975), pp. 3-16.

10 Ahmet Evin, 'Demilitarization and Civilianization of the Regime,' in Metin Heper and Ahmet Evin, eds., *Politics in the Third Turkish Republic* (Boulder, CO: Westview Press, 1994), pp. 23-40.

11 See, for example, Gareth Jenkins, 'Muslim Democrats in Turkey?' *Survival* 45 (no.1: Spring 2003), pp. 45-66.

Appendix I

Election results since 1983
1983 Elections

Parties	Per Cent of Votes	No. of Seats	Per Cent of Seats
ANAP	45.1	212	53.0
HP	30.5	117	29.2
MDP	23.3	71	17.8

1987 Elections

Parties	% of Votes	No. of Seats	% of Seats
ANAP	36.3	292	64.9
SHP	24.8	99	22.0
DYP	19.1	59	13.1
Parties below 10% threshold	19.8		
Parties represented in GNA	80.2	450	100

1991 Elections

Parties	% of Votes	No. of Seats	% of Seats
DYP	27.0	178	39.5
ANAP	24.8	115	25.6
SHP	20.8	88	19.5
RP*	16.9	62	13.8
DSP	10.8	7	1.6
Parties below 10% threshold	0.5		
Parties represented in GNA	99.5	450	100

1995 Elections

Parties	% of Votes	No. of Seats	% of Seats
RP	21.4	158	28.7
ANAP	19.6	132	24.0
DYP	19.2	135	24.5
DSP	14.6	76	13.8
CHP	10.7	49	9.0
Parties below 10% threshold	14.4		
Parties represented in GNA	85.5	550	100

1999 Elections

Parties	% of Votes	No. of Seats	% of Seats
DSP	22.2	136	24.7
MHP	18.0	129	23.5
FP	15.4	111	20.2
ANAP	13.2	86	15.6
DYP	12.0	85	15.5
Independent	0.9	3	0.5
Parties below 10 per cent threshold	8.3		
Parties represented in GNA	81.7	550	100

2002 Elections

Parties	% of Votes	No. of Seats	% of Seats
AKP	34.43	365	66.4
CHP	19.41	177	32.2
Independent	0.96	8	1.4
Parties below 10% threshold	45.20		
Parties represented in GNA	54.80	550	100

Appendix II

Distribution of votes by parties

Parties / Vote %	1983	1987	1991	1995	1999	2002
AKP						34.43
DSP		8.5	10.8	14.6	22.2	1.22
MHP					18.0	8.35
MCP		2.9				
FP					15.4	
RP		7.2	16.9	21.4		
SP			0.4			2.49
ANAP	45.1	36.3	24.0	19.6	13.2	5.11
HP	30.5					
MDP	23.3					
DYP		19.1	27.0	19.2	12.0	9.54
CHP				10.7	8.7	19.41
SHP		24.8	20.8			
HADEP				4.2	4.8	
DEHAP						6.14
MHP				8.2		
BBP					1.5	1.02
GP						7.25
YTP						1.15

Appendix III

List of Political Parties

AKP	Adalet ve Kalkınma Partisi	Justice and Development Party
DSP	Demokratik Sol Parti	Democratic Left Party
MHP	Milliyetçi Hareket Parisi	National Movement Party,
MÇP	Milliyetçi Çalisma Partisi	Nationalist Labour Party
FP	Fazilet Partisi	Virtue Party
RP	Refah Partisi	Welfare Party
SP	Saadet Partisi	Felicity Party
ANAP	Anavatan Partisi	Motherland Party
HP	Halkçi Parti	Populist Party
MDP	Milliyetçi Demokrat Parti	Nationalist Democracy Party
DYP	Dogru Yol Partisi	True Path Party
CHP	Cumhuriyetçi Halk Partisi	Republican People's Party
SHP	Sosyal Demokrat Halkçı Parti	Social Democratic People's Party
HADEP	Halkın Demokrasi Partisi	People's Democracy Party
DEHAP	Demokratik Halkçi Parti	Democratic Peoples Party
MHP	Milliyetçi Hareket Partisi	Nationalist Action Party
BBP	Büyük Birlik Partisi	Grand Union Party
GP	Genç Parti	Young Party
ODP	Özgürlük ve Dayanisma Partisi	Freedom and Solidarity Party
DTP	Demokratik Türkiye Partisi	Democratic Turkey Party
LDP	Liberal Demokrasi Partisi	Liberal Democrat Party
DP	Demokrat Parti	Democratic Party
BP	Baris Partisi	Peace Party
YP	Yeni Parti	New Party
HEP	Halkın Emekçi Partisi	People's Labour Party
IP	Isçi Partisi	Labour Party
IDP	Islahatçı Demokrasi Partisi	Reformist Democracy Party
MP	Millet Partisi	Nation Party
YDH	Yeni Demokrasi Hareketi	New Democracy Movement
YDP	Yeniden Dogus Partisi	Resurrection Party
YTP	Yeni Türkiye Partisi	New Turkey Party
DBP	Demokratik Baris Partisi	Democratic Peace Party
DEPAR	Degisen Türkiye Partisi	Changing Turkey Party
DOGUS	Dogus Partisi	Genesis Party
SIP	Sosyalist Iktidar Partisi	Socialist Power Party*

*Later transformed into

TKP	Türkiye Komünist Partisi	Communist Party of Turkey

Islam, Politics and Democracy in Turkey

David Shankland[1]

Of all Muslim countries, Turkey is known as that which has experimented with secularism, and with democracy, in the most sustained fashion. In detail, the way that this endeavour has unfolded has often appeared extremely complex. Yet, there are some features that, if not exactly constant, do lend the picture more stability than appears at first sight. That Turkey should be a Republic is absolutely accepted: there is no political or mass desire to bring back the Ottoman Empire. That Turkey as a nation should seek to develop economically is also universally welcomed. There are different assumptions of the way consumer society may operate, but there is no generalised suspicion of the development project itself. There also can be no doubt that democracy is permanently established. There have been changes in regulation, crises, new constitutions and coups – all this is well-known – but government by election is regarded ultimately as absolutely the correct way to run a modern society.

Far more contested has been the relationship between government, state and religion. At the outset, the founders of the Republic assumed that it would be possible to introduce a secular system wherein individual faith would be reduced to a personal negotiation between the self and God whilst the organisation and regulation of society would become the domain of human actors. It is to this end that Holy Law, the Seriat, was replaced by European law codes, and the Grand National Assembly formed to represent the will of the nation. The Western orientation of these reforms was mirrored too in the reorganisation of the education system, the introduction of laws governing surname and dress, the adoption of the Western calendar, and of the twenty-four hour clock.

It is sometimes maintained that this series of reforms was in itself anti-religious. In as much as they were aimed against the existing theocratic system, this is indisputably correct. The Republicans were, though, careful to stress that their reforms were not against faith itself, but rather against those who sought to become the mediators between an individual and God. In this they mirrored, or perhaps even were directly influenced by the anti-priestly rhetoric of the French Revolution. Whatever their personal inclinations they certainly made no attempt to declare an atheist regime, and they left the way open for religious activity to develop based on the five pillars (i.e. the expression of faith, prayer, fasting, pilgrimage, and payment of alms), the mosque and the Koran. It is also the case, I think, that the initial reformers assumed that, having established the necessary conditions to assure a modern way of life, secularism would become widely accepted – that even if it might initially be necessary to pass laws guaranteeing secularism, ultimately it would take root permanently.[2]

In practice, those who felt that a secularised Islam would become the established religion have been only partially right. A proportion of the population has indeed been convinced. It is difficult to put any exact figure on this, but it would appear broadly to consist of the longest-established urban dwellers along with those from minority religious faiths, in particular the Alevis, a significant heterodox minority to whom we refer again below. Many professional women, who under the Republic were awarded the franchise and the right to work for the first time, are also amongst secularism's strongest supporters. Geographically, it would certainly not be a mistake to regard the western, Aegean coast as being more supportive of a secular Islam than the more eastern parts of Anatolia. Famously too, the armed forces, in particular the army, regard secularism as an unalterable characteristic of the Turkish Republic.

Nevertheless, as became clear with the introduction of a multi-party system and the first genuinely contested election in 1950, the majority of the population wished for the government and the state to take a much more pro-active interpretation of its religious duties than was first envisaged.[3] While revolutionary calls for the Seriat to be brought back were sharply repressed, the government did respond to this obvious desire by offering far greater support for the training of clergy and the religiously oriented schools that were aimed at producing them. They also permitted foreign exchange to be used for the pilgrimage to Mecca, reopened several important saintly shrines that had been closed and permitted the call to the mosque once again to be in Arabic rather than the Turkish that the early Republicans had insisted upon.

Over the second half of the twentieth century, it turned out that this broadly sympathetic orientation toward orthodox religion, combined with strong pursuit of market-led development, was the favoured position of the majority of the population. This is, even today, what might be regarded the most 'natural' reflection of the mass of Turkish voters, and is represented by such parties as the True Path Party, the Motherland Party, or the Democrat Party. The contrasting more secular, and markedly more leftist (from the economic point of view) orientation that is usually represented by the original and later reincarnations of the Republican People's Party has been unable to win sufficient votes consistently enough to form stable governments.

This basic fact of Turkey's electoral mechanics has had certain profound consequences. While the founding secular reforms have remained substantially in place, there has slowly grown the possibility to pursue a markedly more religious way of life, a development facilitated greatly by gradually expanding government funding for such activities. Channelled often through the Directorate of Religious Affairs, such funding tends to be based on supporting the neighbourhood mosque through providing an imam, upon Koranic schools, on providing funds for religiously-oriented schools, and on subvention for religious publications. From the believers' perspective, such a choice of lifestyle can imply membership of a religious brotherhood, or tarikat, nominally banned but now tolerated. There have emerged also prominent popular movements, such as that based on the works of Said-i Nursi, which seek to reconcile the seeming conflicts between modernity, science and Islam.[4]

In effect, all this has meant that Turkish society, without perhaps being intended explicitly that way at its outset, has become markedly pluralist. In the larger towns and cities at least, those who wish to resort to a less religious way of life have been able to pursue professional lives in similar fashion to those in any other European country. Their recreation and aspirations too have been typical of the Mediterranean nations: centred on good food, dance, music, travel, the occasional glass of wine, beer or rakı, purchasing or building a summer home on the southern coast. The more contemporary emergence of a consumer youth population, one that can be seen reflected in pop culture, or the Eurovision Song Contest held in Istanbul in 2004, is a natural emergence of this established secular orientation. At the same time, however, there can be no doubt as to the commitment to their faith of the broad mass of the population, and there has gradually emerged an affluent middle class who have been markedly more reluctant to make the straightforward distinction between personal piety and public secularism that such an orientation implies.

The rise of Islamist politics

Actively religious, secularist, right, left: all these may be positions adopted within the established canons of the Republic. Many political parties based upon more extremist positions have been founded but then rapidly closed down, whether Islamist, far-right, or revolutionary communist.[5] One figure in particular, however, Necmettin Erbakan, appeared likely to escape this impasse in the 1980s and 1990s. Erbakan is an interesting case study: fluent, even loquacious, he decided to advocate a broad-based appeal to an Islamic way of life, one that would draw in wealthy Islamist supporters and at the same time attract poorer constituents through proposing a new system, the 'just order'. Through his popular speeches, his brilliant rhetoric, and a great deal of hard work, he gradually built up a populist front, known sometimes as the milli görüs, that did indeed succeed in gaining support from diverse quarters.

There are commentators that suggest that Erbakan was permitted certain room to manoeuvre by those in authority, that a public reaffirmation of Islamic ideals was held by them to increase the chances of social peace and decrease the possibility of a sustained move toward communism. Whatever the truth of this, it is the case that Erbakan's third attempt at establishing a major party, the Welfare Party, was not proscribed as firmly as his two previous efforts had been and gradually grew in popularity throughout the late 1980s and 1990s. Their electoral success peaked in 1996, when Erbakan became prime minister in a coalition government. He fell from power soon afterwards, toppled by a combination of elements: some felt that his increasingly aggressive speeches could lead to social unrest, others were worried by his flamboyance. Some too felt that his association with disgraced figures in other political parties did not support his assertion of moral superiority. Above all committed secularists, and the army, were alarmed by his overt calls for sweeping change.[6]

Nearly a decade has now passed since these events unfolded. In retrospect, how can we evaluate his movement? While he is a key figure in Turkish modern history, and he worked untiringly for the reintroduction of Islamic thought and practice, he was also clearly a potentially controversial figure. One problem lay in the rather strong language of his 'Just Order', his text for reform:

'The Slave Order that is part and parcel of the economic system in Turkey did not come about of its own accord. It is a consequence of systematic, planned and deliberate modern colonial initiatives stemming from the imperialist and Zionist forces of this earth. Zionism is a belief, and ideological force whose headquarters are found in America, in the Wall Street Banks of New York. Zionists believe that they are God's true servants; they are convinced that other peoples have been created as their slaves…World imperialism is not just colonising Turkey, but the whole of the Islamic world. The Islamic world's natural resources of all kinds, and above all petrol, are under imperialism's control…'[7]

His comments upon interest rates (which he proposed to ban), industry (which he proposed to bring under total state control) and Turkey's conventional parties, whom he refers to continuously as 'counterfeit', are similarly robust.

Erbakan's forceful approach led many not to take him seriously, maintaining that he was obviously not a competent leader. This, I feel, is a mistake. In fact, the Welfare Party under his leadership organised and regrouped itself extremely efficiently. At a time when Turkey's political organisation was often rather weak, even disorganised, he encouraged the development of electoral and party lists of sympathetic individuals. These helped the party to target their activities effectively. Appealing to those who had fared worse from the transition to modernity, and indeed also to those who were newly forging life for themselves in the city, he stressed very effectively the needless poverty of those who were suffering from hyperinflation, or the corruption of many of those successful in business or government. He also realised very early the importance of local politics: town municipalities in Turkey are directly responsible for a host of urban services even as the communities themselves are growing, developing and changing. Accordingly, mayoral elections tend to be lively affairs in which the electorate are overwhelmingly preoccupied with the establishment and maintenance of their urban infrastructure. The candidate who appears best able to run the town efficiently in sometimes tricky circumstances really often does win. Showing such sensitivity to their local constituents helped Welfare to build up a reputation for grass-roots activism and awareness of their voters' problems, particularly the poorest. This ultimately helped them gain control of both Istanbul and Ankara, the key cities in the modern Republic.

A transitory period

Erbakan finally fell from power in 1997, his resignation precipitated by a meeting of the National Security Council in February that made a number of 'recommendations': amongst them that the religiously-inclined schools (by then catering for perhaps a third of all Turkey's schoolchildren) should be drastically reformed, and that anti-secular activities more generally should be prohibited. In the aftermath of this, the Welfare Party was banned, as was its immediate successor, the Virtue Party. Erbakan was banned from taken part further in politics, and the mayor of Istanbul, a certain Recep Tayyip Erdogan, briefly imprisoned.

At that point, in some ways, there was a feeling that Turkey had drawn back from the brink of a major societal confrontation between the secular and Islamist inclined proportions of the population. This sense of relief was reinforced by the result of the first immediately post-Erbakan general elections. They resulted in a surprisingly stable coalition between the Democratic Socialist Party (nationalist left), the Nationalist Action Party (far-right), and the (by now) smaller Motherland Party (centre right). This meant that the veteran leftist Ecevit became the prime minister, and the figures on the right, Bahçeli and Yılmaz, deputy prime ministers. Whilst this did indeed ensure a diversity of approach, and also presented two fresh parties a chance to be in government, there turned out to be other, major difficulties.

One of the reasons that the previous parties had been skittled out of power was that when Tansu Çiller was prime minister in the 1990s, she had presided over a series of major financial crashes that resulted in a massive devaluation of the lira and stringent government cuts. In order to prevent this reoccurring, and to gain a grip on the very high inflation, Ecevit's government adopted extremely tight control of the money supply, including restrictions on wage compensation to take into account inflation. This meant that civil service salaries, already extremely low, became increasingly inadequate even to maintain a simple standard of life. At the same time, the division of the respective governmental ministries between different parties exacerbated the already prevalent patronage base of Turkish political activity: in other words each party cast a blind eye at the faults of the other as they used the government's money in ways that they felt most beneficial for their supporters' direct needs. In effect, this meant that, in order to maintain support for the government, Ecevit was prepared to overlook a level of political use of government finances that led to an already leaky public purse to become positively punctured. Unable to plug the growing black holes by permitting hyperinflation, and forced increasingly to account for their activities by the IMF, the Turkish banking sector collapsed. The lira devalued catastrophically overnight. America and the World Bank pumped in billions of dollars to avoid a default and a systemic meltdown was just avoided. An electorate, furious with flagrant financial impropriety, which they now associated equally with both the left and the right of the conventional parties, whether larger or small, took its revenge. As soon as elections were called, they turned en masse back to the Islamists, and in 2002, a newly formed party, the 'Justice and Development Party' (Adalet ve Kalkınma Partisi or AKP), swept into power with a crushing majority.

As soon as they were able to resolve the necessary legal complications, the AKP voted Erdogan, the recently imprisoned mayor of Istanbul, their leader. For the first time ever, this meant that Turkey had an elected Islamist prime minister with a rock solid majority, a political platform far more convincing than had ever been achieved by Erbakan. Many wondered whether the army would stage an immediate coup. With such a popular mandate, though, a coup appeared entirely inappropriate and, whatever they felt privately, they held their hand.

The Erdogan government

It is always difficult to write instant history: the government, after all, are still mid-way through their first term in office. There is not the slightest doubt, though, that they have substantially retained the popularity with the electorate that initially brought them to power. There are a number of reasons for this. Indisputably, they were fortunate in inheriting a financial situation that had already developed some discipline under the previous government. This has meant that certain vital conditions: a stable lira, a rising tax income and globally benign interest rates have enabled them to preside over a partial economic recovery.

The government has also been extremely astute in dealing with foreign affairs. At all levels of society, the Turkish electorate are avid followers of the news. They are also attuned to considering Turkey's place in the world. Erdogan's handling of the 2004 Cyprus referendum has been, from this point of view, an absolute triumph. That the northern, Turkish part of the island should accept the United Nations' proposals and the southern, Greek part refuse them has, from the perspective of many in Turkey, placed the nation as a whole irrefutably in a position of the moral high ground. One delighted Ankara civil servant, by no means a supporter of the Islamist movement, said to me in its aftermath: 'The whole world can see that we seek peace, that we are not the ones who have broken the possibility of a settlement'. The government have won similar kudos for its intricate, but ultimately successful withholding of Turkish military support from the intervention in Iraq and, above all, for its clear support of Turkey's membership of the European Union. It would appear then that when the time comes they will go into their re-election campaign with more confidence then any other party: they do not just appear the most popular, but also to many the most competent to govern.

It is possible therefore to see immediately certain crucial differences between the Erbakan and the Erdogan approaches to government. In contrast to the Erbakan government, Erdogan is unequivocally devoted to Turkey's membership of the European Union, a desire that is matched by the majority of the population. He is far less dogmatic than Erbakan, and has pointedly avoided making pronouncements that appear at odds with the established way of running a modern nation's economy. He has no ideological opposition to the West, or to modern technology. He may then be seen as a representative of that moderate tendency within Turkish Islam that has sought to devise ways that religion may be seen compatible with modernity. This has led his party occasionally to be regarded as close to those standard, even familiar centre-right governments that flourished under Menderes, Demirel or Özal. Indeed, it is often pointed out that his government includes many political figures who were prominent under Özal and the Motherland Party.

There are, however, significant differences. Erdogan's party has remained close to its roots in the urban poor. The anthropologist Jenny White, of the University of Boston, has charted brilliantly the way that the AKP public rallies highlight the appalling inequality in Turkey, the direct result of the growing rise in income disparities that have increasingly become a feature of Turkish social life.[8] In turn, the rhetoric of unity that they promote through such public display relies greatly on their use of religious symbolism and they appear to be serious in their pursuit of a greater role for Islam in Turkey's public life. For instance, there is at the time of writing (Summer 2004) sustained governmental pressure on the Higher Education Council, a foundation set up in the aftermath of the 1980 coup that is charged with regulating and protecting the universities. Through a law that is passing through the Assembly, the government wishes to legislate explicitly to change the way that the Higher Education Council permits entry to the university system so as to allow those who have graduated from technical high schools to gain unfettered access to the university system. This sounds a fairly neutral, bureaucratic measure: it is not. The vast percentage of graduates from 'technical' schools are from Imam-hatip schools, that is religiously oriented institutions originally founded to teach mosque prayer leaders but which now cater for a significant proportion of all high school graduates. Whatever view is taken on the bill (and this depends on whether one talks with the secularists or their opponents), the measure is not a neutral one, and opening up this pious route to university would have a profound effect on the shape of Turkish Higher Education.

The AKP can also be extremely tough. It is entirely normal for parties when they come to power in Turkey to replace civil servants within the bureaucracy with their own figures, even those at a very low level in the hierarchy. Here, though, the AKP have been cleaning out the previous staff and reinserting their own supporters with a systematic determination which is quite remarkable even by these norms, even forcing through legislation that has made many older civil servants take early retirement thus increasing the number of openings.

Nevertheless there remain sharp differences between them and their Islamist predecessors. It is widely held that the AKP have taken care to avoid direct rhetorical clashes in a way that would have been quite inconceivable for a Welfare party government. In part, at least, this restraint appears to be due to Erdogan himself, who has consistently emphasised the democratic and modernist orientation of his administration. We have already noted the eagerness to become part of the European Union. This orientation is reflected too in economic affairs. For instance, in a speech to businessmen in London on 28 May 2004, Erdogan emphasised his government's commitment to the free market and stressed the openness of Turkey to foreign investment. He also noted that inflation this year will probably be under his government's target of twelve per cent. This is, given Turkey's recent history of hyperinflation, a genuine triumph.

More generally, the genuine social disquiet that accompanied the Erbakan-led Islamist expansion has not reappeared publicly. For instance, during the Welfare Party's rise in the 1990s, a riot in the centre of Sivas, a town in central eastern Anatolia, headed by what can only be described as extremist agitators led to the deaths by burning of many delegates, whom they regarded as atheists and unbelievers, at a folklore congress. In retrospect, it appears clear that these events were precipitated by a number of factors coinciding: by an intolerance of scepticism toward religion by the mass within the town; by resurgent brotherhood organisations being permitted to operate freely; by the Welfare Party being in power of the town municipality and by an administration reluctant to act to prevent the civil demonstration growing out of control. This meant that religious rioting was able to take over the centre of the city without any other active part of its government being able to impede them. We may contrast this to Erdogan's vastly more sympathetic reaction to the outrages in 2003 in Istanbul, when the HSBC banks buildings and the British Consulate were bombed. Then, he spoke out directly and convincingly against fanaticism. Many felt that he took enormous pains to distance himself from fundamentalism, and were reassured that he did so.

A further example may be found in the field of heritage and culture. There are extremely diverse and unique archaeological remains through Anatolia, dug both by many European countries, and by Turkish archaeologists. These remains derive from many different periods and may have significant political significance. Atatürk envisaged the multi-cultural nature of Anatolia's past as a way of emphasising its non-Muslim, Turkish roots, and this presumption remains an important part of Republican consciousness today. Reacting to this, when Welfare were in power, there was an explicit attempt to impede the study of pre-Islamic archaeology, even an insistence that, for example, permits would only be given for the non-Islamic research if an Islamic monument would be surveyed or studied at the same time. There were also calls from within the Welfare Party for the Byzantine remains of Istanbul to be destroyed to make way for a ring-road around the city.

The AKP has conspicuously avoided such ideological pronouncements, and has been explicitly supportive toward foreign excavations. They have been, as noted, tough: they held up various permits on taking power, and have refused to reissue others. They also have withdrawn some of the government cross-funding for local projects (for example, State Water Works support for rescue excavation in the south-east). They have also combined the Ministry of Culture (which is responsible for 'Western' type activities such as music, dance, museums, theatre as well as excavation) with the Ministry of Tourism. However, each of these activities can be explained through pragmatism rather than prejudice: it is usual for a new government to wish to peruse and control financial disembursements that have taken place during the previous regime. It may be an entirely sensible move to reduce the number of ministries and concentrate on the foreign exchange revenue that heritage tourism may bring. In other words, it appears that the full force of government and bureaucracy are not brought together under a unified ideological umbrella that would intensify or provoke. Taking things point by point as Erdogan appears to do, separates issues, and to some extent defuses them.

Challenges and reform

Erdogan then, has been both sensitive and successful. Nevertheless, religion is an exceptionally complex subject in Turkey, and there is no reason to suppose that in the future the challenges that it poses to any government will be straightforward. Simplifying enormously, it may be suggested that the essence of the problem that Erdogan faces is this. Western Europe is founded upon liberal views. Even though on occasion in various countries within the European Union (at present notably in the United Kingdom) it may appear that these values no longer obtain, in the long term it is extremely unlikely that a commitment to choice within matters of faith, or the right to be sceptical will be quickly dismissed. Memories of religious wars, seemingly eclipsed by the Second World War, are in fact only just beneath the surface of Europe's collective consciousness. To put it another way: any movement away from religious tolerance between groups would be treated as a matter of exceptional seriousness in almost all of the member countries. Politically too, Western Europe is constitutionally based upon secularism. It is certainly the case that the way this secularism has evolved differs slightly in each country, but the practical fact remains that there is consensus that the rules that govern society are made by men, not God.

Herein lies perhaps the greatest of the opportunities, and indeed the challenges that Erdogan has at his feet. Given the space for far greater freedom of conscience within religious matters both from the secular and the orthodox points of view that has emerged organically within the Republic, it will be possible for both the pious and those who simply have chosen not to believe to live alongside one another so long as the present balance is maintained. Erdogan has also consistently called for greater freedom of Christian worship within Turkey, something that in spite of its secular constitution has been notably difficult under the Republic.

There is though, a further question that is nowhere near resolved, and that is how the government and the state may deal with the minority religious group known as the Alevis. The Alevis comprise a sizeable proportion of the Republic's population – it is not clear exactly how great for the census does not ask after detailed religious affiliation. Nevertheless, one may suppose that there are between ten and fifteen million Alevis in Turkey today. Both Kurdish and Turkish in terms of ethnic background, they are from the religious point of view markedly heterodox. They emphasise Ali within their ritual obeisance, and are markedly mystical in their interpretation of Islam's creed.

In the past, this difference of religious approach has often led the Alevis to be persecuted. The situation is further complicated in that whereas only a proportion of the Sunni population were persuaded by the Republic secular reforms, the vast majority of the Alevi population support them strongly. In part this is because they appear to offer the possibility of full citizenship without discrimination by religion. In part though, the way that the Alevi understanding of religion has adopted and changed parallels the Republican reformulation of Islam. In other words, they have been prepared to internalise their faith, to regard religion as primarily a question of private moral values, and are not at all interested in reorganising society along the lines of a religious model.[9] The Alevis, naturally, just as any other religious group, may hold widely differing views. Nevertheless, the evident public reaffirmation of orthodox Islam means that they are vulnerable twice over: First because from the strictly orthodox point of view they are literally unbelievers and heretics. Secondly, because they support a secular Republic within a public political climate that is increasingly against it.

While this has all sorts of obvious ramifications in terms of the way different social groups may be accommodated into the changing face of modern Turkey, in recent months one development in particular has brought this question to a head. This is the extent to which the Alevis themselves are represented within a state institution known as the Directorate of Religious Affairs. This Directorate exists to channel support for religion, and does so at present through printing religious texts, providing mosque prayer leaders, organising religious meetings, providing religious interpretations (fetwas) and so on. It is a large body, one that has had a budget greater than the Ministry of the Interior, and has many tens of thousands of employees.

The Directorate is funded directly from the public purse. However, at present it only provides for one single interpretation of religion, that is Orthodox Sunnism. Their justification of this is that there are many sub-variations of religious interpretation and it is incumbent upon them to recognise no one group more than any other. The Alevis, however, feel that they are forced into a position of funding a religious position that is directly against their own faith. This issue, which has simmered for many years, is likely to become a lively cause of controversy over the coming years as civil society groups representing the Alevis prepare a legal challenge to the state, demanding that their taxes are not be forcibly used in this way without a degree of representation.

One potentially workable solution to this awkward situation might be to institute a flexible 'faith tax' as in Germany, where those who wish for any reason may opt out. It might also be possible to diversify the purposes to which the funds of the Directorate of Religious Affairs are put, though this is in practice likely to be extremely difficult to implement. Erdogan's dilemma is acute in that he can only accommodate the Alevis without major social conflict if he can do two things at once. He will have to permit the expression of scepticism – as indeed is permitted in principle in any European country – and also admit the possibility that there may be more than one way of interpreting religious faith: that no group has the absolute secret of the true way to God. This is an enormous challenge. Should he succeed, he would have shown himself to be a very great prime minister indeed.

Conclusion

In sum then, it would appear that the Erdogan government has succeeded in treating issues on their merits, have been populist yet pursued their own policies without resorting to an overall rhetoric that might destabilise an already tense situation. Nevertheless, there is no doubt that there are irredentist strains that could lead to internal conflict in the future, even civil violence. Whether Turkey will avoid this outcome will indisputably depend on the skill of this and future governments. However, it will depend too on how Europe treats this issue. Increasingly, in order to resolve the political questions surrounding faith, it may be that we will have to revisit our own history, to a time when religious conflict was prevalent and study not just the tragedy of such conflict but also how the solutions were found. Erdogan and his party proclaim that they are open to all ideas, that they are listening, and listening hard. It would be an appalling waste of an opportunity were the West, and the European Union, not to heed this message. Tragedy is not inevitable, and accepting the AKP's overture for closer and constructive dialogue with Europe is perhaps the single most effective way that it may be avoided.

Endnotes

1 The research in Turkey presented here has been sponsored over a number of years by the UK Economic and Social Research Council, to whom I am extremely grateful.

2 For standard works on the early Republic and the secular reforms, see Balfour, J. (Lord Kinross) *Atatürk*, (London: Weidenfeld and Nicholson, 1964); Lewis, B, *The Emergence of Modern Turkey*, (London: Royal Institute of International Affairs, 1961); Lewis, G. *Turkey*, (London: Benn, 1965) and Mango, A. *Atatürk* (London; John Murray).

3 The argument contained in these pages may be found in more detail in Shankland, D. 1989 *Islam and Society in Turkey*, (Huntington; Eothen Press).

4 On Said-i Nursi, see in particular Mardin, S. *Religion and Social Change in Modern Turkey, the case of Bediuzzaman Said Nursi*, (New York; State University of New York, 1989).

5 On politics and religion in the early Republic, see Rustow, D. 'Politics and Islam in Turkey, 1920-1955' in Frye, R. *Islam and the West*, (Gravenhage: Mouton & Co., 1957).

6 This period of Turkish politics is described in Shankland (1989; Chapters Five and Six).

7 Quoted in Shankland (1999 *op cit*; 209-214).

8 White, J. *The Islamist mobilisation in Turkey: a study in vernacular politics*, (Seattle: University of Washington Press, 2002).

9 This issue is treated in more detail in Shankland, D. *The Alevis in Turkey: the emergence of a secular Islamic tradition*, (London: Routledge Curzon, 2003).

The Turkish Economy before the EU Accession Talks

Nihat Bülent Gültekin and Kamil Yilmaz

Introduction

This chapter is a critical assessment of the Turkish economy. We point out policy mistakes and problems rather than only praising the accomplishments. We should therefore remind the reader that Turkey has been on a steady path to modernise her economy since the foundation of the Republic in 1923. If economic performance is judged by growth rate alone, Turkey's record has not been as impressive as East Asian tigers. There have been policy mistakes, errors in the economic development strategies, chronic macro imbalances, and domestic political problems, but Turkey maintained her resolve to build a democratic society and a market economy in a region that has been in continuous turbulence.

It is our conviction that Turkey has the maturity, potential, and experience to build a fast growing modern economy after 80 years of solid and stable progress toward modernity. It is telling that Turkey's economic relations with the EU Customs Union so far demonstrates the resilience and adaptability of Turkish manufacturing industries to rapidly changing conditions during a period with almost no net foreign direct investment.

We see eventual EU membership as a further catalyst for change and reforms to build a modern economy for Turkey that has been the goal of the founding fathers of the Republic. The accession talks with EU that will commence in October 2005 would provide an external anchor and the motivation to accelerate the progress of Turkey into a political and economic success in the region within a decade. With this eventual transformation, the current debate within the EU about the economic costs of Turkish membership will lose its meaning.

An Overall View of the Turkish Economy

Turkey had the 17th largest economy in the world in 2003 with a $477 billion gross domestic product measured in purchasing power parity. In terms of the size of the economy, Turkey ranks as the seventh among the European countries, after Germany, France, the UK, Italy, Spain and the Netherlands. The Turkish GDP is larger than that of many EU member countries because of its second largest population with 70 million people in Europe after Germany. Istanbul alone, with a population of around eight million people, has an economy larger than that of several EU member states. However, with its 2003 GDP per capita at $6,750, Turkey is a low-income country like Romania and Bulgaria among the current and future EU members.

The regional distribution of production and employment opportunities are skewed towards the western regions of the country and especially to the Marmara region that includes Istanbul. Approximately 40 per cent of the total GDP is produced in the Marmara region. As the region has attracted continuous flows of migration over time, the region's unemployment rate, which fluctuates between 12 and 15 per cent, is higher than the country's average unemployment rate of 10.6 per cent.

As in many other developing countries, the structure of the economy has changed substantially since the early 1980s (Table 1). While agriculture used to account for 17 per cent of GDP in the late 1980s, since then its share declined down to an average of 12.4 per cent over the last four years. Whereas industry continued to contribute approximately a quarter of the total production, service sectors have expanded from 56.2 per cent in the 1987-1989 period to 63 per cent over the last four years.

Table 1. Sector Shares in GDP

	1987-89	1990-94	1995-99	2000-03
Agriculture	17.2	15.7	16.0	12.4
Industry	26.6	25.6	24.6	24.7
Services	56.2	58.7	59.5	62.9

Source: State Institue of Statistics

Manufacturing industry accounts for approximately 20 per cent of Turkish GDP and 17 per cent of employment. After the trade liberalisation reforms of the 1980s, Turkey's main export sectors have been clothing and textiles, iron and steel, and food processing. Turkey moved up in the export ladder and by the end of 1990s and most notably after the 2001 economic crisis, there was a sharp increase in the exports of the automotive, the electrical machinery and equipment (electronics) sectors. In 2003 the automotive sector became the second major exporter after clothing and textiles, reaching a total of $7.2 billion.

In terms of value added in 2000, chemical, petroleum and plastic products, with a share of 27 per cent, lead the manufacturing industry followed by clothing and textiles (17 per cent), food, beverages and tobacco (16 per cent), fabricated metal products (8 per cent), motor vehicles and other transport (8 per cent) and basic metal products (6 per cent). In terms of employment, clothing and textiles lead the manufacturing industry with a share of 37 per cent in 2000, followed by food, beverages and tobacco (16 per cent), fabricated metal products (9 per cent), chemical petroleum and plastic products (8 per cent), basic metal (6 per cent), motor vehicles and other transport (6 per cent).

Among the service sectors, domestic retail and wholesale trade, and transportation and communication services each account for 15-16 per cent of GDP. Smaller in size, tourism and finance are likely to make significant contributions to the growth performance of Turkey in the near future. Tourism is a growth industry, but has yet to reach its full potential. Asia Minor, origin and home of major civilisations in history starting with the Neolithic Revolution, has many spectacular natural and historical sights. The tourism sector is dominated by small-scale operations and mostly attracts low budget tourists. In 2003, the average amount spent by foreign visitors was only $700 per person. Despite this Turkey managed to attract 13.7 million foreign tourists and generate $9.7 billion revenue in 2003.[1] Given its linkages with manufacturing and construction sectors and its employment generating potential, tourism will continue to be one of the key sectors for Turkey in the foreseeable future.

The financial sector, another important service sector, has grown substantially since the financial liberalisation that started in earnest in the mid-1980s. Operating in a chronic and high inflation environment for over a quarter of century the Turkish banking sector has invested substantial amounts in new technology. Even though the economic crisis of 2001 was very costly to the banking system, the sector has been recovering rapidly and its potential for future growth has improved after the banking reforms in 2001 and 2002. The sector has attracted the attention of European banks as possible targets of acquisition. With the success of the current disinflation programme one would expect that insurance, long-term credit, and stock markets would further deepen.

While the contribution of agriculture to overall GDP has been declining over the last two decades, one of the critical challenges for the Turkish economy in the next decade will be to transform the agriculture sector into a viable one. The issue is the size of the rural population and employment in agriculture. Agriculture currently provides approximately 37 per cent of employment, and 45 per cent of the population live in rural areas. For a long time the agricultural sector received government support through a myriad of price support systems and subsidised loans from the public sector banks. This support system mostly helped relatively rich farmers. Direct income support programmes, however, are not well established and effectively implemented.

Small and medium-sized, mostly family-owned firms dominate the Turkish private sector. Eighty per cent of the plants in the manufacturing sector have fewer than 100 employees, yet, they account for only 28 per cent of the total production. Large plants with more than 500 employees account for only 3.4 per cent of total employment, but approximately 40 per cent of total production.

Large enterprises are modern organisations with extremely competent management and a highly motivated labour force. They are no different from their peers in any industrialised country. The work ethic is high. Turkey compares favourably with European countries in terms of the availability of a skilled, flexible and business-oriented labour force. IMD's surveys reported in annual Competitiveness Yearbooks show that Turkey's workforce is significantly more flexible, adaptable and entrepreneurial compared with 12 accession countries.

Macroeconomic Policies and the Consequences

Turkey entered the twenty-first century with a stabilisation programme with the IMF after one of the worst balance of payments and banking crises in the history of the modern republic. The crisis was not an accident, but rather a culmination of misguided and populist economic policies followed by successive governments. The economic history of Turkey since 1950 has been a story of chronic macroeconomic imbalances and periodic balance of payment crises with steadily rising inflation. Nearly every decade ended with a major stand-by agreement with the IMF. The average consumer price inflation rate throughout the last 25 years was 63 per cent, widely fluctuating within a band of 20-140 per cent.

Table 2. Macro Economic Indicators

	1995	1996	1997	1998	1999	2000	2001	2002	2003
Per cent of GNP									
Public Sector Borrowing Requirement	5.0	8.6	7.7	9.4	15.6	12.5	15.9	8.0	- - -
Primary Surplus	2.1	1.3	0.0	2.1	-1.9	3.8	6.5	4.6	5.2
Interest Expenditure (Consol. Budget)	7.4	10.0	7.7	11.5	13.7	16.3	22.2	18.8	16.4
Public Sector Debt Stock	37.6	40.3	40.5	41.3	51.8	53.4	97.8	88.8	79.2
Domestic	14.6	18.5	20.2	21.7	29.3	29.0	66.3	54.8	54.4
External	23.0	21.8	20.3	19.6	22.5	24.4	31.5	33.9	24.8
Per cent per annum									
Interest Rate on Bond and T-bills [1]	124.2	132.2	107.4	115.5	104.6	38.2	99.6	62.7	46.0
Inflation (CPI, end of year)	76.0	79.8	99.1	69.7	68.8	39.0	68.5	29.7	18.4
Inflation (CPI, annual ave)	89.0	80.2	86.0	84.7	65.0	54.6	54.4	45.0	25.3
Ex-post Real Interest Rate (CPI-based) [2]	24.4	25.0	12.4	30.7	32.1	10.5	36.0	29.8	27
GNP Growth	8.0	7.1	8.3	3.9	-6.1	6.3	-8.5	7.8	5.9
Real Exchange Rate [3] (CPI based)	100	102.7	109.4	118.5	123.1	136.5	112.5	125.3	136.5
Real Exchange Rate [3] (WPI based)	100	101.2	107	110.1	107.4	114.3	98.3	116.5	126.8
Average Maturity of Borrowings [4]	188	186.6	394	235	502	427	146	201	273

Sources: Turkish Treasury, State Institute of Statistics, and Central Bank of Turkey.

Notes: 1. Net sales value weighted average of the average interest rates of auctions

Ex-post real interest rate is defined as: $(1+i_t)/(1+p_{t+1})-1$. The average interest rate for the t-bills and bonds sold in auctions conducted in 2002 was 45 per cent. As the returns are expected to be realised one year later annual inflation rate at maturity is used to obtain real interest rate.

RER is average of the monthly REER published by the CB.

Net sales value weighted average of the maturity.

Throughout this period, like many developing countries, Turkey followed an inward-looking, import-substituting development strategy. On 24 January 1980, a date generally considered as the beginning of a new economic era, a comprehensive IMF-backed stabilisation programme was launched following a major currency crisis. The immediate objective of the programme was to stabilise the economy by improving the balance of payments and containing inflation. The long-term goal, however, was much more ambitious: to change the structure of the economy funamentally. The first objective was to remove the dominance of the state in key inustries and in banking. The second was to remove the role of the state in pricing and resource allocation processes. Export oriented growth became the key polcy goal. Export oriented policies were later coupled with a gradual liberalisation that started in 1984, and finally culminated in the Customs Union with the EU in 1996.

Since then, much has been achieved. Despite some periodic setbacks and policy mistakes, liberalisation policies changed the structure of the economy. Exports grew from less than US $2.9 billion in 1980 to US $10 billion in 1987 and to more than US $60 billion by the end of 2004. By 1989, Turkey had a liberalised and open economy dominated by a vibrant private sector.

While Turkey successfully liberalised its foreign trade regime, removed price ceilings on goods and services and other distortions in product markets, and deregulated its financial sector long before many Latin American and East European countries, she was not able to attain macroeconomic stability.

Inflation varied widely: from 100 per cent in 1980 it declined to 34.6 per cent in 1986; it increased over time and reached 140 per cent during the economic crisis of 1994. As can be seen in Figure 1, output growth has also been volatile with periods of rapid growth followed by sharp contractions. As the Turkish lira

Figure 1. GDP Growth Rates (1980-2003, per cent per annum)

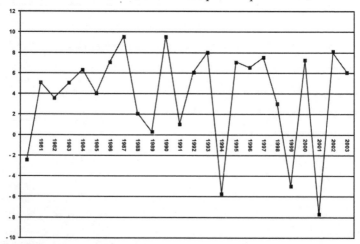

Source: State Planning Organization

lost importance as a store of value, foreign exchange deposits became increasingly important, at times representing almost 50 per cent more than the domestic money supply measure M2 (during the 1994 economic crisis and after 11 September 2001).

The reason for the volatile macroeconomic environment and the high inflation has been the inability of successive governments to deal with the underlying causes of poor public finances. During the 1980s the government's reform efforts focused on external adjustment. The internal fiscal adjustment that was necessary to reduce inflation permanently was never achieved nor seriously attempted. Despite early fiscal successes following a stabilisation programme, public sector deficits soon resumed their cyclical climb. Fiscal dynamics drove monetary and exchange rate policy-mix and set the key parameters for the evolution of the economy and the functioning of financial markets.

The capital account was untimely opened in 1989 at an inappropriate time under unstable macro-economic conditions. Under the open capital account, the Central Bank adopted a managed exchange rate policy to control inflation. When there is no adjustment of fiscal balances, a managed float can be instrumental in keeping the inflation under control only for a while. Eventually, a pegged exchange policy is doomed to fail. Appreciating domestic currency increases the vulnerability of the economy to external shocks and domestic policy mistakes. This process explains the crises of 1994 and 2001 in Turkey.

The economic crisis of 1994 did not alter the course of the fiscal policies. Foreign investors are willing to finance fiscal deficits so long as the Treasury is willing to offer higher and higher yields. In the mean time, a new source of financing was found through the state-owned banks. In a non-transparent and politically regulated banking system, state banks financed the treasury through short term loans. As long as short-term capital inflows continued, the system worked well. Toward the end of the decade, fiscal imbalances turned into stark debt dynamics (see Table 2). The public sector borrowing requirement increased from five per cent of GNP in 1995 to as high as 15.6 per cent in 1999 and the ex-post real interest rates on bonds and t-bills were above 20 per cent, reaching as high as 36 per cent (see Table 2).

After the Russian debt crisis of 1998, external funds began to slow down. As a response, an IMF disinflation programme was initiated at the end of 1999, but it collapsed a year later as much because of the conceptual errors of its design as because of the policy mistakes of the governing coalition at the time.

In February 2001 Turkey experienced the worst economic crisis in its history with a near meltdown in financial markets that eventually led to a drop in GNP by 8.5 per cent in 2001. A short period of turmoil in financial markets took a severe toll on public finances. Government debt increased substantially by 40 per cent of GDP. A new IMF sponsored programme was eventually set in place to address the two bottlenecks of the economy: namely, the government budget deficit and the ensuing government debt, and to rescue the banking system.

After three years of austerity measures, the public sector debt has been brought down from its peak of 98 per cent of GDP at the end of 2001 of GDP to 79 per cent at the end of 2003. Moreover, the banking system seems to be showing signs of recovery after and injection of $40 billion dollars to recapitalise banks in the private and the state sector.

Customs Union and the Integration of the Turkish Economy with the EU

Experience of the Turkish economy after joining the Customs Union (CU) provides insights for its future performance as it integrates with the EU economies. The Turkish economy traditionally had strong trade relations with European markets. Between 1999 and 2003, trade with the current members of the EU and EFTA accounted for 53 per cent of Turkey's exports and 51 per cent of imports. When we include trade with the new EU and remaining candidate countries the share of Europe in total Turkish trade rises to 59 per cent and 55 per cent in exports and imports, respectively.

The overall impact of CU on the Turkish economy has been positive, but less than its full potential. First, there was a small decline in import tax revenues as Turkey lowered tariffs on imports from the EU.[2] Import tariff revenues fell from 2.8 per cent of total tax revenues in 1995 to a one per cent average over the three years 2000-2002. The decline in tax revenues, however, is too small to contribute to the large budget deficits that were the major reason for the most recent economic crisis.

Increased competition in the form of higher imports from the EU forced productivity increases in manufacturing sectors. Sectors such as the automotive, durable home appliances, electrical machinery and equipment had continued to receive protection behind high tariff barriers despite the import liberalisation process that started a decade ago. Total factor productivity (TFP) in the manufacturing industry as a whole had grown by 2.3 per cent per annum during the five years prior to CU (1991-95). In the period from 1996 to 2000 the TFP growth rate increased to 3.2 per cent per annum.[3] Compared to other sectors, productivity growth was higher in import-competing sectors in both periods.

The CU agreement with the EU did not have much impact on Turkish exports in the first five years since the EU had already removed tariffs on imports from Turkey long before the CU went into effect. In addition the EU continued to reserve the right to impose anti-dumping duties on Turkish exports to EU as well as keeping the technical regulation barriers. It is therefore not surprising that Turkish exports did not surge to the EU countries immediately after the CU.

The CU's impact on Turkish exports came with a long delay in a rather subtle way. Deep depreciation of the Lira and the contraction in domestic demand that followed the economic crisis of February 2001 forced domestic producers to search for export markets. As expected, the export volume index increased by 21 per cent in 2001. Exports continued to grow even after the Turkish economy resumed growth in 2002 and 2003 at a rate higher than the period prior to the crisis. The increase in export volume was 18 per cent in 2002 and 22 per cent in 2003.

Better-than-expected export performance in 2002 and 2003 was achieved despite a 25 per cent real appreciation, and even nominal appreciation, of the Turkish Lira during this period. This impressive export performance is in part due to the newly acquired competitiveness of the Turkish manufacturing industries that was forced upon them by the increased competition after Turkey joined the CU.

In a recent paper, Lejour, Mooij and Capel (2004) argue that the economic costs of Turkey's accession to the EU are virtually impossible to assess. It is currently not known under what conditions Turkey will accede. They estimate that the accession of Turkey to the EU will bring economic benefits for Turkey, without exerting a big effect on the EU members. The largest economic gains are likely to be realised through institutional reforms that will increase transparency and thus improve the functioning of the economy as a whole, rather than direct transfers from the EU.

Table 3: Export Volume Index and Growth Rate

	1994	1995	1996	1997	1998	1999	2000	2001	2002	2003
Export Volume	100	107.7	117.1	136.3	151.0	156.3	179.1	217.3	256.7	313.3
Real Growth Rate(%)	- - -	7.7	8.7	16.4	10.8	3.5	14.6	21.3	18.1	22.1
Exports (bil. US$)	18.1	21.6	23.2	26.3	27.0	26.6	27.8	31.3	36.1	46.9
Share EU27+EFTA(%)	54.1	58.6	56.4	53.6	57.1	60.3	58.4	57.6	58.3	- - -
Imports (bil US$)	23.3	35.7	43.6	48.6	45.9	40.7	54.5	41.4	51.6	68.7
Share EU27+EFTA(%)	52.5	53.0	58.3	56.5	57.6	57.7	54.4	51.4	54.7	- - -

Source: State Institute of Statistics and Comtrade Database of the United Nations.

The major disappointment with the CU has been the lack of any change in foreign direct investment (FDI) flows to Turkey. The Turkish side expected FDI flows (especially from Europe) to increase substantially following the full integration of manufacturing goods markets with the EU upon signing the CU agreement. Turkey hoped that multinational companies would take advantage of her geographical location, low-cost yet highly skilled and disciplined labour, and long experience with a market economy.

In the aftermath of the CU agreement, between 1997 and 2000 Turkey received only $875 million per year in FDI flows. In contrast, the Czech Republic, Hungary and Poland who had started the accession talks with the EU in 1997 had received 4.1, 2.0 and 7.0 billion US$ per year in FDI flows. In terms of FDI per capita, the situation looks even worse. In 2000 Turkey attracted $15 of FDI per capita. The same year Poland attracted $105, Romania $50, Brazil $96, Algeria $32, and Ireland $4,750.

It is also interesting to note that whatever small amount Turkey received in FDI flows, only 69 per cent originated from EU countries. In contrast, 79, 80 and 84 per cent of FDI inflows received by Poland, Hungary and Czech Republic during the 1997-2000 period, respectively, originated from EU member countries. As can be seen in Tables A1 and A2 in the Appendix, Turkey has been at par with these three countries in terms of demographics, the business environment, and infrastructure, factors that are crucial for foreign investors.[4]

The track record of the Turkish manufacturing industry in response to the CU has been better than expected, especially when one considers that Turkey received very little financial support from the EU to help ease the adjustment burden. Furthermore, the Turkish economy has been subject to serious economic shocks and natural disasters since then. In 1999 a major earthquake hit the industrial heartland of the country with over 20,000 lives lost. The Turkish economy lived through a banking and a currency crisis and political uncertainties till the November 2002 elections.

But Turkey's economic relations with the CU so far demonstrates dramatically the resilience and adaptability of Turkish manufacturing industries to rapidly changing conditions during a period with almost no net foreign direct investment.

Long Run Demographic Dynamics

The census of population in 2002 estimates Turkey's population at 67.8 million. Behar et. al. (1999) forecasts the population will reach 88 million by 2025 and to stabilise around 95 million by the end of the twenty-first century. The growth rate of population is currently around 1.4 per cent and it is expected to fall gradually to 0.83 around 2020. The fertility rate in Turkey has also fallen sharply over the last two decades to 2.3 children per woman and is predicted to drop to 2.0 in 2010, a figure barely sufficient to maintain the population at its current level.

This rapid demographic change is not a result of population control policies. It is rather a result of couples deciding to have fewer children, reflecting the social and economic development of the country. Turkey completed the demographic transition, that is high fertility and high death rates gave way to a conscious control of birth rate by the population and a decline in the death rate due to rising standards of living. This demographic transition has taken place during the last three decades in Turkey whereas it took place over the course of a century in Europe.

As the population growth slows down, there will be subtle demographic changes. The age composition of the population will change and the process of urbanisation will accelerate. The labour force will increase, family size will decline but the number of households will grow, leading to a larger market for consumer durables and housing despite a stagnating population. Policy makers could now pay more attention to improving the quality of life in urban and large metropolitan areas rather than playing a catch-up game just to provide basic services for a growing population. Furthermore, there is a better chance of improving the quality of education for the young to the level of developed nations.

As the fertility rate falls, the share of the adult population and thus the potential labour force will steadily increase for a while. The rapid growth of the most productive age group of the society is associated with the high economic growth rates experienced in Japan, Taiwan, South Korea, and Singapore since the 1960s, and most recently in China. Turkey is now entering this demographic stage. Turkey could exploit this window of demographic opportunity, which comes only once in a country's history, for faster economic growth provided that she invests in human capital to be competitive in world markets and builds productive capacity to absorb the growing labour force.

Income Distribution

Turkey belongs to a group of countries with extreme inequality of income distribution. The State Institute of Statistics (SIS) conducted two comprehensive income distribution surveys in 1987 and 1994 and a limited one in 2002. A common measure of income distribution inequality is to compare disposable income shares of the households ranked according to the average household incomes (see Table 4).

Table 4: Disposable Income Shares by Households

	First 20%	Second 20%	Third 20%	Fourth 20%	Fifth 20%	Gini Coefficient
1994	4.9	8.6	12.6	19	54.9	0.49
2002	5.3	9.8	14	20.8	50.1	0.44

Source: State Institute of Statistics

In 1994 the poorest 20 per cent of households received only 4.9 per cent of total disposable income, while the richest 20 per cent of households received 54.9 percent. Results are similar for rural and urban populations[5].

The Gini coefficient, a measure of income distribution inequality, was 0.49 in 1994 with a slight improvement to 0.44 in 2002. The Gini coefficient for the best and the worst income distribution inequality among the 12 EU countries is 0.217 for Denmark and 0.345 for Italy respectively for the comparable periods.

In terms of 'market income distribution', that is, the income inequality before state intervention, Turkey is no different from EU countries. When calculated over the income before tax and transfer payments, the Gini coefficient for the European countries varies from 0.42 for Denmark to 0.53 for Italy. In the case of Turkey before tax the Gini coefficient was 0.474 in 1994. The lack of effective tax and transfer policies to alter market distribution is the main reason for Turkey's extremely poor record of after tax income inequality.

Challenges Ahead

With prudent macroeconomic policies in place for the last three years, the Turkish economy shows signs of recovery. Inflation is coming down steadily and the consumer price inflation was finally in single digits in 2004 for the first time in nearly three decades. This impressive disinflation has been achieved without sacrificing growth. In 2003, the economy achieved a growth of rate of 5.8 percent, following a 7.8 per cent growth in 2002. Exports, that grew 20 per cent a year in real terms in 2002 and 2003, continue to grow at a robust rate of 35 per cent (in current US dollars) in the first quarter of 2004.

The Turkish economy has experienced a virtuous cycle for the last three years. But recent macroeconomic successes should not conceal the difficult tasks that lie ahead. The debt overhang is still a major threat for the Turkish economy; it requires fiscal prudence until public sector debt comes down to acceptable levels. The rapid decline in inflation was accomplished by an overvalued Turkish lira and a significant erosion in real wages. It is a challenging task to reach a sustainable growth path while maintaining macro balances. The long-delayed structural and macroeconomic reforms are still necessary for sustainable economic growth.

Lowering inflation and bringing the public sector debt to manageable levels will definitely create the right environment for economic growth and job creation. However, these are necessary conditions but they are not sufficient for a sustained growth performance. After losing a decade with unfinished reforms and economic mismanagement, Turkey is now facing stiffer international competition from the newly emerging economies of India and China. Proximity to European markets is no longer a guarantee for Turkey to increase its market share in Europe.

During the last two decades, per capita GDP growth has been too low to improve the welfare of an average Turkish citizen significantly. As expected, recent surveys show that the main challenge for the Turkish policy makers is job creation. Despite the strong growth performance of the economy during the last two years, the unemployment rate remains high. Per capita growth cannot be sustained in the end unless new jobs are created through more investment and increased value added.

Turkey needs immediate tax reform, not only for higher tax revenue but also for a more equitable distribution of income and wealth to provide the right incentives for economic agents. An informal and unrecorded sector consisting of small firms is a very large part of the economy. While the informal sector may add to the resilience of the Turkish economy in the short run, these small firms do not graduate to become larger and more efficient organisations. The tax burden falls on those in the formal sector or through indirect taxes on the consumers, and thus the tax system becomes very regressive.

One of the most urgent and important tasks for Turkey is to overhaul the education system. Turkey needs to invest in human capital and in education to face the new global competition. Furthermore, reductions and inadequate spending on public education led to the commercialisation of the education system and caused a severe gap in educational opportunities for both the rich and the poor. Policy makers, on the other hand, had been wasting precious time with useless debates on whether girls should wear headscarves at school and on whether graduates of religious schools should attend universities. In order to catch up with the European standards in education, Turkey should start an immediate mobilisation to improve the quality of mass education as she did with the foundation of the Republic. Without those reforms, Turkey's accession to the EU would not have been possible today.

Corruption is a very serious problem in the Turkish economy. While corruption seems to have been on the rise everywhere in the 1990s, and while ethics have never been an issue in international economic relations, the consequences of corruption have been worse in emerging economies where proper traditions and institutions that uphold the rule of law are weak or do not exist. Corruption and disregard for the rule of law in countries that went through the liberalisation process has become endemic, especially when reforms were incomplete and were not backed by proper institutional structure. Eventually, corruption becomes self-sustaining by strengthening those rent-seekers who block further reforms for modernisation and transparency. It is quite surprising that most countries that are so outspoken about basic human rights are so silent on corruption which leads to flagrant violation of the economic rights of individuals and especially of those who are not privileged. Outright corruption and a poor regulatory structure due to indirect corruption through the abuse of power are the main reasons for the high cost of financial sector failure. The cost of bank failures alone was about $40 billion to the Turkish Treasury (the taxpayer) in the last economic crisis. Interlocking relations and vested interests among the business and public sectors, political parties, and the media made corruption so engrained and institutionalised in Turkey that it is almost impossible to undo it without external pressure in the short run.

The political structure in Turkey is another obstacle to structural reform. Party leadership once captured is never given up until the party itself is eliminated like a family owned firm. Leaders maintain positions through patronage and by distributing rents that are captured from being in power. Crony capitalism and the abuse of power once in the office have been the norm. This behaviour has been the reason for the lack of willingness for structural reforms, the source of corruption, and the chronic macroeconomic instability in Turkey. So far no political party has been an exception to this pattern. The only thing that has kept governments in line has been the fear of the inability to roll over the public debt and capital flight, thus a currency crisis. Once that fear is gone and the economy is on the way to recovery, old habits and reflexes emerge again. The current government, despite its rhetoric about reforms, has already demonstrated the same disrespect and mistrust for the newly created independent agencies as its predecessors.

Conclusions

We conclude that Turkey has an economy with significant potential, and it is becoming a modern economy. The country has the experience, resources, an entrepreneurial class and a skilled labour force. Setbacks in the Turkish economy are often due to poor economic management and policy choices. Turkey could reach a sustained economic growth if she adopts a series of structural and macroeconomic policy reforms coupled with political and microeconomic reforms. These reforms require political will more than anything. Because the change in the behaviour of the policy makers is a necessary condition for better economic management and thus better performance, the economy should be run by the rule of law rather than according to political discretion. Moreover, there is a need to build institutions that will make the reforms permanent.

Starting accession talks with the EU in 2005 provides an opportunity and incentive to shift the focus to microeconomic policy measures that are crucial for the viability of the Turkish economy in the end. Eventual EU membership should be a catalyst for change and for further reforms to build a modern economy. The accession talks that will begin in October 2005 will provide an external anchor and the motivation to transform Turkey into an economic success in the region within a decade.

Bibliography

Behar, C., Isık O., Güvenç M., Erder S., and Ercan H., 1999, 'Turkey's Window of Opportunity: Demographic Transition Process and Its Consequences', TUSIAD Publication No-T/99-3-254, Istanbul.

Dutz, M., Us M., and Yılmaz K., forthcoming, 'Turkey's Foreign Direct Investment Challenges: Competition, the Rule of Law, and EU Accession', Togan, Subidey, ed. *Turkey: Towards EU Accession*, Oxford University Press, 2004.

Gürsel, S., Levent H., and Selim R., 2000, 'Individual Income Distribution in Turkey: A Comparison with the European Union', TUSIAD Publication No-T/2000-12/296, Istanbul.

Lejour, A, M, de Mooij, R.A. and Capel, C.H. 2004, 'Assessing the Economic Implications of Turkish Accession to the EU', CPB Netherlands Bureau for Economic Policy Analysis, No 56.

Özler, S. and Yılmaz K., 2003, 'Does Trade Liberalisation Improve Productivity Growth: Plant Level Evidence from Turkish manufacturing Industry,' mimeo.

Togan, S., 1997, 'Opening up the Turkish Economy in the Context of the Customs Union with the EU,' *Journal of Economic Integration*, 12(2), 157-179.

World Competitiveness Yearbook, 2003, IMD – International Institute for Management Development, Lausanne, Switzerland.

Endnotes

1 Once Turkish citizens who reside outside the country are included, the number of total visitors increase to 16.3 million and the total revenue rose to $13.2 billion.

2 Tariffs came down from an unweighted average of 13.5 per cent in 1995 to 3.6 per cent in 1996 (and a median tariff rate of 8.1 per cent in 1995 to 1.2 per cent in 1996) based on sectoral tariff data in Togan (1997).

3 Total factor productivity is the productivity of all factors of production including capital, labour, entrepreneurship etc. It is the residual increase in production that can not be explained by an estimated production function equation. The results are based on preliminary analysis of plant-level data and therefore can be used as indicative rather than finalised productivity calculations. For methodology see Ozler and Yilmaz, 2003.

4 See Dutz, Us and Yilmaz, *forthcoming*, for a more detailed and up to date analysis of the foreign direct investment experience of Turkey.

5 A small improvement is somewhat surprising because Turkey went through two major economic crises and substantial cuts in social programmes as a result. The results might be due to the small sample for the survey in 2002.

Appendix:

Table A1. Infrastructure-related factors - Strengths:

Turkey and Comparable Countries

	Turkey	Poland	Czech Rep.	Hungary
Democracy and business values				
GDP (USD at PPP, 2002)	421	369	154	130
Population - market size (millions)	69.75	38.64	10.27	10.15
Labour force growth (per cent change)	1.93	-0.71	1.47	-0.07
Average number of working hours per year (2002)	2074	1870	2088	1988
Flexibility & adaptability of people (survey)	7.96	4.58	5.53	6.12
Entrepreneurship (survey)	5.96	4.84	5.02	6.59
Availability of competent senior managers (survey)	6.86	5.18	5.07	6.41
Physcial and financial infrastructure				
Internet costs for 20 hours (USD, 2000)	11.4	39.16	42.92	42.61
Adequacy of communications (survey)	6.76	5.26	7.44	6.69
Quality of air transport (survey)	7.02	5.09	7.44	5.41
Efficiency of distribution infrastructure (survey)	5.96	5.29	7.35	5.94
No. of credit cards issued (per capita, 2001)	0.57	0.16	0.23	0.32
Availability of finance skills (survey)	6.94	5.22	5.16	6.00

Note: All measures are from IMD, World Competitiveness Yearbook 2003. The survey measures are all reported on a 0-10 scale, with 10 indicating the most positive perception. (Updated version of Table 7a in Dutz, Us and Yilmaz, forthcoming)

Table A2. Infrastructure-related factors — Weaknesses:

Turkey and Comparable Countries

	Turkey	Poland	Czech Rep.	Hungary
Democracy and business values				
GDP (USD at PPP, 2002)	6036	9550	14,995	12,808
Employment (% of pop., 2002)	29.1	36.1	47.0	37.5
Adult Literacy (% of pop. over 15 yrs)	85	99	99	99
Secondary School Enrolement (in %)	61	88.1	84.3	87.2
Female Labour force (% of tot. labour force)	27.7	45.8	44.2	44.6
Employee training in companies (survey)	4.47	4.18	5.49	5.35
Physical and Financial Infrastructure				
Electricity costs for industrial clients (USD/kWh)	.095	.048	.048	.060
Adequacy of energy infrastructure (surv.)	4.35	6.05	8.42	6.24
Computers per capita (per 1000 people, 2002)	52	114	211	153
Technological coop. between companies	4.39	4.38	6.05	5.35
Easiness of credit flows from banks to business (s)	3.69	3.44	4.88	5.29
Venture capital for business development (survey)	2.67	3.96	4.28	3.88

Note: All measures are from IMD, World Competitiveness Yearbook 2003. The survey measures are all reported on a 0-10 scale, with 10 indicating the most positive perception. (Updated version of Table 7b in Dutz, Us and Yilmaz, forthcoming)

Turkey's Financial Sector – A Practitioner's View of Work in Progress

John T. McCarthy

When asked by his sentencing judge why he chose to rob banks for a living, Willie Sutton, America's famous Depression-era bank robber replied simply: 'Because that's where the money is'. One of the scoundrels in Bertolt Brecht's *'Dreigroschenoper'* (Threepenny Opera) was more circumspect: *'Was ist ein Einbruch in eine Bank gegen die Gründung einer Bank?'* ('What's robbing a bank compared to founding one?')[1]

As in Argentina, Brazil, Indonesia, Russia and elsewhere – recall the USA's saving and loan associations' crisis – the underlying message did not escape attention in Turkey, particularly in the free-wheeling atmosphere of economic liberalisation which characterised the Özal regime of the 1980s. Banking crises in 1984, 1994, 1998 and notably in 2000/2001 affected the Turkish economy seriously and contributed significantly to the risk premium attached to Turkish assets.

Although each crisis brought a reaction for tighter regulation, only after the execution of the Customs Union Agreement (which itself excluded financial services) with the EU in 1995 did the focus of harmonising Turkish banking regulations with the EU's Second Banking Directive become sharper. The Central Bank gained independence from the political influence of the Treasury. Yet it took the shock of the one-two punch combination of the 2000/2001 domestic crises to bring about concrete progress towards reform of the financial system. The EU Council's decision to offer an October 2005 date to Turkey to start the formal accession process – in addition to creating a positive pre-convergence market psychology – will serve to quicken the tempo of financial reforms.

This chapter will look at the principal developments that led to these crises and the changes wrought since.

Even before 11 September 2001, two major political and economic crises (November 2000 and February 2001) had combined to produce a seriously vulnerable Turkish economy. The guiding hand of Washington was certainly helpful in crafting what became a $19 billion standby package arranged by the IMF at the end of 2001. The Fund's response was massive and prompt, evidencing perhaps as much a need on the IMF's part for a quick, apparent success in view of the more recalcitrant problems it faced in Indonesia and Argentina. The election of the current, single-party, AKP government in late 2002 to replace the dysfunctional Ecevit-led coalition, on whose watch the worst of the crises occurred, created a legislative environment conducive to the bold actions necessary to comply with the agreed programme. In December 2004 the IMF tacitly acknowledged the various successes of the Erdogan government. The Fund's $19 billion package was adroitly renegotiated with a new deal for $10 billion containing appropriate mechanism to smooth Turkey's path towards achieving sustainable macroeconomic stability.

Table 1: Turkish Banking System

	Y/E 2000	Y/E 2001	Y/E 2002	Y/E 2003
Commercial Banks	61	46	40	36
State-owed	4	3	3	3
Privately-owned Domestic	28	22	20	18
Foreign	18	15	15	13
Under the State Deposit Insurance Fund	11	6	2	2
Investment and Development Banks	18	15	14	14
Total Banks in System	79	61	54	50

Source: BRSA

In 1999 Turkey had 81 banks. By the end of 2001 the sector had 20 fewer: these institutions were transferred to and variously dealt with by the Savings Deposit and Insurance Fund ('SDIF' – Turkish acronym: TMSF). At the time of writing the system had 50 players, 36 of which are commercial banks and 14 investment or development banks. (There were also a small number of Sharia-based finance houses whose share and contribution to the aggregate system is marginal.) The public sector banks were restructured during 2002 bringing their number down from four to three, and reducing their distorting influence on the money markets and general banking (deposits/loans) activities. (In March 2004, the SDIF announced the merger of the distressed private Pamukbank with the state-owned Halkbank. Whether this reduces the 'pure' state banks further to two from three is arguable.) As with the Central Bank, the intent has been to distance state banks from political pressure and influence. Nonetheless the share of the state-owned banks remains high.

Table 2: Share of state-owned banks and SDIF in total sector (%)

	2001	2002	2003
Assets	43	38	37
Loans	35	21	18
Deposits	53	40	41

Source: BRSA

The restructuring effort has been led by the independent banking supervision and audit regulatory body, the BRSA (Turkish acronym: BDDK, created on 31 August 2000) and the SDIF. Both organisations have earned the praise and confidence of outside stakeholders including the IMF, World Bank and international banks. They have conducted their actions swiftly, professionally – and independently of major political interference. The high ethical and professional standards exhibited by BRSA's management engendered new trust at home and abroad. Rather disturbingly, the AKP government seems to have interfered by orchestrating changes in the senior management of the BRSA in late 2003 as the Imar Bank scandal escalated, this perhaps under pressure from entrenched interests.

Although legal protests have been lodged against some BRSA decisions, by and large, both bodies have contributed to a sea change in the sector, resulting in a sounder financial system. Under the aegis of the BRSA, identification of non-performing loans and a World Bank-inspired restructuring programme (the so-called 'Istanbul Approach'), emphasis on improved risk management systems and asset quality has produced a better capitalised and more finely focused sector.

Macro risks, however, continue to pose a threat to Turkey's banking system. While this also might be the case elsewhere, negative developments in places outside Turkey affect respective local banks' profitability less emphatically. In Turkey, as the experience of the above-mentioned crises shows, the global financial reaction is usually a guillotine-like closing of access to reasonably priced international funding.

In her accession process Turkey will be faced with the combined challenges of continuing to harmonise with EU banking practice plus implementing the tighter conditions which will ensue from the introduction of the Basle II Agreement, notably concerning capital adequacy and risk management. Funding costs for Turkish banks will come under pressure as long as Turkish sovereign credit ratings remain below investment grade. The major issue for all Turkish banks will be to create a steady flow of quality earnings, this at a time when their cost of funds may be rising. Emphasis on improving productivity will also need to be increased.

Banks in Turkey earn money from a few sources, as all banks anywhere: through intermediation of deposits and loans, associated fees and commissions, and through various means of finding and offering more profitable and cheaper intermediation techniques. The level, quality, diversity and sustainability of these sources varies. Among the methods used to make the intermediation function more profitable, running a short foreign exchange position (i.e. borrowing foreign exchange to finance Turkish Lira-denominated assets) has been the most significant. To enhance returns, Turkish banks raised relatively cheap (compared to domestic rates) foreign exchange-denominated borrowings via hard-currency deposits and syndicated loans. The funds so raised were converted into local currency to invest in Turkish Lira assets, a tactic known as the 'carry trade', when such funds were used to finance inventories of government bonds.

This intermediation function has, in the past, been primarily executed though lending to the largest borrower, the government. At the four largest private commercial banks (Akbank, Garanti Bank, Is Bank and Yapi Kredi Bank, this last currently under the administration of the SDIF), who together account for 42 per cent of the total banking system's assets, (and coincidently an equal proportion of deposits) the importance of this source of profit is clear:

Chart 3

	Market Securities Income as per cent of Interest Income			Government Treasury Bills as per cent of Assets		
	2001	2002	2003	2001	2002	2003
Akbank	33	51	62	16	24	27
Garanti	39	57	61	9	7	11
Is	32	50	50	10	14	14
YKB	28	29	29	13	10	10

Source: BRSA

It should, however, be noted that while, at least at the topend of the banking sector, investment in government securities remains a major source of revenue, the recent strength of the Turkish Lira has enabled banks to fund these assets with less reliance on the risky currency mismatch of open short foreign exchange positions. At the end of 2000, the aggregate open position of the banking sector exceeded US$18 billion. By December 2001, the position had reduced to $1.6 billion, $560 million in December 2002, roughly $800 million at the close of 2003 and ended 2004 at about the same level.

With the relative stability established since the 2001 IMF programme, volatility in the markets has declined. Real interest rates on new government securities will also decline owing to the combination of reduced inflation and a strong Turkish Lira. With resulting lower net margins on this carry trade in government paper, banks must shift their focus to developing other sources of profitability.

The other principal aspect of the banks' intermediation function, lending to the private, non-financial sector, has – critically – never been the primary source of revenue for Turkish commercial banks. (Indeed some lending exposure to the private, non-financial sector, as has been painfully discovered since the creation of the BRSA, was lending to group companies owned by or affiliated with owners of the banks themselves. The 'real' lending exposure of Turkish banks to private companies is widely estimated to be only about 20 per cent of Turkey's GDP. This helps to explain the sustained robustness of the private, non-financial sector during and over the frequent periods of crisis. By any standards, the Turkish economy is under-leveraged, a function of the crowding-out effect of government borrowing and the low level of reliance of the private, non-financial sector on bank credit. Following the EU Council's decision of 17 December 2004, it is valid to expect that banking penetration will increase substantially, leading to larger bank loan asset bases, particularly if the government emphasises steps to reduce the role of the informal economy.

Among all banks – state and private, domestic and foreign – there is strenuous competition to lend to the 'blue-chip' corporate sector. Margins on such loans are thus low, forcing banks to seek more lucrative lending opportunities. Currently these are limited to corporate lending to riskier small/medium-sized companies and various forms of consumer lending: mortgages, automobile loans, credit card issuance and general retail lending. Yet such consumer activities comprise still only a small proportion of total banks' assets, accounting for slightly less than 20 per cent of all loans at end-2003. While the system exhibits a generally low level of penetration into retail banking, some banks clearly have identified the need to grow their activities in these product areas, particularly to generate fee and commission income to offset lower net interest income on government securities and low activities in non-financial sector corporate lending.

The drag on profitability represented by the cost of carrying non-performing loan assets ('NPL's'), while significant, is – following the structural adjustments in the system – showing a positive, declining trend. The ratio of NPL's to total loans as measured by the BRSA has declined from 18 per cent at end-2002 to 12 per cent at the end of last year. Conversely, provisions as a percentage of such NPL's have risen from 64 per cent to 82 per cent in the same period. (An interesting, instructive aside: while as a group foreign banks account for slightly less than five per cent of total lending, their gross NPL's are merely 1.4 per cent of the system's total. The systemic damage seems to have been identified and appropriate actions taken: Brecht's scoundrels have been, in the main, caught out. The way forward for Turkish banks is in compliance with Basle II.

Chart 4: NPL's by Banking Groups

TL Trillion	December 2002	September 2003	November 2003
NPL's (Gross)	10,430	9,086	9,015
State	4,545	4,472	4,430
Private	3,335	3,286	3,323
SDIF	2,260	1,029	958
Foreign	112	120	123
Development & Investment	179	179	181
Provisions	6,691	7,043	7,377
State	3,358	3,844	3,908
Private	1,766	2,218	2,479
SDIF	1,366	728	735
Foreign	87	93	96
Development & Investment	114	160	160
Provisions/NPL's (Gross) (per cent)	64.2	77.5	81.8
State	73.9	86.0	88.2
Private	53.0	67.5	74.6

Source: BRSA

But lax regulation and crony-capitalism among politicians and owners of banks (often with no natural ties to banking in their core businesses) may share the blame for the causes of the 2000/2001 crises. The moral hazard created and encouraged by the SDIF's guarantee on deposited funds opened the system to massive abuse. The Imar Bank debacle serves as the prime example of this problem. Again, even if belatedly, the post-crisis management of the system has responded positively. The state guarantee on deposited funds was lifted in the third quarter of 2004.

Recently the Governor of the Central Bank asserted that perhaps the main cause of the 2000/2001 banking crisis could be blamed on the 100 per cent deposit guarantee previously offered by the state. Its continuation, notwithstanding the collapse of even more banks owing to mismanagement, fraud and speculation, has lead to the $77 billion bill (roughly one-third of today's GDP) which will have to be picked-up by Turkish taxpayers in order to restructure the banking system.

Following the establishment of the BRSA, the system's banks underwent a three-layered audit process. Asset quality was independently scrutinised and major non-performing assets identified. Significant reserves have been mandated and established resulting in a better-capitalised system. Cost reductions have been made with the concomitant elimination of branches and employees particularly at the public sector banks. Unfair competition for loans and deposits from the state banks has been reduced and money market volatilities caused by their high level of prior participation have eased, with evident positive impacts on interest rates. Even the scope for foreign direct investment by EU-based banks may have broadened beyond the significant entry of HSBC (via Demirbank) to the involvement of Italy's Unicredito with Kocbank and the smaller purchases of 50 per cent of Turk Ekonomi Bank by BNP and Bank Europa's acquisition of Sitebank. Yet as noted earlier, the challenge for Turkish banks will be to diversify the sources of profitability away from the government securities carry trade to broader forms of efficient intermediation.

Despite the wide use of state-of-the-art IT systems and hardware and a pool of well-educated and skilled financial sector professionals, Turkey's financial markets can in some respects be considered underdeveloped. A broad and deep capital market is still lacking. All economic sectors and stakeholders suffer from this lacuna as a result. Leasing, private pensions, a corporate bond market, a reasonably-priced mortgage market and a legal system conducive to identifying and preserving free title are either insufficiently utilised or only in their formative stages.

Private pensions, in particular, will play a major role in Turkey's financial universe. Generally, economic resources allocated to social security are insufficient in developing countries. Whereas in developed countries roughly 30 per cent of GDP is allocated to social security expenses, Turkey allocates only about nine per cent (including health). The current social security system in Turkey is woefully inefficient. Over-generosity of benefits, 'carrots' offered by politicians and a number of benefit improvements and pervasive misuse/abuse of the system have resulted in a model where benefits cannot possibly be matched by contributions. What is also important is that, today, roughly only 15 per cent of Turkey's population is covered by the existing social security system.

In 2003 Turkey introduced legislation covering private individual pensions, whose aim is to improve welfare levels by providing supplementary income during retirement. Participation in a private pension scheme will be open to anyone over 18 and registered with Social Security. Initially, participation by employers and employees will be voluntary; compulsory schemes can be expected to follow if other countries' examples (Poland, Chile) hold. Contributors will have the right to retirement benefits after the age of 56 and a minimum of 10 years of contributing. After earning the right to retire, contributors may get their accumulated benefits as a lump-sum payment or partial payment or annuity.

Following the 17 December 2004 decision, three majorly important, specific issues dominate activities in Turkey's financial sector. In private pensions, first, 13 licenses have been granted to private pension fund management companies, most of which are affiliated with Turkish banks. Nearly 95,000 participants have contributed to the equivalent of $26 million since late 2003. While at these levels penetration cannot be deemed to have been earthshaking, the potential is massive – particularly if mandatory contributions are, as expected after the conclusion of all IMF structural adjustments under the Standby Agreement(s), enacted.

Second, with the current low inflation (9.3 per cent CPI as of 2004 year-end) and recent macroeconomic stability, the AKP government is expected to complete (in early, 2005) draft legislation establishing a real-estate mortgage system. The positive results of such a system are many, from increased home ownership (a stakeholding in a new 'Turkish Dream'), decreased illegal construction, greater economic activity and employment in the construction and materials sectors, deepened and broadened capital markets and greater balance sheet diversification for the banking system.

The third issue has been the very successful introduction of the New Turkish Lira on 1 January 2005. Again owing to the positive disinflationary environment, by removing six zeros from the (old) TL, this shift, at this time, the government and Central Bank have increased Turkey's confidence and chances for a sustainable success.

It will be the willingness of modern Turkey, after the corrupt, geriatric politics of the 1960s-1990s, to seek and adopt best practices – for example from accounting standards, to laws on leasing, private pensions, bank regulation, to Basle II – that will help her young, dynamic and growing population to close the gap between the performance of the government and the expectations of the electorate.

The time when a lack of transparency and accountability hallmarked the relationships between the governing and the governed is clearly disappearing. The focus on EU accession will exert continued internal and external pressure for reform, including in the financial sector. As their counterparts in the EU 25, Turkey's youth (recall that 46 per cent of the 70.5 million population is below 25), informed and influenced by global media and communications, share heightened aspirations and expectations. A modern, corruption-free and transparent financial sector capable of supporting a more productive macro economy with efficient and rational intermediation of savings for short and long-term development is critically among these.

Endnotes

1 B. Brecht, Die Dreigroschenoper, 3.3. 1928.

The Rule of Law

David Barchard

Human Rights, the Rule of Law, and Enlargement

'The Union is founded on the principles of liberty, democracy, respect for human rights, and fundamental freedoms and the rule of law.' So runs Article 6(1) of the Treaty on the European Union, expressing perhaps the deepest single common instinct of the diverse nations making up the European Union. Total insistence on democratic conditions for member states, present and future, is surely the 'European' issue par excellence on which all Britons, Europhile or Eurosceptic, stand firmly shoulder to shoulder with the EU countries on the other side of the Channel.

Despite the importance of these values, clear tests for applicant countries over the rule of law and the quality of respect for human rights and minority freedoms are relative novelties. Though preliminary guidelines existed in the 1970s, formal tests and criteria emerged only in the 1990s when the EU had to deal with the question of how to admit a group of countries which until very recently had been Marxist single party regimes[1]. In other words they were not so much tests of historical performance over extended periods of time as benchmarks of the point reached in a legal and administrative transition. During the half decade which ended on 1 May 2004 with the Eastern European enlargement of the EU, the Rule of Law and related issues figured prominently at the beginning of the annual progress reports for each country. In one or two cases there were delays along the way, but all of the Ten found 'the Rule of Law' an easy hurdle to clear.

Ironically Turkey – a country where there had been multi-party politics and free elections for most of the previous half-century and which belonged to the Council of Europe and Nato throughout this period – had by far the greatest difficulties. As late as the end of 2003 Turkey had still not managed to satisfy the EU on the preliminary criteria for opening negotiations – and so still had no certainty that its candidacy would ultimately succeed. Not until the Brussels Summit of 16-17 December 2004 did Turkey finally get a somewhat flickering green light, or at least one with an unusual degree of conditionality attaching to it, to open negotiations.

Turks inevitably, and with justification, see this as an expression of discrimination or prejudice against them. But it is, in many ways also a legacy of the 1990s. If the country's earlier human rights record had been less controversial, reservations in 2004 among European public opinion and European responsiveness to 'ethnic-historical' lobbies, such as the French Armenian voters, campaigning against Turkey would have been less strong. Furthermore, because Turkey delayed for so long during the 1990s putting its house in order, the EU scrutinising process has dug ever deeper in the fields of rule of law and human rights and probed for a degree of detail on these matters which might sometimes be embarrassing even for existing members of the EU.

The human rights problem contrasts with Turkey's relatively advanced state of preparedness on other matters which is often greater than generally realised: on the eve of the Helsinki Summit in December 1999 at which Turkey's candidate status was formally recognised, in the opinion of EU officials Turkey was already in a position to open negotiations for almost all the 31 chapters of *acquis communautaire* and to come close to completing negotiations on some chapters.

The focus on human rights in Turkey seemed unsurprising to public opinion in the EU, accustomed to news reports of human rights violations over several decades. Inside Turkey the degree to which a bad human rights image has unfortunately come to characterise the country abroad seems never to have been sufficiently appreciated. This miscalculation very nearly blighted Turkey's application. Successive Turkish governments completely failed to anticipate that human rights issues would sooner or later pose the major stumbling block for accession to the EU. Turkish memories were of the precedents created by lenient treatment from Nato and the Council of Europe, generally prepared to overlook human rights issues between the 1950s and the 1990s. Inside Turkey it tended to be assumed that the real hurdle to EU membership was Greek antagonism. Indeed by the mid-1990s, Turkey's membership prospects seemed to be fading and reached a particularly low point under the Santer presidency. The introduction of the Customs Union at the beginning of 1996, after a quarter of a century of preparation, very nearly foundered in a confrontation with the European Parliament following the jailing of Kurdish activist Members of the Turkish Parliament in the spring of 1994. European Parliament reservations towards Turkey's applications had been awakened by an event a few years earlier when a Turkish Kurdish speaker had actually been prosecuted for remarks he had made to it.

Only at the very end of the decade, at the December 1999 Helsinki Council, did it become evident that, while the membership application would collapse irrevocably if radical changes were not made, if they did take place, the Turkish candidacy would stand a good chance of proceeding. Thereafter the political will for extensive reforms quickly appeared in Turkey. Significant work on legal, constitutional, and administrative changes began in earnest. The process started under the Ecevit coalition (2000-2003) and, to the initial surprise of some observers, accelerated dramatically after the AKP (Justice and Development Party) governments took power in December 2002. The consequence of this was that the Progress Report of October 2004 formally confirmed what EU officials had already indicated for some months: Turkey had finally crossed the line at which negotiations could begin.

A completely new chapter has opened in Turkey's legal and administrative history, comparable with the two earlier main periods of reform in the mid-nineteenth century and under Atatürk in the 1920s. It is perhaps surprising that these have been given relatively little attention inside the EU. They surely deserve to be seen as a remarkable episode of the successful diffusion of democratic legislative standards by the Union.

Europe's 'Unspeakable' Prejudice?

The upsurge in overt racist prejudice towards Turkey and the Turks which erupted in France, Germany, Austria, the Netherlands, and other European countries in the weeks before the Brussels Summit – and the remarkable degree of ignorance of contemporary Turkey which these outbursts exposed – are a warning to tread carefully. Simply because accusations against a nation are couched in moral terms does not mean that they are either true or reputable. Racism typically consists of moral accusations which appear self-evidently true to those who make them, as a glance at Mein Kampf will show: it is by their actual consequences in the real world, not the world of nationalist imagination, that such claims are best judged.

Western Europeans, and others, discussing human rights in Turkey need to be aware of the danger that their approach to the question is framed by prejudices of which they may personally be unconscious. European scepticism, both on Turkey's ability to abide by the laws and moral norms of Europe and on its power to reform itself, has a long pedigree and derives ultimately from the racist Turcophobic literature widespread among French and British liberals in the nineteenth century, one of whose aims was specifically to prevent the growth of friendly ties between Turkey and Europe.

A generation ago such a warning was less necessary than it is today. From the 1920s until the 1970s, though Turkey was a much poorer and in most ways far less libertarian society than it is today, it was widely seen elsewhere in Europe as basically a benign and progressive force thanks to the reforms of Kemal Atatürk in the 1920s and its role as a Nato ally. Since the 1974 Cyprus conflict, nineteenth-century Christian European attitudes towards Turkey have revived.

The quintessence of the European turcophobe tradition is summed up in a few lines from the leading nineteenth-century Oxford historian, E.A. Freeman, one of the founders of modern British historiography and an ardent supporter of Christian nationalist movements in south-eastern Europe. Freeman's comments on Turkey and the Turks in 1877 articulate attitudes which persist in some quarters even today.[2] 'That nothing is to be hoped for from so-called Turkish reforms is a truth which is made clear at a glance alike by the history of the past and by [the] facts of the present.'

'While the West has been ruled by preordained laws, the East knows no government but the will of arbitrary rulers.'

'The whole mistake lies in dealing with the Turks as the civilised nations of Europe deal with one another. ... We have already seen that certain Turks have learned to talk European languages, and to dress themselves up in European clothes. It must always be remembered that this makes no difference [to the innate propensity of the Turks to commit massacres and other cruel acts].' These ideas lie directly behind the claim of the liberal Christian British statesman, William Gladstone, that Turks were 'from the black day when they first entered Europe, the one great anti-human specimen of humanity. Wherever they went, a broad line of blood marked the track behind them.'[3]

Confronted by some undeniably repressive features present on the Turkish judicial and constitutional landscape in the early 1990s, there was an inevitable tendency among some sections of European opinion to ignore the fact that some of the problems were actually extremely recent, being the products of the 1980 military coup, and interpret them sotto voce as manifestations of a 'Turcia eterna', as Freeman had done: non-European, Muslim, alien, brutal, and incorrigible. The weakness of such explanations is that, apart from consisting essentially of morally objectionable racism, they are also incoherent. They do not explain how or why Turkey has in fact changed radically, developing within a couple of generations into a secularised urban industrial society with a multi-party political system.

Turcophobe explanations also ignore the parallels and similarities between Turkey's experience as a late-modernising country and the history of other Mediterranean societies, some of them long incorporated into the European Union, when they made the very painful transition from a traditionalistic agrarian society to an urban industrial one. Ultimately limited and partial vision where Turkey is concerned derives from the fact that too many elite Europeans, no matter which particular athenaeum they sit in, still see the country, as Freeman and Gladstone did, mainly through the falsifying prism of combative regional nationalisms, defined by hostility to Turkey and the Turks and energetic in projecting their visions and their versions of the facts.

The Problem and its Nature

In its Regular Report for 2000, the Commission devoted 12 pages, about 6,250 words, to its review of political issues related to democracy and human rights. It started from the premise that: 'The basic features of a democratic system continue to exist but Turkey is slow in implementing the institutional reforms needed to guarantee democracy and the rule of law.' In the 2003 Report, these sections have expanded to a total of 38 pages and over 15,000 words but this account is written against a backdrop of reforms by the Turkish Government in progress.

How does one make sense of the picture they give? The method attempted here, is first to identify various categories of problem by their origins and then proceed to look at some of the main issues involved.

The first category consists of politically-motivated restrictions on personal individual liberties, political activity, freedom of expression and association, and matters such as the use of indigenous languages other than Turkish.

These restrictions, which generated the most court cases, political prisoners, and claims of human rights abuses, tend to rest on legislation and institutions introduced in two waves of legal and constitutional changes in 1971-73, and 1980-82 by military governments. (Formal restrictions on the use of Kurdish languages in Turkey for broadcasting and other public purposes, for example, date only from the 1982 Constitution. Until the early 1980s, Turkish censuses actually recorded numbers of Kurdish speakers.) The military had been drawn into politics by the repeated inability of civilian politicians to maintain order in the face of rapid social and economic changes. To prevent a further breakdown they created a limited democratic system in which inadmissible activity was clearly defined and they themselves continued to play a part on the sidelines, mainly through two institutions, the National Security Council, and the State Security Courts, in which military representatives sat alongside civilians.

The present situation might have been avoided if bodies such as the Council of Europe and Western Embassies in Ankara had made it clear in the early 1980s that many of the changes were intrinsically undemocratic and relied on concepts of sedition already jettisoned elsewhere. However the main Western European embassies backed the new arrangements even to the point of undermining the local standing of an EU Representative in Turkey who criticised undemocratic practices while the Council of Europe conducted an investigation which in effect absolved the 1982 settlement from the charges levelled against it by libertarians. Western Europe, and arguably Britain in particular, have a measure of responsibility for what followed.[4]

With the return of free elections some of the restrictions introduced by the military vanished very quickly. Civilian politicians and the parties quickly burst the bonds which had been designed for them in particular, but allowed the restrictions on dissident activity to persist. The most important of these were the State Security Courts set up by the military, but proposed before 1980 by centre-right politicians. Under powerful prosecutors and with a panel of mixed military and civilian judges[5], these courts tried persons accused of dissidence and terrorism, smuggling, and narcotics offences.

The second category consists of legal and administrative anachronisms where structures in Turkey have not kept pace with developments in the world as a whole and with urbanisation and industrialisation in Turkey. These are perhaps the widest range of topics, covering such matters as the functioning of the judiciary, the status of women and gender equality, and a host of administrative practices, as well as law on commercial matters. Turkey has a bedrock of constitutional and legal arrangements, mainly derived from the Napoleonic prefectorial government model introduced in the nineteenth century and, in its day, fairly typical among southern and eastern European countries with a style of government basically designed to maintain order in an agrarian society. A certain deference to the customs and values of rural society, particular on issues of gender equality, is discernable, even though patterns of life and behaviour of the 60 per cent of the population living in towns now diverges sharply from countryside communities and even rural society is very different from what it was a generation or two ago. The lassitude shown by the courts and the legal system to 'honour killings' – i.e. murders of female relatives believed to have engaged in extramarital sexual activity – has been widely criticised in this regard.

A third category of problems might be classed as serious political decay. They include corruption, weakness of civilian institutions vis-à-vis the military, and general administrative insufficiency. The roots of these problems are to be sought in the combination of high inflation, rapid changes in demographic patterns, and three breakdowns in four decades of democratic politics, in a country possessing a general social and cultural background of clientelism and patronage familiar in many Mediterranean societies.

A final category consists of cultural and religious issues with deep roots both in Turkish society and, more specifically, the attitudes of local administrators. Many of these related to the conflicts and territorial disputes of the various ethno-religious communities within the Ottoman Empire which are still being played out in international disputes in the region today.

Lifting Restrictions on Political Activity

Though some constitutional and legal reforms were made by Turgut Özal in the late 1980s, the present legal reforms in Turkey essentially began from 1995 onwards as the country's leaders finally realised that its candidacy for the EU would founder unless radical changes were made. They accelerated after the Helsinki Summit in December 1999, speeding up still further after the AKP came to power in November 2002.

Why did the process take so long? There seem to be five main reasons. First, Turkish governments for the decade before 2002 were all weak coalition administrations unable to be decisive. In the latter part of the decade, though most parties shared a consensus over the EU, the government included hard-line right-wing nationalists self-consciously hostile to liberal values. All reforms therefore had to be timid domestic compromises; second, the reforms, particularly in the area of civil-military relations, involved a redefinition of balance between the groups sharing power in the political system; third, almost all civilian politicians, whether of the centre-right or centre-left, basically accepted the claim of the 1982 Constitutional system and its institutions to be an effective bulwark, keeping down the lid on alarming threats: armed Kurdish separatism, radical Islamism, the possibility of general social and political disorder; and, fourth, there was no shared mentality or pool of knowledge with the rest of Europe. The political leadership in Turkey was isolated from the European mainstream with remarkably few friendly contacts with it. During this period visits from European statesmen to Ankara were few and far between while the EU itself often treated Turkey as an unloved peripheral zone, frequently omitting to invite Turkish representatives to EU occasions where they might have been entitled to be present. Finally, potential support for human rights reforms in Turkey after the mid-1980s was weakened by the fairly close identification of human rights campaigners with Kurdish political activism. This was a striking change from the 1970s when metropolitan Turkish lawyers and academics had presided over human rights groups such as the then Turkish local branch of Amnesty International.

All this however is now in the past. If one wants to identify a point at which the legacy of restrictive arrangements created in 1971 and 1982 finally ceased to exist, it came perhaps on 9 June 2004. On this date Mrs Leyla Zana, the Turkish Kurdish activist politician, and her three companions were released from prison at the request of the public prosecutor, after serving just over ten years in prison for contacts with the PKK. The case illustrates the links between Turkish-EU relations and the process of political liberalisation very clearly. All the seven deputies of the Democratic Labour Party (DEP) originally arrested, stripped of their parliamentary immunity, and condemned by State Security Courts in 1994, owe their release to the calendar of the Accession Process. The first three were released late in 1995 as part of the behind-the-scenes deal to clinch the EU's Customs Union with Turkey. By the time of Mrs Zana's release, the legal landscape had changed completely. The State Security Courts were being abolished. Limited broadcasting in the two Kurdish languages and others spoken in Turkey had got underway. Institutions teaching Kurdish had been operating for several months.

These changes remove the restrictions on minority rights which stood in the way of the EU accession. For the Erdogan government they were courageous, even risky, moves which provoked open unrest inside the ruling AKP. Mrs Zana's release coincided with a spate of renewed murders of Turkish soldiers and gendarmes in eastern provinces by Kongra-Gel (the new name for the restructured Partiya Karkiya Kurdistan [PKK] Kurdish Workers' Party). Opinion polls suggested that the majority of ordinary Turks continued to distrust Mrs Zana and tended to regard her calls for a ceasefire as insincere, while a right-wing teachers' union attempted to get a new prosecution launched against her and her colleagues.

Much now depends on both sides, including Mrs Zana and her colleagues, living sensibly and prudently together within the system. The Kurdish issue – which has obvious international ramifications affecting most of the Middle East – is much the most likely to derail the new settlement. European perceptions tended to be shaped by Kurdish émigré groups, many of them not frank about their own use of violence. The Kurds are in a certain sense singularly honoured, for though there are many Muslim nationalities without their own national state on the edge of Europe and beyond, the Kurds are the only one whose nationalist aspirations and complaints on human rights receive the sort of emotional gut support in Western Europe that goes routinely to a diverse range of would-be nationalisms among Christian ethnicities. This is a powerful political card to be able to play: at the end of 2004 it appeared likely that that Mrs Zana and her allies may find continuing to appeal over the heads of the rest of Turkey directly to the European public more tempting than gradualist caution.

Freedom of Expression and the Press

Beyond the changes described so far lies a more fundamental one. In July 2003 anti-terrorism legislation was amended by parliament to drop a clause covering 'propaganda against the indivisible unity of the state' as a terrorist offence, though other laws continue to refer to the state's indivisibility.

During the later 1980s and most of the 1990s, though the mainstream national press faced few if any restrictions on its freedom, articles by political militants attacking the indivisible integrity of the state, the fundamental characteristics of the Republic, and any kind of moral support for organisations regarded as terrorist, remained serious offences to be tried in the State Security Courts. Insults against the state and state institutions were also considered serious offences. (It should be noted that in Turkey, even in civil cases between private individuals, insults are generally considered to be more serious than defamation based on factual inaccuracies or untruths: the exact reverse of the situation in, for example, the UK.)

The lifting of restrictions means that there are now few cases of politically militant journalists being held. (I have been unable to find names of detainees cited at present.) However 'propaganda encouraging the use of terrorist methods' still carries potential sentences of up to five years; insults to the state and threats to its unity could carry a six months sentence. As the 2003 Regular Report put it: 'Non-violent expression of political views beyond these limits is still restricted by a variety of laws and is rigorously enforced.' Powers to confiscate or burn publications on the grounds that they offend people's feelings or exploit their sexual desires have been lifted, but there are attempts, enforced in court, to censor Internet content.

In particular RTÜK (High Board for Radio and Television Broadcasting) enjoys, and uses, powers to fine or shut down TV channels for days or even weeks if their content is deemed by it to offend national or family standards. The 2003 Regular Report notes only that these powers were used against a pro-Kurdish regional channel in eastern Turkey in the summer of 2003, but by Western European standards the use of these blunt instruments against mainstream national TV broadcasters is at least as deserving of comment. The objections these days are not usually to the expression of ideas but to profanity, bad language, border-line obscenity and so on, i.e. matters of social rather than political offence. This is a change. Five years ago, the RTÜK board, (against, it should be noted, the recommendation of its own president) was attempting to block BBC Turkish language broadcasting in Turkey.

Nonetheless comment and discussion in Turkey are clearly wide-ranging, robust, and free. The essential limits are effectively set these days less by the law than by what public opinion (and proprietors) will stand for.

Freedom of Peaceful Assembly

The freedom to engage in marches and demonstrations was severely reduced in Turkey after 1980 when it appeared to be one of the factors which had precipitated the breakdown at the end of the seventies. Whether it is because of the militancy of Turkish protestors or lack of police skills in the field of public order, many Turkish marches and protests are anything but peaceful assemblies. A series of legislative changes easing restrictions on demonstrations has been passed, but protests are still regarded as of dubious legitimacy. In the summer of 2001, after that year's economic collapse, demonstrations against the government were forcibly suppressed. This was a serious check to the democratic process and explains why the coalition had a further 18 months' life and its parties were then annihilated at the polls. In May that year university rectors and other senior academics who demonstrated against proposed changes on the university admission found themselves the subject of a suç duyurusu [formal denunciation] by the Istanbul Police – an appeal to the prosecutor to start legal proceedings. So far no prosecution has been brought.

Freedom of Association

In the early 1990s setting up a club or association in Turkey involved a number of huge and intentional obstacles. They included a constitution or set of rules approved by a prosecutor, the publication of the agenda of the annual meeting, and the presence of a police official at the meeting, while state employees were obliged to obtain written permission from their superiors to join any club or association. Most of these requirements dated back to the 1982 settlement but the roots of these laws can be traced right back to Ottoman times and to government fear of organisations inside civil society outside its direct control, especially if they were formed along religious, ethnic, or radical social lines.

During the 1990s, this picture changed steadily as a result of the rise of non-governmental organisations (mostly based in Istanbul) and the whittling away of restrictions on freedom of association, first in the Constitution and then in laws. The fourth and seventh reform packages (January and August 2003) permit organisations to use any language in non-official correspondence. A Department of Associations now carries out supervisory work which was formerly the responsibility of the police and politically-motivated associations may still experience a greater degree of supervisory interest. Turkey is still some way from the situation in Britain where setting up a club or association is essentially a private matter of no interest to the authorities in normal times, but equally anyone wanting to found an association can do so provided they comply with bureaucratic formalities.

Torture and Ill-Treatment

With the possible exception of minority languages, this is probably the most sensitive topic on the human rights agenda. Legal and administrative measures to combat torture have been introduced at regular intervals over the last fifteen years. How effective have they been? The most recent report of the Council of Europe Committee for the Prevention of Torture, (18 June 2004)[6] notes that 'a vast programme of legislative reforms' is in progress, that even pro-Kurdish human rights groups recognise that in the troubled south-eastern provinces there has been a sharp decline in 'heavy torture', and that problems now centre on occasional incidents of ill-treatment when in detention by gendarmes and on the issue of speedy access to lawyers in certain cases. There are no longer suggestions of systematic torture and the Committee praises the Turkish government's attitude on torture and abuse sufficiently strongly to suggest that it might offer lessons for other governments. Its continuing reservations centre on access to lawyers for detainees, medical checks on ill-treatment, detention conditions, and training of judges and prosecutors. Lack of access to legal advice evidently remains a significant problem: according to the Turkish government figures, of the 7,245 persons detained by State Security Courts in 2004, 4,777 did not request access to a lawyer. During the first four months of 2004, the numbers seemed to be slackening, but nevertheless 959 detainees out of a total of 1,814 held still did not request access to lawyers.

According to government figures, in 2003, 32 Turkish law enforcement officials were prosecuted on charges of torture. Of these four were convicted and six acquitted. In the first four months of 2004, seven officials were prosecuted and four were acquitted; while a total of 89 officials remain on trial in cases pending from previous years. As regards charges of ill-treatment 58 officials were prosecuted in 2003 of whom only 10 were acquitted. During the January to April period of 2004, 11 officials were prosecuted, of whom five were convicted and one acquitted. A further 290 officials remained on trial in cases pending from previous years. These figures give some grounds for supposing that Turkish criminal courts will now replace European tribunals as the primary arenas in which persons claiming to have suffered torture or ill-treatment will be able to obtain redress.

The figures for persons detained by the (now abolished) State Security Courts pose one further question. Generally speaking, though things are changing in the large metropolitan areas, Turkey has far lower levels of reported crime than Western European countries and also fewer policemen per 1,000 of its population than they do. Despite this, the number of detainees held specifically on security offences (about two-thirds of those held by the State Security Courts, the remainder being customs and narcotics-related offenders) seem to be far higher than the numbers of persons detained on terrorist offences in the UK.[7] Turkey, and particularly its south-eastern regions, is of course recovering from a terrorist threat on a scale which no part of Britain has ever experienced, in the course of which around 30,000 people died over a decade and a half.

The Declining Political Role of the Military

Many people in Europe are accustomed to thinking of Turkey as a semi-military regime. Certainly the country has had three military coups since 1960, and in the 1990s the military, though possessing no direct political role, were still an influential autonomous force in society. The armed forces remain attached to the Prime Minister's Office rather than the Ministry of Defence. The role of the military in Turkish society is not simply based on the experience of a series of coups since 1960, but also on the tendency of Turkish civilian society to regard the military as guardians of the last resort, especially against religious fundamentalism, and possessors of organisational ability lacking in civilian society.

The formal power of the military in Turkey during the 1990s was often overstated. The military's most conspicuous involvement in politics was a declaration against Islamism in February 1997. The declaration was a jolt to public opinion and may have played a part in the fall of the Erbakan government several months later, but – contrary to what is often claimed— the government was not directly ousted by the military. Nor did the political parties implement the programme of anti-Islamist measures which the commanders called for. Since 1997, the issue has shifted to when and how full civilian supremacy over the military, who function effectively as an autonomous corporation, will be restored. It is complicated by the desire of much of Turkish public opinion that the armed forces continue to be ring-fenced against Islamist penetration. Any attempt to open the way to the 'Islamisation' of the officer corps or senior commands would provoke a major political crisis in the media and general public and the Erdogan government clearly recognises this.

There is thus a somewhat uncomfortable co-existence. The military as a whole, and senior commanders as individuals, still retain a voice. In the summer of 2004, individual senior army officers were still liable to make public pronouncements on matters such as Cyprus. These did not have a great impact on public opinion. Assessments of the future role of the Turkish military in politics depend on the degree to which the politicians maintain order and stability: in Turkey as elsewhere, the military have been sucked into politics in the past by the inability of civilian governments to maintain order and public security without them. Turkey's present government has no problems in this area and, following the scaling down of the National Security Council, and the scrapping of the State Security Courts, its ascendancy over the military does not seem to be open to serious question. The future of civil-military relations in Turkey, once the country is inside the EU, looks set to follow that seen in Greece, Spain, and Portugal and this seems to be well understood by the Turkish military commanders who have given their endorsement to the process of integration. Equally, if Turkey is excluded from the EU, the prestige of its civilian institutions will be eroded by the rejection with effects that are hard to predict.

Religious Freedoms

The religious system in Turkey these days is clearly in transition. The early Republic combined a secular system with the de facto status of an established religion for Sunni Islam. In practice this meant secularism, of a sort, in political contexts, with traditionalist Sunni expectations in many social ones. Until the 1990s, there were severe legal and administrative restrictions on the activities of Christian churches and in particular on their ability to build or repair churches – and all such activities were subject to permission. The emergence of a large number of 'secularised Muslims' who had little or no religious awareness meant that this anomaly was not even perceived by many senior officials, while they were well aware of social pressures from conservative Sunni groups.

Furthermore, to operate, a religion had to be officially recognised by the state, but in fact in practice it was found that recognition was very nearly impossible to obtain. Even the Roman Catholic Church, which has formal diplomatic relations with Turkey and has been present for hundreds of years in the country, was unable to get recognition.[8]

Long-established churches thus faced the possibility of confiscation if they could not document the ownership of their buildings, while new arrivals on the scene, such as small Protestant religious groups, were wholly illegal and their meetings were subject to possible police raids. Against this, it must be noted that some groups found it possible to work within the Turkish system. During the early 1990s, the Jehovah's Witnesses, treating their difficulties simply as an administrative hiccough, eventually achieved the right to open places of worship and to proselytise.

It is fair to say that these pressures reflected attitudes prevalent several generations ago and were increasingly at odds with the attitude of the majority of the population – nonetheless there were groups in the Ministry of the Interior and some municipalities which tried to enforce the letter of the law. A legal distinction, based on Islamic doctrine, was also made between the 'three monotheistic religions' (Islam, Judaism, and Christianity) and other cults.

The AKP included legislation to enhance the property rights of Christian churches and non-Muslim places of worship in its government programme in 2002 and legislation in 2003. It has since moved to allow training of non-Muslim clergy in Turkey, though legislation for this has not yet been introduced, and this would permit the reopening of the Greek Orthodox seminary on Heybeliada in Istanbul – one of the key Greek demands from Turkey. Since there are now less than 2,000 ethnic Greeks in Turkey, it is not altogether clear how it will function or indeed whether there is any genuine educational need for this particular institution. However it is clearly anomalous that to date all training of religious clergy in Turkey is forbidden – except for the large numbers of Sunni Muslim imams who graduate each year.

The numbers of Christians in Turkey are very small. Over ten million people however belong to the Alevi branch of Islam, a form of Shi'ism which is not officially recognised and enjoys none of the advantages of Sunni Muslims. Alevi children have to attend compulsory Sunni religious instruction in schools and in the longer term EU attention will have to be given mainly to ensuring that these and other non-Sunni Muslim groups enjoy equal rights, an issue which may create social tensions in certain regions.

There continue to be incidents which lay open to question the degree to which religious pluralism is fully accepted even by older members of the secularist elite. In early January 2005, for example, Mrs Rahsan Ecevit, said in the course of a TV programme that Christian missionary activities had increased in Turkey. 'In recent days, they have really grown faster than ever. I think that our desire to enter the EU has an important role in this. Churches are being set up and working in secret closed places…a large number of our Muslim citizens are being persuaded or induced by advantage to convert to Christianity. Of course, as a Muslim I am uneasy at this.'[9] These remarks are scarcely different from widespread Greek and Russian attitudes towards to Western Christian groups such as Catholics or Jehovah's Witnesses. Even so, if correctly reported, the comments nevertheless raise questions about the degree to which religious pluralism is accepted, at least as understood by most of the globe outside the Middle East.

Commercial and Legal Contracts

Turks have long been able to seek redress from the state by suing the government through the Council of State (Danıstay), established in the mid-nineteenth century. Redress against individual officials remains more difficult, though the trend of recent changes is to make them more accountable.

Major changes are under way in the field of commercial law. Turkish commercial law is based, ultimately, on the German Commercial Code, adopted wholesale in 1926 and modified over the years. In many respects however its operations are as cumbersome and overloaded by bureaucracy and shortage of resources as the other branches of the legal system.

One particular point, which applies not only to commercial law, is the relatively weak binding force of contracts. In the public sector it is not uncommon to find salaries and other payments being made late. Legal action was always possible but given the slowness of redress and Turkey's formerly very high levels of inflation, a creditor risked finding that the court would award payment in several delayed instalments in a rapidly depreciating currency. The tradition of late payment of salaries in Turkey stretches back to nineteenth-century Ottoman times when the budget of the Sublime Porte was unable to meet its commitments on a regular basis and soldiers might go for a year or more without pay. Delays today are usually much shorter, but the fact that they happen at all – and that medium level civil servants may be expected to finance costs for travel and other expenses necessarily incurred in the course of their work out of their own pockets – is surely a serious anachronism.

In considering issues of the judiciary, the European Commission and its consultants do not seem to have paid much attention to the central question of remuneration and low overall spending by the government on the justice system. An inefficient and slow moving system, operated by overworked officials (including judges) whose salaries are not commensurate with their responsibilities leads to delays and sometimes to corruption. It also makes judges very vulnerable to local pressures of every sort. As far as businessmen are concerned, this antiquated system is thought to be one of the reasons why foreign investors hesitate to put their money into Turkey.

One landmark as far as businessmen were concerned came on 21 June 2001, when the Grand National Assembly finally passed the Turkish International Arbitration Law No. 4686 ('Law No. 4686' or 'Law enacted as one of the commitments of the Turkish government to the International Monetary Fund and the World Bank'). Another was the new Public Tender law (No 4734) passed in January 2002 which came into force twelve months later bringing Turkish legislation in this area into line with EU practices and aimed at creating transparency, competition and fairness in public tenders. Legislation in areas such as consumer protection, copyrights and royalties, is being carried out under the National Programme for the Adoption of the *acquis*.

Corruption

The economic crisis of 2001, which plunged millions of Turkish families into hardship overnight, exposed serious shortcomings in the banking system and indications of corruption even at senior levels within the system. The rise of corruption follows the rapid growth of the Turkish economy over the last twenty years and the enormous disparity between the kind of money earned by businessmen and the salaries of civil servants and politicians. During the early decades of the Turkish Republic, a very different ethos prevailed and there were cases of senior officials committing suicide when accused of irregularities. By 2001 however such memories were very distant and cut little ice with some politicians. On the eve of the crisis, President Sezer is believed to have been pressing unsuccessfully for the investigation of corruption allegations against at least one member of the cabinet.

Despite the crisis, little if any serious action was taken against corruption at these levels before the end of 2002 when the AKP government came to power. New legislation on public tenders was part of the rescue package negotiated with the IMF in the spring of 2001. But the Ecevit government made little headway over allegations that the Uzan group owed over $2 billion in suppliers' credits to Motorola and Nokia in the USA, and ministers from several parties attended events sponsored by the Uzans. Since coming to power, the AKP has pressed vigorously against banks, businessmen, politicians, and senior ex-ministers and a spate of trials and hearings is getting under way, including the formal impeachment of an ex-prime minister and another minister for corruption. Television channels, banks, and newspapers have been placed in the hands of administrators. A new and stricter period is beginning in Turkish public life.

The pressures creating inefficiency and corruption are very obvious. Though certain 'fast track' contract arrangements for top officials have been created, most public employees still earn only minute salaries and as a result the distinction between regular and irregular payments may get blurred.[10]

Further Reforms of the Judicial System

The removal of anachronistic and repressive legislation to comply with the legal norms and *acquis communautaire* may be only the prologue to the changes to Turkey's judicial system stemming from the interaction between the European Union and Turkey. In September and October 2003 the European Union sent Kjell Bjornberg and Paul Richmond, an English barrister, on a twelve-day visit to investigate the Turkish judicial system and their findings were published in Turkish and English as a 156-page report under the title of 'The Functioning of the Judicial System in the Republic of Turkey'[11]. This document is now being widely read by the legal profession at all levels in Turkey and it is assumed that many of its recommendations will be acted upon. Richmond's views are summarised in a presentation given in April 2004. While praising reforms carried out so far, Richmond expresses uncertainties about their implementation, considers that the structure of the judiciary under the Ministry of Justice makes the former potentially subject to its political will to an unacceptable degree, and believes that too many obstacles still exist for defence lawyers, while the status and powers of prosecutors (close to those of judges) should be reduced. Richmond argues that the international community should be pressing for further reforms in the functioning of the judicial system in Turkey.

Some of Richmond's arguments could be taken as showing a lack of close familiarity with Turkish culture and society. His concern with possible charges for insulting the state, for example, overlooks the fact that litigation between individuals is also often linked with the idea of insult. His views on potential political influence on judges are, as far as I can judge, not well founded. Indeed one of the reasons why the military insisted on martial law courts and state security tribunals was the type of verdicts which tended to emanate from the ordinary courts, suggesting a culture of judicial independence and a prevailing centre-left outlook. Many Turkish lawyers however do welcome the idea of reducing links with the Ministry of Justice and a reduction in bureaucratic red tape and cumbersome procedures.[12] There has been remarkably little outcry so far against the idea of a general reshaping of the country's judicial institutions on the basis of these outside consultancy reports.

A Turkish judge, writing anonymously in Turkish on a legal profession webpage for the benefit of his colleagues, comments that while he generally approves of Richmond's and Bjornberg's proposals, he thinks that some of them could have opposite effects to those intended: reduction of the powers of prosecutors might actually lead to more rather than fewer convictions in some circumstances.

At a more mundane level, it is clear that the quality of justice in Turkey would be improved by things such as greater resources for the judicial system (one of the smallest items on the government's annual budget), a larger number of judges, improved salary conditions and other safeguards for the independence of judges in isolated or small local communities, and greater access to defence lawyers. At present the vast majority of detainees in police stations do not request recourse to lawyers. The number of judges is monitored in the Commission's annual report, which reports a slow increase, while there have been a number of schemes enabling the Turkish judiciary to learn about developments in European law and practice.

Finally, there is some statistical evidence that the judicial system operates more severely in Turkey than in the EU as a whole. In 2001, 84 persons per 100,000 of the population were in prison in Turkey, just below the EU average of 87 per 100,000 and well below the 129 for the UK, but the numbers of offences committed under most categories of crime seem to be well below those characteristic of Western European countries. Whereas 121,370 cases of robbery were recorded in England and Wales in 2001 for example, there were only 2,480 cases in Turkey.[13]

Conclusion[14]

Turkey's application to join the EU has caused a profound and very sudden transformation in its legal and judicial structures, updating an essentially Napoleonic-prefectorial system along the norms of the Union. The tutelary apparatus, introduced in the 1970s and 1980s to counter challenges to the existing political and social order, has now been dismantled and since most reforms in Turkey have always been introduced summarily and then proved durable afterwards, there is little reason to doubt that most of the changes are being implemented and will find permanent expression.

There are several questions which may arise. First, on some issues such as corruption, the reforms are grappling with problems which existing EU members have not always succeeded in overcoming and the scale of Turkey's population and large cities suggests that its future difficulties could be proportionately greater or at least require a greater concentration of resources to contain them. Second, it is not yet altogether clear how Turkish society will fare in the absence of legislation which both ring-fenced it against some genuine threats and promoted order and cohesion in a society which views itself as undisciplined and fissiparous. Turkish opponents of the EU argue that the EU is assisting in the process of removing safeguards against an Islamist takeover. If that is the case, if Turkey evolves into a country more along the lines of Malaysia or Pakistan, (a development which the majority of the population unquestionably do not want), the reforms will have failed to promote democracy and tolerance.

This issue is tied up with a deeper one. It remains to be seen how Turkish rural society – with engrained hierarchical traditionalistic and religious values held both by officials and by the general population – will respond to the pluralist, egalitarian, liberal, and essentially metropolitan values implicit in much EU legislation. While this article was about to go to press, for example, a court in the religiously highly conservative Fatih district of Istanbul reduced a gaol sentence on a husband who murdered his wife from 24 years to six years eight months on the grounds that she had engaged in a lesbian relationship and this was extreme provocation.[15] But this episode exposes an important point. We know of this incident and others like it because they are energetically and indignantly flagged by Turkey's mainstream press which undoubtedly subscribes to the common values of the modern world. If the Turkish media had not been so free, modern in its outlook, and conscience-driven on these matters, there would be no debate on human rights in Turkey.

So pessimism can easily be overdone. It should not be forgotten that ordinary people in Turkish society are already being exposed as never before to these values by modern communications, multi-channel satellite television, and the Internet. The 'global village' has become a reality. The reaction to the changes – whether they are welcomed and absorbed or are regarded as an imposition – depends more than anything else on the degree to which Western Europeans can overcome their own traditional prejudices towards the Turks and subdue the impulse to assist Turkey's enemies and critics without asking searching questions. These

European prejudices and impulses are perceived and understood very clearly even in remote villages in Turkey, yet despite that, according to recent opinion polls, support for EU membership is even stronger than in the country as a whole[16], a sign perhaps that full membership will eventually lay many ancient and otherwise endemic tensions to rest.

Endnotes

1 For a discussion of suggestions that the 'level of conditionality is more demanding than for other candidates' in Turkey's case, see Christopher Brewin, 'Turkey and Europe after the Nice Summit', TESEV 2002.

2 Extracts from E.A. Freeman, *History of the Saracens* and *The Ottoman power in Europe. Its nature, its growth and its decline.* 1877

3 William Gladstone, *Bulgarian Horrors and the Question of the East;* 1876, p.17.*Lessons in Massacre,* 1877, p.76.

4 These comments are made on the basis of personal observations as a British newspaper correspondent in Ankara in the 1980s.

5 The military judges were dropped in May 1999 at the time of the trial of Abdullah Öcalan.

6 CPT/Inf (2004) 16, *Report to the Turkish Government on the visit to Turkey carried out by the European Committee for the Prevention of Torture and Inhuman or Degrading Treatment or Punishment (CPT) from 7 to 15 September 2003*, Strasbourg June 2004.

7 I have found exact comparisons difficult to make because the Turkish statistics are more readily available on the Internet than the British ones, but a crude contrast may be drawn. In 2003, a total of 4,498 persons were held by the former State Security Courts in Turkey, whereas between 11 September 2001 and 31 January 2004, in the UK (excluding Northern Ireland), 544 individuals were arrested under the Terrorism Act 2000 of whom only 98 were eventually charged. Detainments for Northern Ireland would probably add only a few more hundred detainees over the same period.

8 The Vatican Embassy in Ankara several times tried unsuccessfully to obtain recognition for the Catholic Church in the 1990s. Even the establishment of a new bishopric required official permission.

9 Hürriyet, 4 January 2005.

10 See David Barchard: 'Society and Bureaucracy: The Civil Service' in *Turkish Transformation; New Century, New Challenges* Ed. Brian W.Beeley, London 2202, p. 217-8.

11 *Türkiye Cumhuriyetinde Yargı Sisteminin Isleyisi— Istisarî Ziyaret Raporu* (Commission of the European Union) Brussels 2003. Also 'Turkey – A Presentation on the Independence of the Judiciary and the Legal Profession in Turkey' Centre of the Independence of Judges and Lawyers in Conjunction with the World Organisation Against Torture, 15 April 2004.

12 *The Legal System,* Mesut Çakmak, *Financial Times World Report*, December 10, 2002.

13 Gordon Barclay and Cynthia Tavares, *International Comparisons of Criminal Justice Statistics 2001,* Home Office London. (The comparison is hampered by absence of overall crime figures from Turkey. In certain categories Turkey does have significantly higher rates of crime in absolute numbers than the UK. In 2001, there were 1,050 homicides in the UK, 867 in Germany, and 1,047 in France, but 1,550 in Turkey, though this last figure includes attempts. Turkish rates for homicide in the capital city however are comparable to those of Western European cities, suggesting that there is a strong rural component involved.)

14 For a leading NGO's summary of the situation in December 2004, see 'A Crossroads for Human Rights? Human Rights Watch's key concerns on Turkey for 2005'. New York 2004. Available on http://www.hrw.org/english/docs/2004/12/15/turkey9865.htm

15 NTV news: 'Lezbiyen iliski 'ağır tahrik' sayıldı'; http://www.ntvmsnbc.com/news/303671.asp.

16 *Halkın yüzde 94.5'i AB'yi istiyor* ['94.5 per cent of the people want the EU.'] NTVMSNBC News, 2 June 2004.

Does Civil Society Matter?

Hakan Altinay

The key question about any field is whether it matters. In other words, would an analyst studying EU-Turkey relations miss out on anything, if he/she were to omit civil society? I will argue in this chapter that civil society has mattered in EU-Turkey relations, and any analysts interested in this relationship would omit civil society at their own peril. I will try to prove this argument by looking at a specific period, namely 2002-2004, and the efforts of pro-EU forces in Turkey. After offering a description of the work of pro-EU civil society, I will also dwell on what they could not do. At the end, I offer some observations about the larger context and trends that are associated with Turkish civil society's performance.

Let me start by describing the work of four major actors: IKV (Economic Development Foundation), TUSIAD (Turkish Industrialists' and Businessmen's Association), TESEV (Turkish Economic and Social Studies Foundation), and Avrupa Hareketi 2002 (European Movement 2002). IKV, or the Economic Development Foundation, was founded in 1965 after the signing of the Ankara Agreement with the EEC, at the initiatives of the Istanbul Chamber of Commerce and the Istanbul Chamber of Industry. Other than the Chambers of Commerce and Industry of Istanbul, the Union of Chambers, Maritime Chambers and Stock Exchanges of Turkey (TOBB), the Istanbul Stock Exchange (IMKB), the Union Banks of Turkey (TBB) and the Assembly of Turkish Exporters (TIM) are among its important members. IKV defines its general mission as 'closely monitoring the European integration process'.[1] More specifically, the main mandate of IKV has been to promote business partnerships that have served as an essential basis of economic integration. In this context, IKV has acted as the 'national counsellor institution' for small and medium enterprise-oriented EU programmes such as Europartenariat, Medpartenariat, and Interprise. Over the years, IKV also produced detailed sectoral analyses of economic integration with the EU for a large variety of sectors.

When economic integration and the Customs Union were the central focus of EU-Turkey relations in the mid 1990s, IKV was the main pro-EU voice in Turkey. As enhanced integration in general, and the Copenhagen political criteria in particular, became the make-or-break issue, IKV was notably aloof. Monitoring EU political reforms by IKV has not been detail-rich, and essentially involved a checklist without discussing whether these legislative changes went to the heart of the matter. This can be best explained by IKV's diverse constituent circles, who themselves were not all on the same wavelength concerning the political criteria.

If not a very forceful agent of change in terms of demanding political reforms, IKV nevertheless played an indispensable role in mobilising Turkish civil society in expressing their general support for Turkey's EU vocation. In more than one instance when Turkey seemed stuck with spinning wheels, IKV choreographed one public statement after another that put Turkey back on track. The main vehicle for these statements was 'The Turkish Civil Society Platform,' more commonly known as 'The Turkey Platform,' which IKV coordinated. 'The Turkey Platform', a gathering of 240 NGOs to convey the determination of the Turkish people to integrate with the EU, revealed a 'Common Declaration of the Turkish Civil Society' in October 2001 with the catchy slogan of 'Turkey's Place is in the European Union. We have no time to lose'. The platform gathered on 7 October 2002 for the second time, this time to make a call upon the European Union: 'Turkey has proved her decisiveness. It is now the EU's turn'. [2]

The two declarations of the Turkey Platform were successful in describing what Turkey wanted loudly and clearly. It was symbolically significant and representative of the solidarity among Turkish NGOs. Full-page advertisements in all newspapers, organised by IKV at critical times, marked important milestones during the last three years as Turkey progressed into near-complete compliance with the letter of the Copenhagen political criteria.

If one needs to point to possible weaknesses of IKV activism, one can argue that at times one needed more than a determined statement that 'Turkey wants EU membership and hence should carry out the reforms.' IKV identified the end goal, but remained vague about what Turkey needed to do to get there. IKV also did not substantiate the desirability of the reforms with anything other than the argument that 'these are what the EU wants and since we are determined to become a member, we should just do them.' The works of TUSIAD and TESEV were more conversant with local priorities and sensitivities, and provided more authentic arguments.

One less recognised contribution of IKV is to have acted over the years as a school or a factory of EU specialists and EU enthusiasts. We cannot fail to mention, for example, the quiet but critical role that its current Executive Director, Sebnem Karaucak, played in the European Movement 2002.

Currently, IKV is carrying out two information dissemination projects, both with the support of the EU Commission. The first of these projects is aimed at increasing the awareness and understanding of the Turkish business world regarding the implementation of those chapters of the EU *acquis communautaire* having a direct impact on the economy and business life. This is being done through a total of twelve seminars in Istanbul and Ankara to extend *acquis*-related information through the training of their representative organisations' experts. The other project, though similar to the first, is more embracing of Turkey's needs: To organise seminars to be held in 24 different cities all over Turkey, and to raise the awareness and understanding at all layers of society on the aims, scope and implementation of the pre-accession process as well as its effects on economic, political and social life. This project is important for IKV since this is one of the few projects that IKV is carrying out beyond its normally restricted scope of economic integration.

Another business organisation that has devoted substantial energy to EU-Turkey relations is TUSIAD. TUSIAD is thought to be the organisation of big business, and is a member of UNICE (Union des Industries de la Communauté Européene), BIAC and UMCE; it has offices in Brussels and Berlin. While itself not completely homogeneous, TUSIAD membership has been more forcefully behind Turkey's EU aspirations. Unlike IKV, TUSIAD's determination has included taking less-than-popular positions on specific political reforms, and most recently on Turkey's policy on Cyprus. One has to recall, in this context, TUSIAD's 1997 report, 'Perspectives of Democratization in Turkey.' The 1997 report is a homegrown manifesto of full democratization that TUSIAD updated in both 1999 and 2001; It closely resembles the Accession Partnership Document of 2000 by the Commission. This is an important reminder that the political reforms in question were indeed authentic aspirations of the Turks. Before the European Union recognised Turkey as a candidate, TUSIAD chose to highlight the notorious legislation restricting Freedom of Expression, the mandate of State Security Courts and the make-up of the National Security Council. While I do not have much empirical basis, my hunch is that TUSIAD's principled embrace of democratisation is not dissimilar to the grand compromise we saw in Spain in the late 1970s and early 1980s. TUSIAD, with its 1997 report, demonstrated that it can and does rise above the narrow interests of its members, and while the move was not reciprocated by other sectors in society, it signified a larger conviction about the possibility of a non-zero sum gain along the European lines, and must have opened the door for various sectors of society to congregate around the common goal of EU membership.

Another institution whose efforts have been instrumental in galvanising Turkey's drive to overcome its hesitation about difficult political reform issues is TESEV. Now arguably the premier think tank in the country, TESEV has a history of addressing difficult issues that Turkey faces: in the highly polarised environment of the 1960s and 1970s, TESEV advocated a European style social market economy. In the 1990s, transparency and civil liberties become critical issues for TESEV. In the context of EU-Turkey relations, TESEV's most important contribution was a research project called 'European Union Survey: Turkish Public Opinion on the European Union.' Carried out in June 2002, the project analysed subgroups of public opinion regarding their support for the political reforms required by the EU.[3] The timing of the TESEV project is significant. Unlike today, in the summer of 2002 it was unclear whether Turkey possessed the determination to go through with the tough political reform issues. Elimination of the death penalty was a serious stumbling block. After 15 years of violent conflict, and the conviction of the man widely held responsible for this conflict, Turkey was being asked to resist the temptation of going through with the conviction and the execution of the most dreaded man in the country. The image of the 'Mothers of the Martyrs' was frequently invoked to underline how unacceptable forgoing Ocalan's execution was. The government and the parliament of the time were hesitant in the face of the presumed opposition to this move, especially given the looming general elections. It was in this context that TESEV's research confirmed not only that 74 per cent of the public was in favour of EU membership[4], but that large sections of the public were in favour of the required political reforms. On the burning issues of the death penalty, TESEV's research showed that there was no strong correlation between 'being a victim of terrorism' and 'supporting the death penalty'. According to the study, 43 per cent of the subjects who had not lost close relatives or friends because of terrorism approved the unconditional abolition of the death penalty. Contrary to assumptions that this percentage would be much lower among those who did lose loved ones to terrorism, the research showed that this was not the case. In fact, the percentage for this latter group was 44 per cent, slightly higher than the general public. Along with IKV's networking efforts and European Movement's 2002 creativity, which I will discuss next, TESEV's critical intervention was highly instrumental in getting Turkey to make the first major leap of faith. The successive reform packages became easier once the initial leap was made.

TESEV was also instrumental in the debate on Cyprus. In the autumn of 2003, at a time when there was much confusion and disinformation about the Annan Plan, TESEV translated the PRIO (Peace Research Institute of Oslo) account of what the Annan Plan involved into Turkish, and convened a meeting of the Greeks and Greek Cypriots in Istanbul for a comprehensive debate on the Cyprus question. In doing so, TESEV's demonstrated that, as a civil society organisation, it could be very independent and courageous, and help deepen the debate on Cyprus.

The least institutionalised of the four civil efforts that I set out to cover is Avrupa Hareketi 2002, or European Movement 2002. The movement was started by a handful of EU enthusiasts, such as Cengiz Aktar, Mehmet Altan, Eser Karakas, Sebnem Karaucak, and Berna Turkili. The core group assumed a low public profile throughout, and the Movement came to be known through its communication strategy. AB Hareketi 2002 was founded on 9 May, Europe Day, with a statement signed by people from all walks of life. The Movement was marked by a stunning organisational capacity, extraordinary creativity, and enormous media attention and public response.

European Movement was a civil society initiative born out of the recognition that Turkey's EU bid stood at an irreversible crossroad in the summer of 2002, when urgent reforms were required in order to meet candidacy obligations, and to demonstrate the political will of Turkey. European Movement 2002 was conceived at this crucial moment in time; the founders felt that one needed to do everything possible to mobilise the 74 per cent support lent by Turkish society for Turkey's accession to the EU. The Movement enlisted *pro bono* services of advertising agencies and production companies; they persuaded the print and broadcast media to provide them massive free-of-charge advertisement space. What the Movement lacked in financial resources, they made up with aggressive networking and agile organising.

The emblem of the Movement, a rushing star, symbolised, in the Movement's own words, 'the urgency attached to the task lying ahead and the vigour in the campaign to set in motion a largely inert legislature and to follow through the implementation of reforms'. The Movement received tremendous public support. Carefully using the advantage of being a popular initiative, the Movement enlisted many high profile individuals in the Turkish public eye including academics, artists, civil servants, media representatives, businessmen and self-employed people. The slogan of the movement was 'Baska yarin yok', which can be roughly translated as 'there is no other tomorrow'. For a period of roughly three months in 2002, from early May to early August, the movement was highly active with enormous media coverage; European Movement commercials were aired frequently: Turkish coffee was pictured almost spilling over, with the caption: 'We are about to be too late'. Cars with 'European Movement 2002' stickers were everywhere. It seemed like all neighbourhoods in Istanbul had one of the street banners of the European Movement.

The Movement also placed a huge clock in front of the parliament running backwards: 'The clock is ticking', symbolic of the little time Turkey had left. The clock was put in place on 1 August, and it put enormous pressure on the parliament to work faster. The parliament passed the laws concerning the fulfilment of the Copenhagen criteria two days later, on 3 August. The Turkish Parliament voted to abolish the death penalty, to legalise education in native languages, and to safeguard the freedoms of expression and association among other things. It might very well be that if it weren't for the pressure of the Movement, the Turkish Parliament might not have passed the laws so expeditiously, especially given the looming early general elections, and the much more pressing need to carry out re-election campaigns.

The Movement also recognised the importance of being active in Europe. Realising that ' a successful campaign in favour of this goal cannot be limited to domestic politics', the Movement organised a series of gatherings, which aimed to bring together European decision -makers with European intellectuals who recognised the importance of Turkey vis a vis the Union. Apart from arranging meetings in Europe's capitals, the Movement organised a Brussels performance in November 2002. Supporters of the Movement arranged a special flight from Istanbul to Brussels only for this occasion. Sezen Aksu, a mixture of between Madonna and Joan Baez, had done a series of immensely popular performances that autumn in several Turkish languages. European Movement 2002 arranged for her to give her last performance in Brussels. The major goal of this activity was to encourage the participation of various European diplomats and commissioners in the audience, and to a certain extent, the show was a success. After Brussels, the Movement decided that it had fulfilled its mission and dissolved.

To be sure, there is a larger circle of pro-EU, NGOs and other civic organisations than these four described above. Let me at least briefly mention some of them: The Association for Liberal Thinking (LDD), based in Ankara, for example, did an authoritative study of what Turkey needed to do for freedom of association, and its work was seminal for several reform packages. We were delighted when the current AKP government appointed the author of this LDD report, Vahit Bicak, as the president of the Human Rights Office at the Prime Ministry, a decision that many wholeheartedly applauded. Although considerably later than business organisations, labour union confederations such as Hak-Is and DISK have linked up with their opposite numbers in the EU. Helsinki Citizens Assembly Turkey was always a persistent voice for the political reforms. AEGEE made sure that we did not forget the youthful side of EU-Turkey relations. We should also mention EU missionaries such as Cengiz Aktar and Ahmet Sever, who, through their TV programmes and popular writings, made possible several leaps forward in comprehension and appreciation of EU membership among the general public.

These are some of the things that pro-EU NGOs did in the last few years. Yet an assessment of them as a social actor or force for change also needs to address what they could not do: most activities by these groups were initiated by a sense of urgency or even emergency. These moments are often marked by extraordinary bursts of activism, energy and creativity, but these episodic flairs have been interrupted by long periods of inactivity. We need to be more strategic, and have more staying power.

Pro-EU NGOs seem to share the more general fixation with legislative changes, and have been relatively uninterested in the implementation of the reforms. Admittedly, monitoring implementation of reforms requires a greater organisational capacity than monitoring the legislative changes, and yet we need to build this capacity. In discussing the reforms, Turkish civil society has been uninterested in the practices of the Member States or the experiences of other candidates. One notable exception to is the Istanbul Policy Centre of Sabanci University which has translated into Turkish the work of the EU Accession Monitoring Project, EUMAP[5], that has done comparative studies of reforms in Central and Eastern Europe. The Istanbul Policy Centre has also organised the Turkish section of the gender equality report of EUMAP. The next theme of IPC studies will be media plurality. This is an exciting development as Turkish civil society is no longer a passive recipient of norms developed before its time, but in certain cases has been an active participant in the development of these norms.

All the efforts I have discussed above are urban and elite-dominated. In a more thorough strategy, one would have expected the pro-EU NGOs to render the EU integration project more intelligible to larger sections of the Turkish body politic. One exciting project that we are aware of is Bilgi University's effort to capture the experience of the Turkish Diaspora in France and Germany, and to render the EU idea accessible through the eyes of the Turkish Diaspora for their brethren at home.

If one challenge to civil society efforts that want to see Turkey as a member of the EU is that of EU-sceptics in Turkey, a greater challenge is Turkey-sceptics in the EU. With the notable exception of TUSIAD reaching out to business groups in Europe, there has been a glaring absence of engagement on this track. One could argue that the challenge at home was more pressing, and that now that Turkey seems firmly on track to realise the political criteria, more attention will be paid to the European front. And yet, there was no reason why Turkish civil society did not organise a Europe-wide campaign to ask for Giscard D'Estaing's resignation, for example, when it became so clear that he was out-of-sync with the political authority that asked him to lead the Convention.

One manifestation of under-engagement with Europe is the absence of any meaningful debate about the European Convention in Turkey. It is unfortunate that Turkish civil society has been uninterested in this seminal process, and has not ushered in a parallel discussion in Turkey. If Turkey is to be a bona fide member of the European body politic, it needs to have active participants in its deliberations, rather than passive importers of its ways[6]. At a minimum, in the case of the European Convention, Turkish civil society may have made an interesting contribution to the so-called 'God debate' in the Convention.

I should also note, however, that civil society in the EU has been slow to engage with its counterparts in Turkey. Amnesty International registered its Turkey affiliate in 2002; European Stability Initiative is scheduled to open an office in Turkey in the near future. Policy institutes such as CEPS in Brussels, CER in London, FASOPO in Paris, SWP in Berlin, CESPI in Rome and Elcano in Madrid all have Turkey in their research agendas of 2004. There are three other exceptions to this under-engagement: The Greens in the European Parliament held their annual meeting in Istanbul in October 2004, and the meeting ended up being a joyous demonstration of the solidarity of the Greens with Turkish civil society. Similarly, No Peace Without Justice, together with the Liberal Group in the European Parliament, organised a Turkey event in the European Parliament in December 2004; in this highly symbolic event, the room that was often the venue of debate on Turkey, hosted on that day people from Turkey and in Turkish. MEPs Daniel Cohn-Bendit, Joost Lagendejk and Emma Bonino could not have made the Turks feel any more welcome as equal partners if they tried. Both events have taken their rightful place in the annals of civil Europe.

The initiative that was most remarkable, however, was the Independent Commission on Turkey[7]. This self-appointed group of European dignitaries worked for six months between March and September 2004, deliberated all the tough questions regarding Turkish membership, visited Turkey and reported on their findings through their report. The report has been widely read and discussed, with 25,000 hard copies and 20,000 downloads from the Internet site. The Independent Commission has been a beacon of how Europe can be very fair and diligent in the pursuit of the truth, and as such has gained much praise both in Europe and in Turkey.

To sum up, the most outstanding achievement of Turkish civil society has been to articulate the European aspirations of the general public through multiple formats and channels. This has been done through IKV's institutional coalitions, TUSIAD's demands for principled reform positions, European Movement's street-smart ways, and TESEV's public opinion surveys. These efforts have produced results: Eight reform packages by three different governments in the last three years have been made possible in substantial part due to these efforts.

In its efforts, Turkish civil society has been less strategic and more episodic than one would like. While we should expect more for Turkish civil society in terms of strategic thinking and engagement with Europe, we should also recognise that we are talking about a fairly new, young field. Ambassador Lake reminded us in his report of 1998 that there was very little of this sort of activism when he first came to Turkey in 1991. The organisational capacity and financial resources of these organisations have grown significantly since then, and this is a process that will and should continue. If Turkish civil society can retain its organisational agility, as it develops its financial and organisational capacity, as well as its links with its counterparts in the member states, it can be an even more formidable force of change in Turkey.

Endnotes

1 http://www.ikv.org.tr/ikv-eng/ikv-eng.html

2 'Common Declaration of the Turkish Civil Society', signed by numerous Turkish NGOs, can be accessed from http://www.ikv.org.tr/ikv-eng/activities/activities.html

3 'European Union Survey: Turkish Public Opinion on the European Union', June 2002, Ali Carkoglu, Refik Erzan, Kemal Kirisci, Hakan Yilmaz- Bogazici University, TESEV Research

4 Spain may be the country that Turkey has the most in common in terms of its trajectory. The highest recorded support for EU membership in Spain prior to 1986 was 51%.

5 For more information, visit www.eumap.org

6 One very notable exception to this has been Kemal Dervis, whose theories on future of Europe are original contributions the pan-European debate. For more detail, see 'Vision of Europe,' *Turkish Policy Quarterly*, v.3, n.3 (Fall 2004)

7 The Independent Commission on Turkey was formed by Martti Ahtisaari (Former President of Finland), Kurt Biedenkopf (Former Prime Minister of Saxony), Emma Bonino (Former European Commissioner, Member of the European Parliament), Hans van den Broek (Former Foreign Minister of Netherlands, former European Commissioner), Bronislaw Geremek (Former Foreign Minister of Poland, Member of the European Parliament), Anthony Giddens (Former Director of London School of Economics and Political Science), Marcelino Oreja Aguirre (Former Foreign Minister of Spain, former Secretary General of the Council of Europe, former European Commissioner), Michel Rocard (Former Prime Minister of France, Member of the European Parliament) and Albert Rohan (Former Secretary General of Foreign Affairs, Austria) For more information, visit www.independentcommissiononturkey.org

Women in Turkish Society

Nicole Pope

Turks are rightly proud of the fact that women in their country were legally given equality and obtained the right to vote earlier than many of their Western counterparts. Important reforms benefiting women were indeed introduced by Atatürk in the early days of the Republic. The Civil Code of 1926 abolished polygamy and gave women the right to divorce and get custody of their children.

But these early reforms do not reflect the whole picture. Eight decades after the birth of the Turkish republic, millions of Turkish women are still not fully aware of their rights, let alone in a position to exercise them. Although women from the educated elite have reached positions of power in the public and the private sector, particularly in Istanbul, Ankara and Izmir, Turkey is still a strongly patriarchal society where discrimination against women is endemic, and participation of women in the political life of the country remains minimal.

In recent years, however, civil society has grown more vocal and brought greater awareness of issues affecting women, such as domestic violence. Pressure from women's groups challenging traditional perceptions of women is gradually opening the way to social and legal changes.

Before the Republic

The introduction of the new Civil Code in the early Republican era brought Turkish women legal rights, but they had not waited for the advent of the Republic to demand greater freedom. A lively women's movement had already emerged in the second part of the nineteenth century. The late Ottoman period was characterised by political reforms introduced as a result of growing European influence and a desire to modernise the empire in all areas. It is therefore hardly surprising that Ottoman women too felt the impact of social changes that were happening in Western Europe.

In the second half of the nineteenth century, women's magazines promoting education and greater rights for women started to appear. The first one, Terakki-I Muhadderat (Progress of civilisations), was published in 1869, and it was soon followed by some forty other publications aimed at a female readership. One of the most radical magazines was published by the Ottoman Association for the Protection of Women's Legal Rights; it was openly feminist and employed an entirely female staff.

Women's associations, founded to support women's education or their right to work, scored a few early victories. In 1897 women were admitted into the workforce as salaried employees, and a university for women was established in 1914.

Women also became active in the budding nationalist movement and took to the streets to demonstrate against foreign occupation. Halide Edip, who became a leading figure of the War of Independence and a famous writer, founded The Society for the Improvement of Women in 1908. She had first-hand experience of the discrimination faced by women: her first husband's decision to bring a second wife into the household, after nine years of marriage, led to their divorce. Halide Edip, who later married Dr Anan Adivar, organised relief for families suffering from the consequences of the war and dedicated much of her life to the improvement of education for Turkish women. She is best remembered for the fiery speech she gave at a famous meeting in Sultanahmet in 1919, mobilising the women of Istanbul against the occupation of Izmir.

The Republican Era

The reforms introduced by Atatürk undoubtedly gave many Turkish women an opportunity to escape from the constraints of tradition, but they also paradoxically curbed the momentum of the women's movement.

The new Civil Code had brought Turkish women rights that some of their Western sisters did not yet enjoy, but it also produced a sense that women had now achieved their aims and activism was therefore redundant. The early women's movement was replaced by state-sponsored feminism that focused more on furthering republican ideals than on challenging traditional perceptions of women.

Women who were able to take advantage of Atatürk's reforms were in fact only a small minority, usually from wealthy families or relatives of members of the Kemalist establishment. Atatürk's adopted daughter, Sabiha Gökçen, was a fighter pilot in the 1930s. Secular, republican women were seen as a symbol of Turkey's modernity. This is still the case today: the way a woman dresses is often perceived as a gauge of modernity. As we shall see, the official definition of modernity has been challenged in recent years by young women wearing the türban, the Islamic headscarf tightly wound around the head that first appeared in the streets of Turkey's big cities in the early 1980s.

Women from the educated urban elite are now doctors, lawyers or bankers, and many of them have reached high level positions previously occupied only by men. Female participation is 33 per cent in the civil service, 36 per cent in academia, 19.7 per cent in law and 33.8 per cent in medicine.[1] But in rural parts of Turkey, the reality remains very different. According to a UNDP report published in 1999, 22.4 per cent of women are still illiterate compared with only 5.9 per cent of men despite the fact that primary education has been compulsory since 1924, and only 2.8 per cent of women have university degrees. Women still constitute the majority of the workforce in agriculture, and most of them receive no salary for their labour.

The low level of participation of women in politics is a good illustration of the complacency that set in after initial achievements. A year after women were granted the right to vote and be elected to the national assembly in 1934, women won 18 parliamentary seats, or 4.6 per cent of the total, in general elections. Instead of increasing, this percentage declined over the following decades before taking a slight upward swing again, but the current level shows that women still have very little say in the running of the country. In the present parliament, voted into power in November 2002, only 4.4 per cent of deputies are women, a ratio that leaves Turkey behind countries such as Pakistan (20.6 per cent), Malaysia (11.5 per cent), Syria (9.7 per cent) or Sudan (8 per cent)[2]. Turkey did have a female prime minister, Tansu Çiller, from 1993 to 1996, but the current government led by Recep Tayyip Erdogan has only one woman minister. The coalition that preceded the arrival in power of the Justice and Development party, led by leftist Bülent Ecevit, had none.

For decades, the political establishment showed little enthusiasm for a review of the 1926 Civil Code, which was progressive for its time, but still left women in a subordinate position within the home where the husband ruled as official head of the family. These provisions were in contradiction to the spirit of the Constitution, which granted all Turkish citizens, men and women, the same status. A first step was taken in 1988 when a bill was introduced to facilitate divorce, and another improvement was recorded in 1990 with the lifting of the law requiring a woman to get her husband's permission to get a job. But Turkish women had to wait until the adoption of a brand new Civil Code in 2001 to get equal rights within the family.

Between enshrining rights in the law and giving women the power to exercise them, there is a wide gap that Turkish officialdom has not done enough to bridge. In rural areas, particularly in south-east Anatolia, women are still commonly believed to be the property of their father or their husband. Although the law states clearly that girls cannot be married without their consent, many young women are still coerced by their family into marrying relatives or men they have never seen, often much older. The 1999 UNDP report showed that only 25.9 per cent of Turkish women were free to choose their spouse and 22.6 per cent were married to relatives; official figures also indicated that 28.6 per cent of marriages involved the payment of bride money (baslik) to the girl's family. [3]

Although the 1926 Civil Code banned polygamy, many men in rural Turkey, again particularly in the east and south-east, have more than one wife. In a study conducted in south-east Turkey by Pinar Ilkkaracan, of the association Women for Women's Human Rights,[4] 10.6 per cent of marriages in that region were shown to be polygamous, a situation that usually causes the women involved a lot of distress. The majority of the marriages surveyed had been arranged (61.2 per cent), while one in 20 were cases of berdel, or exchange of girls between two families.

Second wives or kuma, who have only contracted a religious marriage in front of an imam, have no rights in the eyes of the law. In fact, children born to second or subsequent wives are often registered as being born to the first, and only legal, wife. But concubines are not the only women whose marriage is unregistered: 19.6 per cent of the women who were the focus of Pinar Ilkkaracan's research had only had a religious marriage even if they were first wives, and therefore had no official documents proving their married status.

In the decades that followed the foundation of the Republic, there were social improvements and women gained wider access to education and to jobs, but little significant legal progress was achieved, although maternity leave was regulated in 1945. In the 1960s and 1970s, women became more active again, but mainly within the framework of leftist organisations. Often these political groups considered women's issues as 'secondary issues' to be automatically solved by a Marxist revolution. Following turbulent years marked by fierce fighting between right and left, the 1980 coup led to a major crackdown on leftist groups and silenced civil society in general.

Women activists, however, started organising with renewed vigour after this dark period of Turkey's history.

One of the issues they highlighted, until then a social taboo rarely discussed, was violence against women. Domestic abuse is widespread in Turkey. Various studies show that more than half of Turkish women suffer violence at the hands of their male relatives. According to a recent study carried out by two women's groups in Diyarbakir, wives in south-east Turkey get beaten for a variety of reasons ranging from 'looking out of the window for too long', 'saying hello to a male friend on the road', 'spending too much time talking with shopkeepers' or 'the way they dress'.[5]

The campaign against violence gained momentum in 1987 after an Anatolian judge quoted the old saying 'a woman should always have a stick on her back and a baby in her womb' in an infamous case, to justify the use of violence by a husband. A book entitled *Let Them Hear You Scream* was published and the Purple Roof Shelter was opened in Istanbul in 1990, followed two years later by a Women's Library in Istanbul. Gender studies programmes were also established in universities. In 1998, a new law on the protection of the family introduced measures to protect women and children from domestic abuse.

A split developed in the 1980s and grew in the 1990s between secular and Islamist women, centred on the türban or Islamic headscarf. The issue is a complex one. As long as the headscarf was worn mainly by peasant women in rural Turkey, or by grandmothers and cleaning ladies in big cities, it aroused little passion. The Islamic headscarf surfaced as a divisive issue when daughters of the Anatolian bourgeoisie started wearing it in universities. Secular Turks, and the state establishment, see the türban as a sign of women's lower position in Islam and therefore believe it must be kept out of public offices and universities at all costs. They don't object so much to the headscarf being worn in a traditional fashion, tied with a knot under the chin, but they perceive the türban, pinned around the head and covering the neck, as a symbol of political Islam. Others argue that the türban is simply a more fashionable way of covering the head, favoured by urban young women who want to distance themselves from their mother's traditional past.

The young Islamist women who demonstrated for the right to keep their head covered were indeed very different from women of the previous generation. Far from being submissive, they loudly claimed the right to become lawyers, doctors or engineers. Ironically, in the early 1980s women played a more active role in the Welfare Party, led by Islamist Necmettin Erbakan, than they did in secular parties. At the head of the women's wing of the Welfare Party in Istanbul, lawyer Sibel Eraslan managed an army of 18,000 volunteers who ran the mayoral campaign of Recep Tayyip Erdogan in 1994, establishing a party presence in each street and neighbourhood of the metropolis. Their strategy proved successful and Erdogan was elected mayor of Istanbul, but the female cadres of the party, perhaps seen as too powerful, were later sidelined by the leadership of the party and replaced by more traditional deputies' wives or relatives.

The polarisation in the society reached a peak during the brief tenure in office as prime minister of Necmettin Erbakan of the Welfare party in 1996-1997. Secular Turks were alarmed by the arrival in power of Turkey's first Islamist prime minister. The combined pressure of the army and civil society eventually forced Erbakan to resign in June 1997. In 1999, Merve Kavakçi, a newly elected deputy of the Virtue Party (successor to the now-banned Welfare Party), caused an uproar when she walked into parliament with her headscarf to take the oath of office. Hounded by the secular establishment, she was never allowed to take her seat and was in fact stripped of her Turkish nationality after it was discovered she also had American citizenship. Her case is now under review at the European Court of Human Rights.

Tension between secularists and Islamists is no longer as high today as it was at the time, but the türban remains a divisive issue. Several incidents revealed the disapproval of the state institutions after the Justice and Development party (AKP), sometimes described as a 'muslim democrat' party, came to power in November

2002. Although the AKP had no veiled women among its candidates, the wives of many of its officials, including Emine Erdogan, the prime minister's spouse, cover their head. A scandal erupted in November 2002, when the newly elected speaker of parliament Bülent Arinç, in accordance with protocol, turned up accompanied by his wife, who was wearing a headscarf, to bid the presidential couple farewell as they departed on an official visit abroad. On the eightieth anniversary of the Turkish Republic, President Ahmet Necdet Sezer invited opposition deputies to attend the official reception at the presidential palace with their spouses. Members of the ruling party whose wives were covered, however, were invited alone.

Is the türban an affront to the modern image of the Turkish republic? Secular Turks believe it is. On the other hand, it could be argued that forcing deputies' wives to stay at home or denying thousands of young women hoping to embrace a professional career the right to get an education is also in contradiction with the modernising mission of Atatürk's republic and does little to improve women's rights.

An important study carried out by Prof. Binnaz Toprak and Dr Ali Çarkoglu, published by TESEV in 2000[6], showed that only 27.3 per cent of Turkish women do not cover their head when they go out, although most of them wear a traditional scarf rather than a türban. The study also revealed greater tolerance for veiled women than was expected: 66.6 per cent of respondents said female civil servants and university students should be allowed to cover their head.

The Current Situation

Turkish women have scored important victories in recent years; 126 women's organisations formed a joint platform to lobby for a new Civil Code, which was eventually introduced on 1 January 2002. Under the new Civil Code, women finally have equality with their husband, who is no longer the head of the family. Spouses share responsibility for the children and the running of the household. The minimum age for marriage was set at 18 for boys and girls, whereas the previous code allowed girls to marry as early as 15. In practice, however, under-age marriages only sanctioned by an imam remain common in rural areas.

One of the most important amendments in the Civil Code concerns the division of marital property in case of divorce. Until the new law was introduced, separation of property was the default option and women only kept assets registered in their own name if the union was dissolved. While educated women often took the precaution of ensuring that the marital home, the family car or other assets were registered in their name, many wives were not in a position to assert their rights and were left dispossessed after the collapse of their marriage.

Since the new Civil Code came into force, all assets acquired during the marriage are held in common and therefore equally divided in case of divorce, unless couples choose another option when they wed. A last minute amendment was made by members of parliament apparently keen to protect their own assets, who changed the wording of the law to prevent the new rules being applied retroactively to existing marriages. Nonetheless the adoption of the new code was a major success for Turkish women.

Strengthened by this victory, women's organisations went into battle to ensure a planned new Penal Code did not contain articles discriminatory to women. A Women's Penal Code Platform was formed to lobby for change, but initial amendments they had been suggested to the Justice Ministry were not taken into account in the first draft submitted to parliament. Working for months in close cooperation with the sub-commission charged with reviewing the draft, women's activists, led by organisations such as Women for Women's Human Rights/New Ways, eventually convinced lawmakers to amend crucial articles, thus altering the way Turkish women are perceived by the law. After much debate, and a last minute hitch caused by a government suggestion to add an article criminalising adultery, which caused such an outcry that it was abandoned, the new Penal Code was finally adopted by parliament on 26 September 2004 and will come into force on 1 April 2005.

Old patriarchal concepts such as 'chastity', 'honour' and 'morality' were removed while concepts such as marital rape and sexual harassment at the workplace were introduced for the first time. In the new code, sexual offences are no longer considered to be committed against 'society' and 'public morality and family', but as 'crimes against individuals'. The Women's Penal Code Platform was adamant that two controversial articles, allowing rapists to have their sentence postponed or suspended if they marry their victims, be repealed. Underlying these articles was the notion that a girl who has been raped is damaged beyond repair and will not find a husband. Traditionally, it was believed to be in the interest of the society, and the girl's family, to put a legal stamp of approval on the act of violence committed by the rapist against his victim. Needless to say, few victims were consulted in the matter and even if they were, the pressure of their environment often made it impossible for them to object.

In October 2003, Professor Dogan Soyaslan, who teaches at Çankaya University Law Faculty and is an adviser to the Justice Ministry, triggered a national debate when he defended these articles in the media and insisted they should be maintained. 'Nobody wants to marry someone who is not a virgin ... Those who say otherwise are liars. If her virginity is broken, she must marry him', he was quoted as saying. His comments are a good example of the deep-seated prejudices women still face in Turkish society. Virginity and chastity remain central elements of traditional perceptions of women in Turkish society, but feminists insist these notions should have no place in law. Virginity tests will no longer be allowed, although judges will be able to order genital examinations to prove a crime has taken place.

In the introductory part of the Penal Code, definitions were also changed to remove the distinction between a 'woman' and a 'girl'. In 1990, Article 438, which reduced sentences for rape if the victims were prostitutes, had already been repealed. These developments are particularly important because the new Penal Code will offer better protection to women. They are also a welcome sign that Turkish civil society is getting organised and has the power to influence policy.

Women's groups are now active not just in Turkey's western cities but also in regions such as south-east Anatolia, where women are still trapped by repressive customs. The Ka-Mer association, founded by Nebahat Akkoç in 1997 in Diyarbakir to provide education to women and tackle the problem of domestic violence, is now a leader in the fight against so-called 'honour killings', which claim the lives of dozens of women every year.

Several high profile cases extensively covered by the Turkish media have recently drawn public attention to these crimes, usually committed as a result of a cold-blooded decision by the 'family council' when a girl is deemed to have sullied the family 'honour'. The case of 35-year-old Semse Allak was particularly gruesome and caused public outcry in Turkey. The young woman, who had become the second wife of a married neighbour after he made her pregnant, was savagely stoned by her relatives. She later lost the baby she was carrying and eventually died in June 2003, after seven months in a coma. Members of Ka-Mer paid her daily visits in hospital and supplied the medicine necessary for her treatment. When her family refused to claim Semse's body after she died, a long procession of women carried the young woman to her last resting place.

In February 2004, Güldünya Tören was killed partly as a result of negligence by the authorities. The young woman, from a village in the Bitlis region of south-east Turkey, had given birth to a baby boy a few weeks earlier. Fearing for her life after her pregnancy was discovered, she had sought the protection of the police and, after negotiations with her relatives, was placed in the care of a retired imam from her region. But her brothers later came to collect her, allegedly to go and visit a relative. Instead, Güldünya was shot in the street by her 17-year-old brother. The young woman, only wounded in the leg, was taken to hospital where, left without police protection, she was shot dead a few hours later by her brothers who had returned to finish the job.

These cases have drawn criticism from Europe and prompted some soul-searching in Turkey. In 2003, Article 362 of the Penal Code, which granted reduced sentences for 'honour' crimes, was abrogated as part of a series of reforms introduced to boost Turkey's European Union membership bid.

Although the removal of this controversial article and subsequent amendments to the Penal Code are important improvements, they are not sufficient to change traditional perceptions of women. Training programmes are also needed to sensitise the judiciary and the security forces to gender and human right's issues. Turkey became a signatory to the Convention on the Elimination of All Kinds of Discrimination against Women (CEDAW) in 1985 and ratified this convention on 19 January 1986, but the authorities have not done enough to protect women.

The new Turkish Penal Code is an important step in the right direction. Although 'crimes of honour' were not specifically mentioned alongside 'crimes of tradition' in the category of aggravated crimes carrying a life sentence, the new Penal Code no longer allows the excuse of provocation to be used in cases of murders committed in the name of honour. Conservative judges had in the past often invoked 'unjust provocation' under Article 51 to reduce the sentences of 'honour' killing offenders by up to two thirds, therefore accepting the notion that a woman's sexual behaviour – or, in some cases the fact that she was raped – could incite her male relatives to kill her.

Aside from the legal framework, mechanisms also need to be put in place to provide better protection for girls and women under threat. There are only a few women's shelters in Turkey, and many more are needed to address society's needs.

Crimes of 'honour' and domestic violence are now hotly debated, and condemned in the media. On 25 November 2004, the Turkish government launched a comprehensive awareness programme to combat domestic violence, enlisting the help of famous footballers and actors to pass on the message to the public. Training and education programmes will be given to a wide section of the bureaucracy, including judges and policemen. With the backing of UNFPA, the government is setting up plans to make all army conscripts aware of domestic violence.

Sensitivity to women's issues is clearly increasing in Turkish society and pressure is growing for the government, the social services, the police and the judiciary to play a more active role in preventing discrimination and violence. A private programme launched by Ka-Mer to prevent 'honour' killings before they occur saved over 20 lives in just over a year, and showed that early intervention and mediation efforts can be effective.

Better access to education and employment would also help improve the situation of Turkish women. In 2003, the Turkish Ministry of National Education and UNICEF launched a girls' education campaign to encourage parents to send their female children to school with the help of the private sectors. 'In some provinces over 50 per cent of girls between seven and 13 do not attend school while in rural areas over 60 per cent of all girls between 11 and 15 have not even enrolled.'[7] The programme, Haydi Kizlar Okula (Girls, let's go to school), aims to close the average gap of seven per cent between girls and boys enrolled in primary education in Turkey by the end of 2005.

Within the framework of its South-eastern Anatolian Project (GAP), the Turkish government also runs some 30 community centres in the south-east that provide services in the areas of education and training, health, income generation, social support and cultural-social activities to women and girls over 14.

Lack of funds is often a major obstacle to the development of programmes for women. KAGIDER – the Women Entrepreneurs Association – is hoping to remedy this situation by establishing a national women's fund that will mobilise resources from the local and international community, and distribute grants to

NGOs working to improve the economic, social and political status of Turkish women and their communities.

These initiatives will undoubtedly bring progress, but to get heard women also need better representation at the political level. Organisations such as Ka-Der were founded to support women candidates, but participation of women in politics remains low. This state of affairs is often attributed to a lack of interest on the part of women but, as a recent study by Prof. Binnaz Toprak of Bosphorus University and Prof. Ersin Kalaycioglu of Sabanci University[8] shows, Turkish women are only marginally less interested in politics than their male counterparts. If interest was the criterion, women should have at least a third of the seats in parliament. The research suggests Turks want women to be given more opportunities to take an active part in society: 83 per cent saw the fact that women are less educated than men as an obstacle to Turkey's development. More than 65 per cent of those surveyed believed women were not given the opportunity to enter politics, and 74.3 per cent said the number of women in the national assembly was insufficient.

To change the status quo, the authors of the report suggested declaring a 'Women's Decade' and are introducing an official policy of affirmative action, with quotas for women candidates on electoral lists and in the public service, as well as better childcare facilities to allow more women to work.

On 7 May 2004, the Turkish parliament approved a series of Constitutional amendments designed to satisfy EU demands for greater democracy. Article 10 of the 1982 Turkish Constitution previously ruled that 'all individuals are equal without any discrimination before the law, irrespective of language, race, colour, sex, political opinion, philosophical belief, religion and sect, or any such considerations'. A paragraph was added stressing that 'women and men have equal rights. Ensuring equality between women and men is the responsibility of the state'.

This amendment, however, falls short of giving the authorities the legal means for a policy of affirmative action since the Constitution in theory does not allow for discrimination, even for a good cause. The opposition Republican People's Party (CHP) suggested adding a clause opening the way for temporary measures aimed at redressing gender imbalances, but this proposal was overwhelmingly rejected by conservative deputies from the ruling party.

Turkey is currently undergoing important political changes, motivated largely by the desire to join the European Union. Official accession talks are now scheduled to start on 3 October 2005 and women's issues are expected to be on the agenda in the course of the lengthy process that will lead Turkey to EU membership. As the country moves toward a more democratic system, it is imperative that women are not left behind. Social perceptions are changing but they need to be backed by robust policies guaranteeing women representation at all levels in the society.

Endnotes

1 'Women in Turkey 2001', August 2001 Directorate General for Status and Problems of Women, Ankara 2001; quoted in UNICEF, *A Gender Review in Education*, 2003.

2 Toprak Binnaz and Kalaycioglu Ersin, *Türkiye'de Kadınların siyaset, üst yönetım, ve is yasamdaki konumu*, TESEV and Open Society Institute 2004.

3 UNDP, 'Women in Turkey', 1999.

4 Ilkkaracan Pinar, Exploring the Context of Women's Sexuality in Eastern Turkey, in *Women and Sexuality in Muslim Society*, Women for Women's Human Rights (WWHR) 2000.

5 NTVMSNBC.COM, *Kadin dövmey bahane çok*, March 4, 2004.

6 Toprak Binnaz and Carkoglu Ali, *Religion, Society and Politics in Turkey*, TESEV 2000.

7 UNICEF, Haydi Kizlar Okula programme description.

8 *Toprak Binnaz and Kalaycioglu Ersin, Türkiye'de Kadınların siyaset, üst yönetım, ve is yasamdaki konumu* TESEV and Open Society Institute 2004.

The Security Dimensions of Turkey-EU Relations

William H. Park

Introduction

Any commentary on Turkish security considerations must begin with the country's location, both geo-strategically and also because it straddles so many cultural and political fault lines. Turkey is simultaneously part of, or borders, Europe, the Middle East, and the Mediterranean, the Balkan, Black Sea and even Caspian regions. It is geographically Eurasian, Islamic by faith but officially secular, and broadly European in outlook and aspiration. It abuts such troubled regions and countries as the Caucasus, Iran, Syria and Iraq. It shares a linguistic and cultural root, if not much history, with a Turkic world that embraces the former Soviet Central Asian states, Azerbaijan, and a number of minorities in the Middle East, Balkans, and former Soviet Union. With the collapse of the Soviet Union, Turkey increasingly provides an outlet for the people, trade and, not least, the energy resources, to its north. Turkey is fast becoming an oil and gas energy highway, with pipelines from Iraq as well as various locations in the former Soviet Union.

Ankara's diplomacy has increasingly reflected the complexity and diversity of Turkey's geopolitical circumstances. In addition to its membership of the North Atlantic Treaty Organisation (Nato) and other essentially Western institutions, Turkey has long been a member of the Organisation of Islamic Conference (OIC) and the essentially Islamic Economic Cooperation Organisation (ECO). Turkey took the lead role in the establishment of the Black Sea Economic Cooperation Organisation (BSEC) in 1992, and the Black Sea Naval Cooperation Task Group (BlackSeaFor) in 2001. In late 2002 Ankara initiated the formation of the loose group of Regional Countries bordering Iraq that have since been co-opted by the

UN in the search for a viable future for post-Saddam Iraq. Since the mid-1990s Ankara has developed a close relationship with Israel, which has not always helped its somewhat patchy relationships with the Arab world. Turkey belongs to the Mediterranean Forum, formed in 1994, and has played a leading role in the multiplicity of groupings concerned with the Balkans – the Stability Pact, the South-East European Cooperation Process, the Multinational Peacekeeping Force for South-Eastern Europe (SEEBRIG) established in 1999, and so on. In addition to its intense bilateral relations with Azerbaijan and Georgia, Ankara forms part of the Minsk Group set up to mediate the conflict over Nagorno-Karabakh, and works hard to cultivate the Turkic countries of Central Asia.

Turkey and the West during the Cold War

This multilateral and multidirectional quality of Turkish foreign policy has more fully taken shape since the Cold War. During the Cold War, economic, political and cultural relationships with the Soviet space were largely frozen, and Turkey's value to the West derived largely from a location that offered a southern flank in the containment of an expansionist Moscow.[1] Turkey was also valued for the contribution of its armed forces which, with US help, were impressively modernised and currently stand at almost 50,000 strong, constituting the second largest in Nato after those of the US. The deployment on Turkish territory of intermediate and battlefield range nuclear forces, Nato air and naval forces and associated bases, and surveillance facilities and operations, demonstrated the country's role as a Cold War strategic asset. Turkey was also valued for its proximity to the Middle East, a region that was a recipient of Moscow's attentions and whose oil featured ever larger in the security interests of the world's industrialised states. Ankara's direct relationships with Middle Eastern states were generally cool and sometimes frosty throughout much of this era.

Turkey's utility to Nato in its policy of containment dovetailed with Ankara's need for protection against an expansionist Soviet Union, manifested by Soviet pressure on both the Straits and on Turkey's north-eastern Kars and Ardahan provinces. Turkey also aspired to be fully accepted as part of the post-World War Two Western community. Turkey's determination to modernise, to 'join' the West, and generally turn its back on Anatolia's Islamic root and Middle Eastern past dates back to Kemal Atatürk's aspirations for his new-found Republic. The Cold War offered Turkey the opportunity to institutionalise and give substance to this impulse. Ankara's contribution of a combat brigade to the US-led military campaign in the Korean War represented a Turkish down-payment on Nato entry, whilst its domestic experimentation in democracy, started in earnest in 1950, can similarly be regarded as part of the country's endeavour to westernise. Turkey joined the Organisation of Economic Cooperation and Development in 1948, the Council of Europe in 1949, Nato in 1952, became an associate member of the European Economic Community (now EU) in 1963, applied for full membership of the EU in 1987, became a West European Union (WEU) associate member in 1991, and in January 1996 entered into a Customs Union with the EU. In December 2004 the EU decided to open accession negotiations with Turkey, to start in October 2005.[2]

Turkey and the US, post-Cold War

With the Cold War's demise, it was initially thought that Turkey's strategic utility would decline. However, US preoccupation with Iraq, from the 1990 annexation of Kuwait until the 2003 removal of the Ba'athist regime in Baghdad, again elevated Turkey's geo-strategic value to Washington. During the crisis over the Iraqi annexation of Kuwait, Ankara closed the pipeline carrying Iraqi oil through Turkey to the Mediterranean, permitted the use of bases on Turkish territory for US bombing raids against Iraq, cooperated with the trade sanctions policy against Iraq, and deployed a substantial military force on the Iraqi border. Ankara's cooperation against Iraq, which represented a break with the Turkish Republic's preference for non-involvement in Middle Eastern affairs, aroused considerable unease amongst officials and the public alike in Turkey, including the powerful military establishment. It reflected the then-president Turgut Özal's single-minded determination to ensure Turkey's post-Cold War value in US eyes, and ensured that Turkey would be regarded as pivotal in Washington's approach to Iraq specifically and the Middle East generally.

Subsequent to the liberation of Kuwait, access to the Nato base at Incirlik enabled the establishment of a 'no-fly-zone' over northern Iraq by US and UK (and initially French) forces from 1991 until recently. In the wake of the overthrow of Saddam Hussein's regime in 2003, Incirlik has again been useful in supplying and rotating US troops deployed in Iraq. The post-9/11 'war on terrorism', in which the November 2003 Istanbul bombings made Turkey a 'front line' state, Washington's suspicion of Iran and Syria, general regional instability, and Turkey's emergence as a conduit for gas and oil pipelines, have also helped sustain Turkey's post-Cold War pivotal status in US eyes.

Turkey has played a constructive alliance role in other ways too, engaging actively in Partnership for Peace (PfP) training missions, agreeing to the establishment on Turkish territory of an anti-terrorist training centre and a tactical air training centre, for example. Turkish troops are also amongst the most utilised in Nato, or anywhere else for that matter. Since 1993, Turkey has been a regular contributor to peacekeeping and other multilateral military missions, including in Somalia, former Yugoslavia, Albania, Georgia, Kuwait, Hebron, East Timor and Afghanistan, where Turkey took over command of the International Security Assistance Force (ISAF) from the UK in 2002, and again in February 2005. In November 2003 a Turkish offer of 10,000 troops to assist the US-led coalition in peacekeeping duties in Iraq was withdrawn only in the face of Iraqi, and particularly Kurdish, opposition.

However, with the removal of Saddam Hussein and thus the need to contain him, there has also been cause to question the strategic utility of Turkey's geographical location. The 1 March 2003 vote in the country's National Assembly that refused US access to Turkish territory as a launch pad for an invasion of northern Iraq reminded Washington that Turkey could obstruct as well as enable its access to this vital region.[3] The vote also hinted at a possible weakening of the Turkish General Staff's (TGS) domestic political role. If true, this would be a significant development because the TGS had served as the main conduit in Turkey of Washington's policy preferences. It also served as a reminder that even the TGS could not be guaranteed to see eye to eye with Washington where issues of Turkish national security were perceived to be at stake. In fact, this had long been a truth, and one often overlooked in Washington. After all, the TGS had not been enamoured of Özal's support for Washington in the 1990-1991 crisis.

The realisation that Washington and Ankara do not share perspectives on the Middle East has been reinforced by subsequent developments. Ankara remains uneasy about the US adventure in Iraq, and angry and frustrated at the perceived failure to reign in Iraq's Kurds and to quell the activities of those remnants of the Kurdish Workers Party (PKK) based in northern Iraq's mountains. Furthermore, Turkey's relations with Syria have warmed substantially, and its contacts with Iran are at least businesslike and respectful. These flirtations with members of the 'axis of evil' have met with Washington's ardent disapproval.

Indeed, Turkey's perspective on Iraq is in tune with those common to the region, and the Justice and Development Party (AKP) government that came to power in November 2002 values and seeks to improve Turkey's relationships in the broader Middle East region. The AKP does not share Turkey's Kemalist inclination to turn its back on the immediate neighbourhood wherever possible, but instead prefers to engage actively and constructively with it. Intensification of US pressure against Turkey's neighbours, such as the trade embargo imposed on Syria in May 2004, or the tough approach to Iran's nuclear programme, have not met with Ankara's sympathy. Ankara's AK government has also exhibited a much greater readiness to criticise, and even fall out with, Israel. Strong anti-Americanism is now a marked feature of Turkish public opinion surveys, and government figures are frequently openly critical of US policies. These developments have raised doubts in Washington, and especially the Pentagon, concerning Ankara's reliability as an ally.

Of course, Washington might yet emerge chastened by its Iraq experiences. In the meantime, however, US and Turkish approaches to the region's problems have indubitably diverged. Indeed, Ankara's position more closely resembles those found in Paris and Berlin. Although Turkey will surely remain a valued ally, the US-Turkish relationship looks set to alter its parameters, and acquire a less exclusively military dimension.[4] US Assistant Defence Secretary Paul Wolfowitz for one has speculated on how US-Turkish relations might in future be based more on their shared commitment to the development of a democratic, modernising Islamic world.[5] Indeed, the AK government sympathises with current US thinking about the political and economic failings of the Islamic world.[6] In the context of Washington's Greater Middle East Initiative, Turkey might at last begin to serve as the model of a democratised, westernised but Islamic state that Washington has longed for it to be.[7] Paradoxically, however, this might partly come as a consequence, and be reinforced by, a less close US-Turkish relationship. Recent domestic political changes in Turkey, which in particular have seen an apparent demotion of the military's key role in Turkish security policy, will deny Washington a major means of influence over Turkish policy.

Turkey, Europe and Security

This is important, because hitherto Turkey's Nato membership has largely taken the form of a Turkish-US bilateral strategic alliance, and has had 'hard' security considerations at it heart. Europeans, with some exceptions, generally acquiesced in Turkey's membership of the alliance in the interests of containment of the Soviet Union in Europe and at the behest of Washington. Only the UK and France have consistently maintained a broader engagement with security issues beyond Europe itself. It is also worth recalling that the UK's initial post-WW2 preference, and that of many senior figures in US administrations too, was that Turkey should become part of a Middle Eastern rather than European security architecture. Turkey was not then considered as European either geographically or politically.[8] The Christian Democratic end of the European political spectrum continues to this day to query the validity of Turkey's claim to be 'European', an outlook that could yet derail Ankara's bid for EU membership.

Furthermore, and in addition to the general reluctance to focus on broader security issues, Europeans have not always sympathised with Turkey in its regional difficulties. Turkey's European Nato allies imposed an arms embargo on Turkey in the wake of the 1974 invasion of Cyprus, as did the US of course. Arms deliveries were also held up in protest at Turkey's military incursions into Iraq during the 1990s in pursuit of PKK activists there, or where such weapons might be used in Turkey's domestic military campaign against the PKK. Indeed, European criticism of Ankara's approach to its Kurdish problem, and the human rights contraventions associated with it, have been far less muted than those of Washington. On the eve of the US-led attack on Iraq, and much to Washington's annoyance, Germany, France and Belgium refused to sanction a transfer of Nato AWACS, chemical and biological detection teams, and Patriot missiles, to Turkey, confirming Turkish doubts as to the reliability of their European Nato allies. Europeans are also less impressed than is Washington with Turkey's relationship with Israel, but share with Washington an influential Armenian lobby whose activities often serve to undermine sympathy with Turkey.

Until the April 2004 referendums on Cyprus, in which the Greek side of the island voted against the UN settlement plan and the Turkish side voted for it, European sympathies with respect to Cyprus have generally been with the Greek side, even if the explanation is not unrelated to the fact of Greek EU membership.

The EU allowed the ethnically Greek part of the island to accede to the Union in May 2004 even in the absence of agreement on reunification and in the wake of the Greek Cypriot 'no' vote in the referendum on the UN plan. Indeed, the EU had even hinted, in its 1999 Helsinki Declaration, at possible Turkish non-accession as a consequence of the failure to reach agreement on the island's future. Since the April 2004 referendum, there is far greater sympathy in Europe for the Turkish and Turkish Cypriot predicament, not least because the AK government pushed so hard for acceptance of the UN plan. Nevertheless, the Cyprus issue too retains the capacity to derail Turkey's EU accession bid.[9] If a settlement is not forthcoming, even were blame for such a failure is not placed at Ankara's door, it would be problematic for the EU to accept as a full member a country militarily occupying part of the territory of an existing member. From within the EU, Nicosia, even if not Athens, will surely seek to maximise Turkish discomfiture.

More significantly, and notwithstanding the Nato-wide Cold War consensus on the need to contain the Soviet threat in Europe, the EU's security culture as it has evolved is at odds with that traditionally associated with Turkey as well as with that of the US. After the Second World War, Western Europe set out to so construct relationships between its constituent states, and most especially France and Germany, in the hope that the rivalry and wars that had bedevilled modern European history might in future be avoided. In effect, the key to achieving this goal was to 'desecuritise' relationships in Europe, and instead to base future progress on economic integration, transparency, social and cultural interpenetration, good governance, civilian control of the military, political consensus building, and the adoption of common values such as democracy and pluralism, the rule of law, and respect for human rights and minorities. Ultimately, a measure of political union might even be achieved, implying a readiness to dilute national sovereignty.

With the collapse of Europe's Cold War divisions, and the concomitant requirement to define what 'Europe' now meant in order that a strategy for enlargement to the east could be developed, these prerequisites for membership were more formally laid out in the Copenhagen criteria of 1992, to which aspiring EU members were expected to adhere. For the former communist states of Central Europe, keen to throw off the residues of communism and 'return' to a Europe to which they rightfully and naturally belonged and from which the Cold War years had artificially separated them, the Copenhagen criteria – and comparable partnership agreements with Nato that similarly formed the pathway to expanded membership – offered a clarifying road-map.

For Kemalist Turkey, however, with its political system left unchanged by the Cold War's demise, the Copenhagen criteria threatened possible exclusion from the EU. Turkish politics have long been characterised by routine military involvement in the political process, in order to safeguard the official secularism that was Atatürk's legacy, to campaign against expressions of Kurdish political and cultural identity as well as against the PKK's bloody separatist war, and to impose order whenever turbulence threatened Turkey's weak democratic culture and institutions. Freedoms of speech, political activity and assembly have been constrained, and Turkey's political culture remains relatively authoritarian, centralised, and intensely nationalistic. Indeed, in the months and years immediately preceding the November 2002 AKP election victory, incorporating the so-called 'soft coup' against the Islamic-led coalition government of Necmettin Erbakan in 1997 and the Defence White Papers of 1998 and 2000, the domestic political role of the military and the identification of ethnic separatism and religious fundamentalism as the major threats to Turkey's security had become even more pronounced.[10] This is a form of politics quite unlike that which has evolved in mainstream Europe.

Furthermore, Turkey's intense jealousy of its territorial integrity, sometimes referred to as the 'Sevres complex', and its sensitivity to external 'interference' in its domestic affairs, are also somewhat at odds with the political culture of Western Europe. So too has been Ankara's ready resort to the threat or use of military force – on Cyprus in 1974, Iraq on a number of occasions in the 1990s, against Syria in 1998, and during the crisis over the planned deployment of Russian S300 missiles in Cyprus in the same year. Although many would argue that Ankara's 'hard' approach to security is primarily a consequence of its problematic neighbourhood, incidents such as these nevertheless indicate how divergent the security cultures of the EU and Turkey have appeared to be.[11]

As a 'civil power' reliant far more on its economic and political influence and appeal than on its military prowess, and still unproven as an effective security actor externally, the EU is best seen as a security 'community' than as a security 'actor'. As such, its membership is arguably more repelled by Turkey's proximity to troubled and turbulent regions than it is attracted by Turkey's pivotal geopolitical location. Ankara and Washington have frequently failed to appreciate this when they have sought to impress the EU with Turkey's qualifications for EU membership by highlighting its strategic significance.[12] Many in the EU are not greatly attracted by the prospect of acquiring Iran, Iraq, Syria or the Caucasus as neighbours because the EU has neither the capacity nor the desire to cope with the problems such a dangerous neighbourhood might bring. Some have argued that the EU's interests would be better served by preserving Turkey's role as Europe's security 'insulator' from the problems of the Middle East.[13]

European Security and Defence Policy

Differences between the EU and Turkey over the European Security and Defence Policy (ESDP) reflected, among other things, this divergence in security culture and perspective and are worth revisiting in order to illustrate this divergence. For the EU, the launch of the ESDP in 1997 was both an expression of the EU's aspiration to achieve greater political union and 'actorliness' in its external dealings, and a means to address low key threats to stability around its periphery or within its reach and spheres of interest. It is an aspiration in keeping with the EU's normative approach to security issues, and its desire to extend the values of the European security community model. The ESDP's Petersberg tasks, adopted by the West European Union (WEU) in 1992, of humanitarian missions, crisis management and peace support operations, and the Headline Force Goals agreed in 1999 for the creation of a EU Rapid Reaction Force, are quite modest. The material progress made by the EU, whose members continue to under-resource their armed forces and between whom consensus is not easily arrived at, has been similarly modest. The fact that during 2004 the EU took over responsibility for military peacekeeping in Bosnia and has also been able to launch a long-range – and largely French – mission in the Eastern Congo, does not alter the essential modesty both of the EU's aspirations and its achievements.

Yet Ankara's initial reaction to the ESDP initiative was fierce, inspired both by an assumption that the EU was seeking to challenge Nato as Europe's hard security actor, and by the consequence that Turkey would thereby be excluded from a key component of Europe's emerging security architecture. Given too that 13 of the 16 'hot spots' identified by Nato were located broadly within Turkey's vicinity, Ankara argued that the EU might engage itself in crises in which Turkey had a stake but no right to be consulted. Ankara was particularly concerned that Greece and, in time, Cyprus too, would be able to recruit the EU in their struggles with Turkey over Cyprus or the Aegean. Ankara's outburst prompted a bout of intense diplomatic activity by London and Washington in an endeavour to square Turkey's position with the EU's plans.[14] As a carrot, Ankara declared at Nice its willingness to commit to the EU's proposed Rapid Reaction Force a minimum of 5,000 troops, 36 F-16s and air transport and maritime vessels in the event of the EU devising more inclusive mechanisms for non-EU participation in ESDP decision-making. On the bright side, this offer – and the impact of Turkey's ambitious force modernisation programme launched in 1996[15] – indicate the potential enhancement of EU military capabilities that Turkish membership could eventually offer.

If one appreciates that the EU is highly unlikely for the foreseeable future to be either willing or able to act without or against the vital interests of a key Nato ally such as Turkey, then one can more easily perceive ESDP developments as benign. However, Ankara's security culture, its nationalistic sensitivities, and its mistrust of the EU led it to the conclusion that the ESDP represented a wilful determination to marginalise Nato and exclude non-EU members. In the event, London and Washington were eventually able to satisfy Turkish grievances with the so-called 'Ankara document' agreed in December 2001, that incorporated mechanisms for more inclusive consultation with non-EU Nato allies, a commitment to exclude Cyprus as a non-Nato and non PfP state from the ESDP's agenda, Turkey's right to a say and to participation in any ESDP activities in its region, and an undertaking that ESDP missions would not come into conflict with any Nato ally.

In the face of Greek obstruction, it was not until the end of 2002 that a form of words acceptable both to Greece and Turkey was arrived at, thus opening the way for a lifting of the Turkish veto on EU recourse to Nato assets if needed, and for Turkey to contribute to ESDP missions if desired and on a satisfactory basis. The exclusion of Cypriot ports and airfields from ESDP missions was, however, offered by the (Greek) Cypriot government as a reason for the 'no' vote in the referendum on the UN settlement plan for the island in April 2004. The ESDP episode demonstrated the scope for increased EU-Turkish tension should Ankara's endeavour to join the EU fail. It also confirmed for many that Turkey would function as an Atlanticist 'trojan horse' inside the EU if it were allowed to become a member.

EU Accession?

Thus, the significance of the December 2004 EU decision to open accession negotiations with Turkey cannot be overestimated. The domestic reform programme introduced by the AK government, and by the Bülent Ecevit-led administration that preceded it, and designed to make the country ready for accession negotiations, has been impressive in scope.[16] Most notably, it saw the introductions of reforms to the military-dominated National Security Council (NSC) aiming to convert it from an executive into a purely advisory body. Defence spending has been opened up to parliamentary scrutiny. The military-dominated State Security courts have been abolished. The state of emergency has been lifted throughout the entire south-east of the country. Military representation on the country's media and educational boards has ended. Laws easing the restrictions on Kurdish language broadcasting and education have also been introduced.

Whether the reforms, or more importantly their implementation, will prove sufficient to satisfy the EU remains an open question, notwithstanding the December 2004 decision. Many have their doubts, and the December decision was grudging, contentious and qualified. In effect, Turkey has been put on an explicit 'good behaviour' notice by the EU, and the ten or more years that the accession negotiations are expected to take will surely offer ample opportunity for Ankara to displease its EU doubters. Furthermore, France and Austria, perhaps to be joined by others, are set to hold referendums on Turkish accession, an unprecedented approach to EU enlargement. Popular and elite unease with the prospect of Turkish accession could yet make itself felt through this medium. The road ahead still contains numerous pitfalls, and it might not be Turkey that is found wanting. Many in Europe remain opposed to Turkish entry on 'civilisational' as well as economic, political, and security grounds.

Few doubt the impact the AK government has had on the tenor of Turkish politics. Should it remain in office, and if Turkey continues along its recent reformist path, the country might eventually evolve into a 'normal' modern European state. The future Europe-Turkey security nexus will hinge considerably on Turkey's domestic development. There are grounds for pessimism, however. For example, the military's domestic political influence has traditionally relied on more than constitutional provision and its former capacity to dominate the NSC, and has often been expressed less formally, through a combination of threats, civilian self-censorship, legal and constitutional interpretation, a fragmented political culture, and genuine popularity and respect.[17] Even in the wake of the reforms, laws and constitutional clauses that place limits on freedom of speech and political activity remain in place. There is too a continuing tension between the Islamic-inspired AK government and the Kemalist establishment concerning the nature and extent of Turkey's secularity, as evidenced by the dispute over educational reform in the early summer of 2004. The Kurdish issue and Cyprus are also sources of tension between Turkey's Kemalist establishment and the AK government.

Indeed, the Kurdish issue, now inextricably bound up with developments in Iraq, also offers grounds for pessimism. The threat posed by Turkey's Kurdish separatists, whether based in Turkey or Iraq, substantially reduced in the wake of PKK leader Abdullah Ocalan's incarceration in 1999. In the summer of 2003, Ankara introduced a limited and temporary amnesty for Kurdish activists, and a compensation programme for Kurdish victims. The June 2004 release from prison of four Kurdish former members of parliament, including the Sakharov peace prize winner Leyla Zana, and the shift amongst Turkey's Kurdish leadership towards political engagement and peaceful change, all hint at more benign possibilities.

However, although for a number of years now violent incidents have been relatively few in number and small scale, there has been a marked increase since the PKK lifted its unilateral ceasefire in June 2004. In any case, it is not certain that the EU-inspired reforms aimed at liberalising the laws governing political activity or cultural and linguistic expression either go far enough or will be sufficiently implemented to encourage disaffected Kurds into the mainstream of Turkish society. There remains intense opposition in Turkey to any adoption of more mainstream EU approaches to minority rights and identity politics, and this will not go unnoticed in the EU. Kurdish ethnic identity and a sense of grievance remain intact, and a continuation of the conflict in its more violent manifestations could set back Turkey's democratisation, and EU accession, prospects.[18]

For the AK government, which lobbied strongly to achieve a settlement of the Cyprus problem, EU accession has been the policy priority. Its calculation appears to have been that the obligations of EU accession offer the best opportunity to entrench the political rights of Islamists and Kurds, and to contain the obstructive power of state institutions, including the military. Furthermore, the 'good governance' that the AKP leadership hopes will emerge from its EU-related reform programme, its remarkably successful management of the economy, and its anti-corruption campaign, might similarly help marginalise the traditional political and bureaucratic establishment, and thus reinforce the AKP's domestic popularity as well as meet the EU's requirements. Paradoxically, this development has cast elements of Turkey's 'westernising' Kemalist establishment in the role of critics of the AK government's success in Europe. Although lip service is paid to EU accession, much of Turkey's secular political elite remains wedded to the 'Sevres complex', a prickly brand of nationalism, security consciousness and paranoia that frequently elides into anti-European sentiment. Should these elements regain political power in the near future, a successful outcome to the EU accession negotiations would appear less likely.

On present trends there are good reasons to suppose that Ankara's security policy might align with the EU's mainstream more and more. This will in part stem from a process of 'socialisation' into Europe's security culture, in which Ankara might increasingly adopt the 'security community' approach. Present relations with Greece, the AK government's approach to Cyprus, and its bridge-building approach to regional diplomacy, are all indications of this. In its approach to regional issues, such as engagement with Syria and Iran, Ankara often has more in common with Europe than with the US – at least under the AK government. A politically weakened TGS, which has so often set both the tone and content of Turkish security policy and played a key role in the centrality of the security relationship with Washington, would also free Ankara's civilian politicians to explore European as well as regional alternatives. There might be more material calculations and consequences too. Currently, around 80 per cent of Turkey's arms purchases are from the US. This would be expected to shift in Europe's favour.

A US bent either on its present unilateralist course – not least in ways that insufficiently take account of Ankara's regional security interests – or perhaps inclined towards disengagement as a consequence of failure in Iraq, could also encourage a cementing of EU-Turkish relations. Ankara's future security relationship with Europe hinges considerably on US policy and on Nato's future. Again paradoxically, Turkey's path towards Europe in security terms could be eased considerably were the recent bleak state of transatlantic relations to show signs of improvement.[19]

Problems on the Horizon?

Should Turkey's neighbourhood implode as a consequence of continued chaos in Iraq, other possibilities emerge. The future of Iraq, and particularly its Kurdish north, looms large as a security concern in Ankara. Ankara continues to fear that Iraq and the entire region could unravel, not without reason, and is concerned at the prospect of a more or less sovereign Kurdish entity emerging from Iraq's present chaos. Turkish anguish would be intensified still further if the Kurds were to succeed in their desire to incorporate the Kirkuk oilfields, currently lying beyond the Kurdish Regional Government zone. Although Iraq's Kurds have worked constructively within the US-established Iraqi Governing Council (IGC) and Interim Government, and offered reassurances that they intend to remain part of Iraq, as a minimum the Kurds have continued to demand in the wake of Saddam's overthrow much of what they enjoyed for a decade before – that is, a very high degree of autonomy. They are especially loath to put their future welfare in the hands of a chaotic, theological, or Arab nationalist Iraq. Yet, as the January

2005 elections approached, each of these outcomes appeared more likely than the establishment of a democratic and federal Iraq.[20]

The AK government appears no less exercised than the TGS and Turkey's Kemalists generally by such possibilities. Syria, Iran, and other regional powers also fear such an outcome, and it is not beyond the bounds of possibility that Turkey and other regional powers might feel they have no option but to intervene militarily in Iraq to forestall the emergence of a de facto Kurdish state or in some way establish control over events.[21] Iraq's neighbours could act in unison or competitively. In a worst case scenario in which the Iraqi state crumbles, Ankara could also be drawn towards the option of establishing a kind of Kurdish 'protectorate' in northern Iraq, as a means of limiting its autonomy, establishing a 'firebreak' between itself and a chaotic Arab Iraq, managing the interrelationship between Turkish and Iraqi Kurds, and even obtaining access to the region's oil. Continued Sunni Arab resistance to a Shi'ite dominated Iraq could pit much of the Arab world against Iran, and this too would undermine regional stability and prove compromising to Turkey's regional relationships.

For the time being, the hope of EU accession and US strategic sponsorship function as inhibitors on Turkish adventurism. Should Iraq fall apart, particularly if it should follow in the wake of a US pull out from the country, or should Ankara fail to get satisfaction from the EU, such constraints would be removed. In any case, intense regional turbulence could prompt a return of 'traditional' forces and politics in Turkey, putting back the prospect of EU accession. Europe is unlikely to prove tolerant of Turkish difficulties with Iraq, certainly if the Turkish response to them is to intervene more actively and militantly. Domestically, the military would once again return to the forefront of Turkish politics, positive developments in the handling of Turkey's domestic Kurdish dilemmas would surely be reversed, and Turkey might again show a more nationalistic and militaristic face to the world. In such circumstances, Ankara might seek to develop its regional relationships more broadly, in the Middle East, perhaps the wider Islamic world, the Caucasus, Central Asia, Russia and the Ukraine. It might find itself pushed back into Washington's arms, particularly were Iran to emerge as a rival to Turkey for influence and control in Iraq. Turkish external policy could incorporate elements of each of these alternatives.

Conclusion

Over 50 per cent of Turkey's trade is with the EU, with which it also enjoys a Customs Union and from which the bulk of its inward investment comes. These are facts of Turkey's existence. Furthermore, Turkey's relationship with the EU is one in which the more dynamic elements of Turkey's society and economy will continue to have a stake. Following a period of anger and reflection, such difficulties with the EU would in all probability in time be papered over by a drift back towards the pursuit of Turkey's European 'destiny'. We should also note that the EU too has begun to think more creatively about the scope for establishing zones of stability and friendship around its periphery that fall short of membership but which extend the benefits of Europe's stable security community and its economic might. The 'special relationship' with Turkey of which some of Europe's Christian Democrats are so enamoured could emerge as a viable alternative to Turkey's complete estrangement form Europe. Turkey could conceivably, if reluctantly, come to occupy a halfway house in its relationship with the EU for some time into the future.

For Turkey, times are rarely dull. But there could have been few moments in the history of the Republic that are more momentous than the present. The future of Turkey's US relationship, its European destiny, the stability of its neighbourhood, its own domestic evolution, and even its territorial integrity, all appear to have arrived simultaneously at or close to a point of intense sensitivity. There is an almost ungraspable contingency and a deeply complex interdependency surrounding Turkey's current predicaments. Predicting the future of Turkish security policy, even in the relatively short term, is thus especially fraught. The one given in Turkey's security landscape is its geopolitical location. This does not determine Turkey's security policy in any particular direction, but it does ensure the country's vulnerability to developments around its borders and even beyond. Furthermore, a Turkey bereft of strategic utility to Washington, or remaining outside Europe's security community, might find the safety net against its own economic mismanagement withdrawn, its domestic political stability more vulnerable, its military less well armed, and its behaviour in Cyprus, Iraq or with respect to its own Kurds – or, in the Middle East, its relationship with Israel – less tolerated. Turkish security policy must avoid the country's isolation, but this is not entirely in Ankara's hands.

Endnotes

1 For a brief overview, see Bruce Kuniholm, 'Turkey and the West since World War II', in *Turkey between East and West: New challenges for a rising regional power,* edited by Vojtech Mastny and R. Craig Nation, (Boulder, Colorado: Westview Press, 1996), pp.45-69.

2 For an account of the evolution of Turkey-EU relations, see Meltem Muftuler-Bac, 1999, 'The never-ending story: Turkey and the European Union', in S. Kedourie, (ed), *Turkey before and after Atatürk: internal and external affairs,* (London: Frank Cass, 1999), pp.240-258. See also Gamze Avci, 'Turkey's slow EU candidacy: insurmountable hurdles to membership, or simple Euro-scepticism?', *Turkish Studies,* 4(1), 2003, pp.149-170; and Ziya Onis, 'An awkward partnership: Turkey's relations with the European Union in comparative-historical perspective', *Journal of European Integration History,* 7(1), 2001, pp.105-119.

3 For an account of events leading up to the vote, see Bill Park, 'Strategic location, political dislocation: Turkey, the United States, and Northern Iraq', *Middle East Review of International Affairs (MERIA),* 7(2), June 2003, pp.11-23.

4 For considerations of US-Turkish relationships in the context of differences over Iraq, see Barak A. Salmoni, 'Strategic partners or estranged allies: Turkey, the United States, and Operation Iraqi

Freedom', *Strategic Insights* II (7) July 2003, at www.ccc.nps.navy.mil/si/july03 ; and Soner Cagaptay, 'Where goes the US-Turkish relationship?', *Middle East Quarterly,* XI(4) Fall 2004, pp.43-52.

5 See the transcript of his January 2004 CNN Turk interview with leading Turkish journalists, www.dod.mil/transcripts/2004/tr20040129

6 For an indication of this, see Abdullah Gul, 'Turkey's role in a changing Middle East environment', *Mediterranean Quarterly,* 15(1), Winter 2004, p.5.

7 For some interesting thoughts along these lines, see Graham E. Fuller, 'Turkey's strategic model; myths and realities', *The Washington Quarterly* 27(3) Summer 2004, pp. 51-64; and Mohammed Ayoob, 'Turkey's multiple paradoxes', *Orbis,* 48(3), Summer 2004, pp.451-463.

8 See, for example, Cihat Goktepe, *British foreign policy towards Turkey 1959-1965,* (London: Frank Cass, 2003), pp.7-25.

9 For thoughts on this, see Semin Suvarierol, 'The Cyprus obstacle on Turkey's road to membership in the European Union', *Turkish Studies,* 4(1), 2003, pp.55-78; and Nathalie Tocci, 'Cyprus and the European Union accession process: inspiration for peace or incentive for crisis?', *Turkish Studies,* 3 (2), 2002, pp.104-138.

10 See Umit Cizre, 'Demythologising the National Security Concept: the case of Turkey', *Middle East Journal,* 57(2), Spring 2003, pp.213-229.

11 See H.Tarik Oguzlu, 'The clash of security identities: the question of Turkey's membership in the European Union', *International Journal* 57(4), Autumn 2002, pp.579-603 for a deeper discussion of this; and Gulner Aybet and Meltem Muftuler-Bac, 'Transformations in security and identity after the Cold War', *International Journal* 55(4), Autumn 2000, pp.567-582.

12 See Bruce Kuniholm, 'Turkey's accession to the European Union: Differences in European and US attitudes, and challenges for Turkey', *Turkish Studies,* 2(1), Spring 2001, pp.25-53.

13 This idea is articulated in Barry Buzan and Thomas Diez, 'The European Union and Turkey', *Survival,* 41(1), Spring 1999, p.47.

14 For accounts of Turkey-EU differences over ESDP, see Bill Park, 'Turkey, Europe, and ESDI: inclusion or exclusion?', *Defense Analysis* 16(3) December 2000, pp.315-328; Antonio Missiroli, 'EU-NATO cooperation in crisis management: no Turkish delight for ESDP', *Security Dialogue,* 3 (1), March 2002, pp.9-26; Sebnem Udum, 'Turkey and the emerging European security framework', *Turkish Studies* 3 (2), Autumn 2002, pp.69-103.

15 For details on this, see Elliot Hen-Tov, 'The political economy of Turkish military modernisation', *The Middle East Review of International Affairs (MERIA),* 8(4) December 2004.

16 Information can be obtained from the Turkish Foreign Ministry at www.mfa.gov.tr

17 See Gareth Jenkins, 'Context and circumstance: the Turkish military and politics', Adelphi Paper 337 (London: International Institute for Strategic Studies, 2001).

18 For an exploration of alternative approaches to Turkish-Kurdish relations, see Murat Somer, 'Turkey's Kurdish conflict: changing context, and domestic and regional implications', *Middle East Journal,* 58 (2), Spring 2004, pp.235-253.

19 For speculation on the future of the transatlantic relationship, see Ivo H. Daalder, 'The end of Atlanticism', *Survival,* 45 (2), Summer 2003, pp.147-166; James B. Steinberg, 'An elective partnership: salvaging transatlantic relations', *Survival,* 45 (2), Summer 2003, pp.113-246; and James Thomson, 'US interests and the fate of the Alliance', *Survival,* 45(4), Winter 2003-4, pp.207-220.

20 For speculation concerning possible Iraqi futures, see the Middle East Briefing Paper 04/02, published by Chatham House in September 2004, 'Iraq in transition: vortex or catalyst?'.

21 For speculation on Turkey's future options with respect to Iraqi Kurdistan, see Michael Gunter, 'The consequences of a failed Iraqi state: an independent Kurdish state in northern Iraq?', *Journal of South Asian and Middle Eastern Studies,* XXVII(3), Spring 2004, pp.1-11; and Bill Park, 'Iraq's Kurds and Turkey: challenges for US policy', *Parameters,* XXXIV(3), Autumn 2004, pp.18-30.

On The Future of US-Turkish Relations

Mark R. Parris

Future historians may well see the period 1997-2002 as the high-water mark of modern US-Turkish bilateral relations.

During those years, America and Turkey achieved a level of cooperation that was unprecedented in scope and intensity, and that is unlikely to be repeated in the foreseeable future.

The 'Strategic Partnership' …

Turkey and the US had been important to one another throughout the Cold War era. But the relationship during that period was essentially one-dimensional. Washington looked to Ankara to hold down Nato's longest land border with the Soviet Union; Ankara relied on Washington both to provide the military wherewithal to carry out that mission and to legitimate (directly and through its leadership of Nato) Turkey's credentials as a 'Western democracy'.

That basic bargain was called into question with the collapse of the Soviet Union. Turks experienced a profound identity crisis as they debated whether Ankara could retain its traditional importance to American strategic planners. In Washington, the 45-year defence relationship began to fray under pressure by interests hostile to Turkey (i.e. Greek, Armenian and human rights critics). By the mid-nineties, major arms transfers (assault helicopters, frigates) that would have been non-controversial when there was a Soviet threat had been stopped in their tracks by Congressional holds, and relations between the two allies had taken on a distinctly scratchy tone.

The second half of the decade saw this deterioration arrested and, ultimately, reversed. A number of factors were responsible:

First, on a whole series of high-profile regional security issues, not only did American and Turkish assessments overlap, but Turkish support emerged as critical to Washington's prospects of success in achieving its own goals. Examples included Bosnia, Nagorno Karabakh, Kosovo, and Caspian energy transport.

Second, on the range of transnational issues (drugs, people-smuggling, money-laundering, WMD proliferation) that demanded increasing attention as the bi-polar world of the Cold War receded, Turkey's geography inevitably made it part of any successful interdiction strategy. An entirely new set of agencies in Washington acquired an interest in Turkey, expanding bilateral cooperation beyond traditional military-to-military channels, and in many cases bringing to the table significant resources to expand Turkish capabilities.

Third, Turkey's warming relationship with Israel in the late nineties both underscored the commonality of US and Turkish strategic vision and garnered Turkey powerful new allies in Washington which, over time, insulated Turkey from attacks by its traditional adversaries there.

Fourth, the liberalisation of Turkey's economy in the early nineties, the consequent leap in growth which followed, and the prospect of investment and business opportunities in connection with ambitious privatisation and infrastructure development plans put Turkey on the map for the American business community. Turkey was formally declared by the US Commerce Department one of ten emerging markets of priority interest to the United States, and corporate America began to emerge as a new constituency for closer US-Turkish ties.

Fifth, Turkey's vision of becoming a member of the European Union ran sharply aground at the December 1997 Luxembourg EU summit, when Ankara was accorded a status different in important respects from other aspirants. The reaction in Turkey was strongly negative, emotional and broadly-based. The relationship with America was left in the eyes of many Turks as their only meaningful claim to be 'Western'.

The result was that by late 1999, US-Turkish relations were qualitatively different from what they had been at the beginning of the decade. A relationship that had been one-dimensional and based on Nato security commitments had become multi-faceted and dynamic. A relationship that had been the whipping boy of special interest groups in Washington had gained the support of a diverse, growing and influential set of interlocking constituencies in Washington. Perennially difficult issues like Cyprus, Turkey's relations with Greece and Armenia, and human rights remained on the agenda. But the new breadth and depth of the relationship allowed them to be discussed in other than zero-sum terms, and strengthened advocates in Ankara of innovative approaches.

Formal recognition that the relationship had reached a new level of maturity came with President Bill Clinton's November 1999 visit to Turkey. To prolonged, repeated applause from Turkey's Parliament, he declared the US and Turkey to be 'strategic partners', a term applied at the time to a very few close US allies, notably Israel.

... And Its Limits

There was every reason to expect the US-Turkish strategic partnership to flourish under the Republican administration that took office under George W Bush in January 2001. Republicans had traditionally been more 'pro-Turk' than their Democratic counterparts. Bush's father, George H W Bush, had had a close relationship with then Turkish President Turgut Özal. Senior members of or advisors to the new administration, notably Under Secretary of Defense Paul Wolfowitz, were noted for their strong support for Turkey; at the State Department, Under-Secretary Marc Grossman was a former Ambassador to Ankara and an architect of the 'strategic partnership'.

Indeed, 'strategic partnership' seemed in the opening months of the new Administration to be well-founded. When, in February 2001, Turkey's banking sector collapsed, precipitating its worst economic contraction since World War Two, Washington supported an IMF bail-out package, despite having criticised the Clinton administration's past resort to such remedies. Following the September 11 attacks later that year Turkey's Prime Minister Bülent Ecevit was the first leader of a Muslim country to express unequivocal support for America's response. He would subsequently override public opposition to send Turkish troops to Afghanistan to command the International Security and Assistance force (ISAF).

Iraq

In retrospect, the opposition of the Turkish man in the street to sending forces to fight the Taliban should have been a warning light that there were limits to strategic partnership, at least from the Turkish perspective. Those limits became much clearer when the issue became regime change next door in Iraq.

Convincing Turks of the wisdom of removing Saddam Hussein by force of arms would have been a tall order under any circumstances. Unlike virtually all other regional issues that the US and Turkey addressed during the late nineties, Iraq was one where the two sides' strategic assessments fundamentally diverged.

Turkey had been badly hurt in both economic and security terms by the first Gulf War and its aftermath. While it had allowed American warplanes to fly out of Incirlik airbase during the nineties to enforce a no-fly zone over northern Iraq, Ankara maintained diplomatic relations with Saddam Hussein's regime, and progressively loosened border controls on trade funded by illicit oil exports. When the Clinton administration in late 1998 was forced by Congress to adopt a policy of 'regime change', Turkey's reaction was tempered only by evidence that the shift was largely rhetorical. Saddam was the devil Turks knew. They saw far more risk than opportunity in seeking to remove him.

The new Bush administration had a very different view. They had campaigned on a platform of removing Saddam and, unlike Clinton's team, seemed to mean it. After the September 11 attacks, it became progressively harder for Ankara to ignore the reality that its 'strategic partner' was prepared to use force to change the government of its neighbour. President Bush reportedly told then Prime Minister Ecevit as much in January 2002, and Wolfowitz and other administration officials over the succeeding nine months briefed Turkish military and civilian officials in increasing detail on how this would be done. While polling consistently showed overwhelming majorities of Turks opposed to war with Iraq, the conventional wisdom in both Ankara and Washington as the year proceeded was that Turkey would ultimately have to cooperate with the US in order to safeguard its interests in Iraq.

The conventional wisdom failed adequately to take into account three related factors.

The first was the early November 2002 victory in Turkish national elections of the Justice and Development (known by its Turkish acronym, 'AK') Party. The heir to several previously banned Islamic political parties, AK had campaigned as a secular party dedicated to taking Turkey into the EU and to rebuilding the economy through implementation of commitments to the IMF. But its core constituency was even more opposed than the average Turkish voter to using force against another Muslim country.

The second was the nature of AK's leadership upon assuming office. While Turkey's proportional representation translated the party's 34 per cent plurality into a virtual three-fifths majority in Parliament, only a handful of AK's deputies had ever before held elected office. Moreover, since the leader of the party, Recip Taip Erdogan, had been excluded from the election because of a prior ban on political activity, he was not a Member of Parliament, and thus could not become prime minister. A caretaker government led by party Deputy Chairman Abdullah Gul was formed to run the country during the few months it was anticipated would be required for Erdogan's status to be regularised. As a result, AK entered office with a temporary, make-shift administration with little practical experience in government at the national level and even less in high-wire diplomacy.

The third was a singular failure on the part of the Bush administration to understand the extent to which AK's victory had changed dynamics on the Turkish side. This led to a series of perceptual, tactical and ultimately strategic errors that compounded the difficulties of securing Turkey's cooperation with Washington's war plan. Time and again over the course of the winter, American and Turkish representatives at every level seemed simply to be unable to communicate with one another. If Turkish missteps were at least in part a function of inexperience and domestic politics, the American side's are harder to explain.

Ironically, the AK leadership did, in fact, reach the conclusion foreseen by the conventional wisdom: that Turkey's interests left it no choice but to cooperate fully with Washington on Iraq. A 1 March 2003 parliamentary motion that would have authorised Turkey's government to permit US forces to invade Iraq from Turkey received more 'yes' than 'no' votes. But a technicality (which counted abstentions in the total number of votes cast) deprived the motion of an absolute majority, throwing US war planners into despair. Themselves surprised by the outcome, AK leaders sought to correct the mistake, and would almost certainly have done so, when their efforts were overtaken by Washington's time-line for going to war.

Turkey would later provide important support for America's war effort in Iraq in terms of over-flight and other access. Nonetheless, the prevailing sense in Washington after 1 March was that the Turks had let America down. 'Strategic partnership' with Turkey largely dropped from the Bush administration's lexicon.

But there was more irony to come.

As the Bush administration over the course of the late spring and early summer of 2003 began to realise that the problem of bringing security to Iraq would be a harder task than originally anticipated, it began a concerted effort to enlist troop contributions from third countries to take pressure off thinly-stretched American forces. When (now Foreign Minister) Abdullah Gul visited Washington in late July, the Americans formally presented a request that Turkey send a contingent. Turkey's AK government, still smarting over the embarrassment of the previous 1 March, undertook to respond 'in a positive spirit'.

On 7 October, despite continuing popular opposition to US policy in Iraq, (now Prime Minister) Erdogan used important political capital to move a new authorisation motion through his government and Parliament with dispatch. It was an impressive display of personal leadership, which put to rest any doubts lingering from 1 March about Turkey's – and AK's – reliability.

Unfortunately, the Americans, out of deference to their new Iraqi partners' reluctance to see forces from neighbouring Turkey enter Iraq, proved unable to take 'yes' for an answer. After an embarrassing interval, Ankara announced that it would not, after all, be sending troops to help out the Americans.

Beyond Troops

The debates in March and October over troops to Iraq – in one case, American; in the second, Turkish – dominated discussion of US-Turkish relations during AK's first year in power. That was probably inevitable, given the stakes involved on both sides. American pre-war expectations that its 'strategic partner' would ultimately deliver were very high; the disappointment, when it did not, correspondingly deep. On the Turkish side, resentment that what most viewed as an illegitimate war in Iraq should be made the test of a 50-year partnership was similarly intense. In the second-half of 2003, polls showed that a large majority of Turks saw the United States as the greatest threat to world peace – a dizzying turn-around after decades in which America was consistently seen as Turkey's most reliable friend abroad.

How permanent was the damage to US-Turkish relations? And will those relations be fundamentally different in the future than during the period of 'strategic partnership'?

From the vantage point of late 2004, the answers – at the state-to-state level – would appear to be, respectively: 'Not very.' and 'Yes.'

Whether or not one chooses to use the terminology of 'strategic partnership', the Turkish-American relationship seems likely to remain 'strategic' for both parties for a long time to come. More often than not, the two countries will find themselves partners.

From Washington's standpoint, a war on terrorism with no clear end in sight and with important roots in the Muslim world means that:

America's strategic focus for the foreseeable future will inexorably be drawn to the area around Turkey; and Turkey's status as the world's only Muslim society with a functioning, secular democratic political system and close ties to the West potentially gives it a special place in America's strategic calculus.

The first point implies that, as the Bush administration or its successor struggles to come to grips with the implications of what it has termed (and made) the first war of the twenty-first century, it will repeatedly find itself confronting the reality that it must either work 'with' Turkey or 'around' Turkey. In almost every case, Washington seems likely to find 'with' a more satisfactory solution than 'around'.

The second point implies that the United States has an abiding interest in a successful Republic of Turkey. The key word here is 'successful'. A Turkey enmeshed in domestic turmoil or crippled by economic debility will simply be one more difficult case for Washington to deal with an already problematic region. But a Turkey that is democratic, prosperous and internally harmonious will be an important fact in the long-term struggle with those determined to foment a clash of civilisations.

From Turkey's standpoint, whatever frustration and disillusionment may have been generated by mutual miscues and false starts over Iraq during 2002-2003, it is hard to imagine how prolonged estrangement from Washington could serve the interests of a state with such a perpetually challenging set of neighbours and regional issues. Even when – and perhaps especially when – Washington is not, in Turkish eyes, acting wisely, a meaningful bilateral dialogue is Turkey's best hope for influencing American perceptions and behaviour in its neighbourhood.

It should have come as no surprise, therefore, that the final months of 2003, by any measure the toughest year in US-Turkish relations since the Cyprus crisis of 1974, concluded with a flurry of high-level bilateral defence and economic meetings, announcement that Erdogan would make his first visit to Washington as prime minister in early 2004, and confirmation that President Bush would come to Turkey later that year. Looking forward, Washington and Ankara both saw the importance of making 2003 an anomaly, rather than a trend. Following George Bush's brief visit in June 2004, US-Turkish relations seemed firmly reestablished on sound footings.

Qualitative Changes?

But to focus on the return to greater 'normalcy' in US-Turkish relations would be to miss an important part of the picture. The fact is that the debate over Iraq from late 2002 through late 2003 largely obscured two major changes in the underlying dynamics of the bilateral relationship that took place during the same period.

On the American side, the fundamental change came with the overthrow of Saddam Hussein.

When Saddam disappeared in April 2003, so did the relevance of a concept that for over fifty years had made Turkey unique in Washington's eyes: 'containment'. Containment of the Soviet Union was of course the core of American foreign policy for more than four decades after the end of World War Two. Containment of Saddam Hussein was a top priority for US foreign policy for another decade after the Soviet Union's collapse. Turkey was essential to both objectives. That enabled Turkey from 1946 to 2003 consistently to box above its weight in Washington in terms of the quality and level of official and other attention it commanded. Turkey's role in containing first the Soviets and then Saddam promoted it from the dozens of 'important' countries routinely handled by State Department desk officers to a more select first tier.

The next phase of US-Turkish relations will be unique in the recent history of the two countries in that – with the possible exception of a nuclear-armed Iran and the special case of international terror (see below) – there is from Washington's perspective no overarching strategic threat to contain from Turkey. Circumstances will certainly arise where Turkish cooperation is useful (e.g. in future efforts to broker an Israeli-Palestinian peace or sort out the situation in the Caucasus). Circumstances will certainly arise where Turkish cooperation is important (e.g. in the long-term battle against al-Qaeda and its affiliates). It is difficult to envision circumstances, however, in which Turkey's contribution will be essential in the same, compelling operational sense that it was in containing the Soviet Empire or Saddam Hussein.

On the Turkish side, the big shift is a function of Turkey's evolving relationship with Europe.

It is probably no coincidence that the banner years of modern US-Turkish relations were those – after the late 1997 Luxembourg EU summit – in which Turkey's relations with Europe were most uncertain. In any case, the EU's 'correction' at its 1999 Helsinki meeting, and especially its December 2002 Copenhagen decision to give Turkey by the end of 2004 an up-down decision on opening membership negotiations, have brought Europe forcefully back to the top of Turkey's national agenda. A commitment to bring Turkey into the EU was at the core of the AK Party's November 2002 general election victory. It has remained AK's highest priority today. Overwhelming popular support for that goal has given AK the parliamentary majority and self-confidence necessary to pass reforms that have already radically transformed Turkish politics and society, including in such previously taboo realms as the status of Turkey's military.

'Europe' can only loom larger as Turkey and the EU begin negotiations on Turkey's membership. A likely result will be Ankara's becoming more attuned to European views – and, consequently, some gaps between US and Turkish perspectives. Taking such issues as Iraq, Iran, Syria, and the Israeli-Palestinian dispute as measures, Ankara's positions across the board are today closer to those of most EU capitals than to those of the Bush administration. This reflects a dramatic reversal of the situation just short years ago, when Turkish officials regularly contrasted the closeness of US and Turkish strategic analyses to those of most Europeans.

So What?

Are these changes (the end of 'containment' as a trump card for Turkey on the American side, and a growing preoccupation with Europe on the Turkish) of any real consequence in terms of the future of US-Turkish relations? As so often during periods of transition, that depends.

It is possible that Turkey's perpetually 'event rich' neighbourhood, combined with the course of the war against international terror, will push Ankara and Washington together often enough and over issues important enough, in the next few years that it may be difficult, as a practical matter, to demonstrate that the end of 'containment' as a driving force in the relationship makes any real difference. The key variable, however, will more likely be the agenda of international terrorist organisations, rather than attitudes in Ankara and Washington.

In that regard, the fact is that, while Turkey's October 2003 vote to authorise the dispatch of troops to Iraq was a necessary step in straightening out ties between Washington and Ankara, it was the terrorist bombs that went off in Istanbul in late November of that year that put Turkey firmly back on the side of the angels, as far as the Bush administration was concerned. It was no accident that Erdogan's Washington visit, which had been under discussion for months, firmed up promptly after the attacks, or that the Vice Chairman of the US's Joint Chiefs of Staff was in Ankara two weeks later for discussions on closing down residual anti-Turkish terrorist havens in northern Iraq. al-Qaeda's decision to make Turkey a front in the war against terror at a stroke restored Turkey in Washington's eyes to something like the stature it enjoyed during the Cold War and the effort to contain Saddam Hussein. To the extent that Turkey remains a target, its stock will be higher at senior levels of the US government than would otherwise be the case.

A harder question to answer is how significant a role, after the tensions of 2003, Turkey will be prepared to play in an anti-terror script still written in

Washington. A hint may have come in paired events during the same week in late December 2003: on the one hand Turkey agreed to a Nato request to provide helicopters (although without Turkish markings or crews) for efforts to expand ISAF's capabilities beyond Kabul; on the other it pointedly refused a request by State Department Under-Secretary Marc Grossman to agree in principle that US forces might in the future use Incirlik airbase without prior approval by Turkey's parliament. The message seemed to be that, while Ankara is anxious to get US-Turkish relations onto a more positive footing, it is not writing any blank checks.

The extent to which Turkey's wariness of too close an embrace by Washington becomes more pronounced could, of course, be profoundly affected by the EU's December 2004 decision to set a date for the start of membership negotiations. A red light might well have left decision-makers in Ankara feeling they had no choice but to move closer to the US generally (à la post-Luxembourg, 1997). Instead, the prospect of starting negotiations in 2005 will add a powerful political stimulus to the gravitational pull Europe already exerts on Turkey by virtue of economics and geography.

On balance, Washington will take satisfaction from that outcome. One occasionally hears the arguments, generally in American neo-conservative circles, that closer Turkish-European ties will inevitably be at American expense, that Europe is in any case simply leading the Turks on, and that Turkey would be best advised to abandon its European vocation altogether and associate itself more closely with the United States. Whatever truth there may be in such arguments, they are trumped by two stark facts: (1) America's most compelling post-September 11 interest in Turkey is that it succeed; and (2) a Turkey that is seriously engaged in becoming 'Europe' cannot fail. Thus the Bush administration's persistent (if at times maladroit) pressure on EU countries to give the Turks a date.

The Bottom Line

Where does this leave us? As Turkey and the EU begin the long process of defining their common future (and, indeed, as America and Europe consider the future of the trans-Atlantic relationship), US-Turkish relations remain in flux. They have shrugged off the shocks of 2003 and leaders on both sides have reaffirmed a desire to return to traditional patterns of cooperation. Best intentions on both sides to the contrary, however, there are solid grounds to question whether the relationship will revert as smoothly or as completely as many hope to the cordial, broad-gauged cooperation that reached its peak under the rubric of 'strategic partnership'.

Instead, one can anticipate that US-Turkish relationship will henceforth 'work' differently in subtle but important ways. Over a whole set of criteria ranging from protocol matters, to decisions on future economic or military assistance, to putting American diplomatic muscle behind problems of importance to Ankara (like the Baku to Ceyhan pipeline project), odds are that Turkey will have to struggle harder than in the past to gain the attention of senior US decision-makers. Washington, for its part, is likely to find Ankara more selective in associating itself with American positions.

Each country, in short, is likely to become more 'normal' for the other. Events in the region, international terrorists and the EU can affect the parameters of this new dynamic. But the bottom line will be a different kind of relationship from the one that Washington and Ankara shared from 1945 to 2003. 'Strategic partnership' may have been as good as it gets.

Realities and Perspectives – A Greek View on Turkey's European Ambitions

Yiannis Papanicolaou

The Attitudes and the Strategy

The Greek view on Turkey's European ambitions can only be understood in the wider perspective of Greek-Turkish relations. For Turkey and the Ottoman Empire expansion towards Europe and the West was always an old dream. Turkey began 'westernising' its economic, political and social structures in the nineteenth century. However, westernisation meant the harmonisation of modern Western civilisation with indigenous patterns of Turkish-Islamic culture.[1]

Following the First World War and the proclamation of the Republic in 1923, Turkey chose Western Europe as the model for its new secular structure. Thus the ambition of Turkey to join the EU dates from 1959 when it made its first application to the European Common Market. Since 1981, the date of Greece's entry to the EU, Greece had always vetoed Turkey. It was only at the summit in Helsinki in 1999 that Greece lifted its veto on Turkey's candidature in the hope of improving its bilateral relations. In the changing climate of international relations during the post-Cold War period, it was perceived that Greece had more to gain if Turkey was not isolated from Europe.

Turkey has always been a central issue of Greece's foreign policy and is the driving force behind Greece's security and foreign policy priorities and initiatives. Greece has always perceived Turkey as a serious threat and a major security concern. Relations between Greece and Turkey have constantly evolved under the shadow of the unwavering effort of the Turkish government to become a regional power. In the framework of that effort since 1973 the Turkish government has adopted an attitude of challenging Greek sovereignty in the Aegean. The Turkish government insisted that its claims should be discussed in the framework of comprehensive bilateral negotiations, and agreements be reached in the form of a package deal, the whole procedure taking place without preconditions or reference to International Law and Treaties. The Turkish challenge was assessed in Athens as aiming at a condominium in the Aegean. The position of the Greek government is that discussion with Turkey is welcome and necessary on objectively existing issues but only on the basis of international law and existing Treaties. Therefore Turkey's participation in the EU could ameliorate bilateral relations since Turkey would have to accept certain rules according to the European Union's *acquis*. The Europeanisation of Turkey is perceived as an opportunity for Greece to defend its sovereignty.

Therefore the historic decision that the EU took during the Summit of the EU Heads of State and Government on 16 and 17 December 2004 to give the green light for the opening of negotiations with Turkey on 3 October 2005 was perceived by the Greek government as a strategic choice to secure a high degree of stability in the region and progress in Greek-Turkish relations. The conclusions of the Presidency specified that resolutions of disputes should be carried out in conformity with the principles of and in accordance with the United Nations Charter.

The Issues

1. The Delimitation of the Aegean Continental Shelf

Let me first present a brief overall setting of the Greek-Turkish disputes. This is important in order to explain better the position of Greece concerning the European ambitions of Turkey.

The Aegean Continental Shelf is the only objectively existing issue between Greece and Turkey. The Greek position is based on the 1958 Geneva Convention on the Continental Shelf (Article 1) and on the 1982 United Nations Convention on the Law of the Sea (Article 121) as well as on Customary International Law Article 1 of the 1958 Geneva Convention on the Continental Shelf that should be regarded as crystallising the rules of Customary Law, accepting that the islands have a continental shelf on the same footing as land territory [2]. Turkey did not ratify any of the aforementioned Conventions mainly because the Conventions recognise that islands are entitled to their own continental shelf. Turkey's refusal to ratify the Conventions was in accordance with the Turkish government's policy, ie, their refusal, since 1973, to recognise that the Aegean islands are entitled to their own continental shelf.

In view of changing international conditions and of Turkey's wish to join the European Union the issue of the continental shelf has been the object of exchanges of views at the level of the secretaries-general of the Greek and Turkish Foreign Ministries, over the last one and a half years. The danger for Greece is that in order to decide on the width of the continental shelf, the Court will have to take into consideration the width of the territorial sea and thus involve itself indirectly on the issue of the Greek claim to a 12-mile territorial sea.

2. The Turkish Challenge to Greek Sovereignty in the Aegean

Territorial Waters

Greek territorial waters extend to six nautical miles. Yet Greece claims the right to extend them to 12 nautical miles if and when it might decide to do so, as allowed under the 1982 United Nations Convention on the Law of the Sea.[3] This claim is opposed by the Turkish government which has threatened on several occasions to resort to war in the case that such an extension of Greek territorial waters was decided upon. This is a violation of the Charter of the United Nations, which forbids the use of force or the threat of the use of force as a means of settling international disputes.[4] It is to be noted that although Turkey has not signed the UN Convention on the Law of the Sea, she has extended her own territorial waters to 12 nautical miles both in the Black Sea and the Mediterranean.

Air Space

For the purposes of air navigation control Greece fixed by law, in 1931, the width of its national air space to 10 nautical miles, i.e., four nautical miles beyond the limit of her territorial waters. Since 1974 and in the framework of her overall policy towards Greece, Turkey challenges the 10 nautical mile air space by systematic violations and put up objections to the discrepancy between the territorial waters and the territorial air zone or, as Turkey calls it, Greece's national air space.[5] Massive armed military aircraft formations penetrate deep into Greek air space almost every day even beyond the six nautical mile limit. Moreover, Turkey challenges Greece's authority to coordinate civil and military air navigation and flight safety within the limits of the Athens Flight Information Region (FIR.), as fixed by the International Civil Aviation Organisation (ICAO.).

Demilitarisation of the Eastern Aegean Islands

Turkey challenges the right of Greece to maintain military forces and to defend the eastern Aegean islands against Turkish threats, claiming that these islands have been demilitarised by international treaties. However the notion of militarisation lost its ground after the creation of Nato. It is hard to believe that Turkey should invoke unilateral demilitarisation within the Nato Alliance.[6]

The Imia Crisis and Its Aftermath

The Turkish challenge of Greek sovereignty in the Aegean reached a dangerous climax when the Imia (Turkish: Kardak) crisis broke out on 26 January 1996. Turkey used military force to back her claim to the Imia rocks by briefly landing troops on Greek territory and risking a war with Greece. The then Turkish Prime Minister Tansu Çiller spoke of 1,000 and later of 3,000 islands, islets and rocks of unspecified status, thus challenging Greek sovereignty. The then Foreign Minister Emre Gonensay introduced the theory of the so-called grey zones, the status of which has not been specified in international treaties. The Turkish President Demirel claimed that 937 islets and rocks in the Aegean belonged to Turkey, in its capacity as successor of the Ottoman Empire.[7]

In fact Article 12 of the 1923 Lausanne Peace Treaty cedes to Greece all islands and leaves to Turkey only such islands, islets and rocks, which are situated less than three nautical miles from the Asiatic coast.[8] When the 1947 Peace Treaty of Paris ceded the Dodecanese to Greece, Greece inherited the rights and obligations of Italy in as far as those islands were concerned by virtue of Article 14 paragraph 1 of the Treaty.[9] Italy and Turkey had proceeded in a very accurate delimitation of their border along those islands in 1932 and signed a Convention on the matter, registered with the League of Nations in 1933.

It has to be noted that the sea border between Greece and Turkey has not been traced with the exception of the border along the Dodecanese. In 1949 Turkey proposed a meeting to that end. Later in 1955 and 1956, Greece proposed the creation of a joint Committee, in order to trace the border 'north of the Dodecanese'. This delimitation of the borders was proposed in order to complete the one of December 1932.[10] The tracing of the border has not yet taken place. That however does not cast any doubt on Greek sovereignty as described by the 1923 Peace Treaty of Lausanne.

Cyprus

Recent History

Under the pretext that the Greek Junta violated the Treaty of Guarantee, Turkey invaded the Republic of Cyprus in July 1974, occupied 36 per cent of the Republic's territory and forced the Greek-Cypriot population of the occupied north to flee to the south and become refugees in their own country. The Security Council condemned Turkey to no avail but failed to take action. Turkey settled more than 50,000 colons from Anatolia in the occupied north and also stationed 30,000 heavily armed troops plus local ones there.

According to the official Greek view, the question of Cyprus is not a bilateral problem between Greece and Turkey.[11] It remains an international question, which, however, has cast a heavy shadow on the relations between the two countries and has brought them more than once to the brink of armed conflict. In November 1983, the leadership of the Turkish Cypriot Community declared the independence of the Turkish Republic of Northern Cyprus which was condemned by the Security Council and recognised only by Ankara. Ever since, Turkey acts on the assumption that two equal and independent entities exist in Cyprus and demands that this situation be recognised and taken into account in the framework of any solution.

An event of momentous importance in that respect was the whole process of Cyprus's membership of the European Union. Since 1995, Greece's foreign policy was based on progressively 'Europeanising' the Cyprus problem and Greece's relations with Turkey. [12] Turkey first tried to prevent the accession of Cyprus to the Union. Then she changed to an attitude more compatible with her own wish to join the European Union and with the fact that her efforts to prevent the accession of Cyprus proved at the end to be fruitless. Turkey saw that its road to Europe was passing through a solution of the Cypriot problem. It was an obstacle which always negatively influenced its relations with Europe. Nevertheless, Turkey has always insisted on her demand for recognition of the so called Republic of Northern Cyprus as an equal partner to any settlement in the framework of a Confederation between two independent states and to the right of intervention in Cypriot affairs by virtue of the Treaty of Guarantee.

The Annan Plan

An element of particular importance was the plan of the Secretary General of the United Nations, Kofi Annan, put forward in November 2002 prior to the signing of the Accession Treaty of the ten new members of the European Union at the Athens Summit in June 2003. Sir David Hannay, the British Special Representative for Cyprus, conceived the plan with US encouragement and approval. The Annan plan foresaw certain territorial arrangements in favour of the Greek Cypriots as bait to induce them to accept its other provisions. The previous Greek government accepted it only as a basis for negotiation. The government of Cyprus was very apprehensive of its weaknesses and found itself in dire straits. Having no other way out it reluctantly accepted it as a basis for negotiation.

The accession of Cyprus to the European Union took place at the Athens Summit in June 2003 and constituted a setback for Turkish diplomacy. However the entry of Cyprus into the EU has activated the interests of the Turkish Cypriots who have a post-Kemalist tendency. There are two tendencies, the Turks who are pro-European who are menacing those who want to continue in the tradition of Kemalism and those who are negative to the European tendency. The pro-European tendency sees that it is not possible to define the world's geopolitics of the twenty-first century in terms of conventional power politics.[13] On the other hand the Kemalist view does not like the profoundly interventionist character of the European project. For them the entry of Cyprus into the EU is a trap for Turkey and they believe that if Turkey joins the EU this will be the end of the Turkish state. It would not be in Greece's interest for this position to prevail.

After the bilateral talks in Cyprus failed and the talks on reunification were declared inconclusive, the plan was then submitted to separate referenda on 24 April for approval by the Greek Cypriots and the Turkish Cypriots. The Turkish Cypriots accepted the plan by 65 per cent while the Greek Cypriot side rejected it by 76 per cent. According to the Greek Cypriots, the proposed solution by Kofi Annan was more responsive to the Turkish Cypriot demands and that was the reason they turned it down.[14]

Recent Developments

The President of Cyprus, Tassos Papadopoulos, stated that it is in the interest of Cyprus that Turkey becomes a European state. Thus he did not veto the start of negotiations with Turkey, although the latter is still not recognising Cyprus. On the other hand, Athens is attempting to protect the fragile Greek-Turkish rapprochement from fallout from the Cyprus stalemate and is disconnecting the Cyprus issue from Greek-Turkish relations because it may lead to wider regional fallout.[15]

With the accession of Cyprus on 1 May, Europe has now inherited the problem. During the summit of 16 and 17 December 2004, Turkey refused to recognise Cyprus. However, in the Presidency conclusions the following statement is included, 'the Turkish Government confirms that it is ready to sign the Protocol on the adaptation of the Ankara agreement prior to the actual start of negotiations'. [16] For some this is an intention towards de facto recognition and normalisation of relations because the recognition of Cyprus cannot be legally averted. Nevertheless, it is in the interest of all for a solution to be found in order to reunite the island because any further prolongation of the problem will continue to poison relations among all involved. Many think that Europe should have been, from the beginning, more pro-active for a solution. 'After all Europeanisation in the field of a conflict settlement and resolution is a process which should be activated and encouraged by the European Union'.[17] The way Europe will handle Cyprus will have other repercussions in cases such as Kosovo, Bosnia or FYROM in the Balkans.

The Impact of Turkey's Accession in Europe

Before lifting its veto to Turkey's candidacy to the EU, Greece made many efforts to ameliorate its relations with Turkey. Greece has no reason and no interest to feed Greek-Turkish relations with tension. The Greek government have always been seeking to create a climate of détente in order to bring about some kind of change in the attitude of the other side of the Aegean.

The Effect of Turkey's Europeanisation on Greek-Turkish Relations

In recent years Greece has constantly and actively supported Turkey's integration in Europe on condition that Turkey meets all the prerequisites other candidate countries were expected to meet. The Simitis administration moved away from the so-called strategy of 'conditional sanctions' to the one of 'conditional rewards'. Greece abandoned its veto within the EU institutional nexus.[18] European orientation would eventually promote a process of Turkey abandoning its 'aggressive behaviour' towards Greece and the adoption of international law and agreements thus adopting a more European way of behaving.[19]

Greece can only gain from the Europeanisation of Turkish society and the dissemination and further strengthening of European civic values in Turkey. Turks will live as citizens of Europe. European integration offers another opportunity to go beyond the narrow understanding of sovereignty and exclusionist national development strategies. Greeks and Turks would then increase their economic, social and political interdependence which would render conflict unthinkable as an option in the future.[20] Membership of the European Union thus implies a constant reconciliation of national interest and standards.

A stable, democratic, and peaceful Turkey with a market double the size of that of all the other Balkan countries combined, with strong ties to Greece would be the best partner for the joint construction of the new European, Balkan and Near Eastern order.[21] Greek and Turkish entrepreneurs are thus busy exploiting the tremendous development, investment, and trade opportunities in the area's newly evolving market economies. There is important potential for a Greek-Turkish partnership in promoting Balkan business development with several projects involving both Greece and Turkey.[22]

There has already been some progress on cooperation between the two under the aegis of the South-East Cooperation Initiative (SECI) and the Black Sea Economic Cooperation (BSEC).[23] The interstate agreement signed by Greece and Turkey to construct a pipeline which will facilitate the supply of natural gas from the Shah Deniz field in Azerbaijan and provide Turkey, Greece and the entire EU with a feasible alternative capable of satisfying their increasing energy demand is a good example of the potential to develop common interests between the two countries. There are also other connections and other potential suppliers. Iran has already been discussing eventual deliveries of gas to Greece via Turkey.[24] Greece and Turkey have understood that it is in their interest to cooperate. Globalisation and the increase of competition that flows from it oblige every country to bundle its forces.

The Question of European identity

For many, the identity of Europe is based on a common cultural heritage, with foundations in ancient Greece, Christianity, and the Europe of the Enlightenment. However if Europe ends where Christianity ends what about the Bosnians? What about the Albanians? What about the Arab Muslim immigrants? It seems that for many Muslims living in the European Union, the common European culture is based on Christianity; 40 per cent of the Turks also think that the EU is a Christian club.[25] However, Christianity, with its roots in Judaism, was also a Mediterranean, non-European religion. However, there are other Muslims who do not believe that Europe is a Christian club. They are living in the EU and insist that there is a Europe's Islam which depends much on the adoption of a form of Islam that embraces an international morality and values consensus, an Islam which accepts democratic civil society, pluralism and the separation between religion and the state.[26] This is an expression of Euro-Islam and wants to be part of Europe.

In post-modern Europe, the most contradictory inspirations can be united because nothing is fixed any more in a given cultural belonging: each individual likes to visit, without obstacles, a Chinese restaurant or a Mexican one and likes to try a French or an Italian specialty. He can go from jogging to religion. There is a 'Europe of cultures' rather than of a 'European culture'. If Turkey joins it could provide a unique cultural and historical dimension to the Union, bringing back patterns of Turkish and Islamic culture and smoothing the friction between different tendencies in the north and the south of Europe. The concept of Europe will no longer be considered by some as starting with the coronation of Emperor Charlemagne which was always underlining the Western character of Europe. For some 'Europe goes from the Atlantic to the Urals' also seeing the Russian Empire as part of the European system. However, one question arises: can we deny this solidarity to those who wish to subscribe to this common European order wherever they may live in Europe?

It would be a mistake if the EU appears more open to the east at the expense of the south. The south already has borders with Turkey. After all, the distance from Athens to Ankara is shorter than the distance between Athens and Poland. Greeks have more in common with Turks than with Poles. Since 1950, Europe has achieved very much that could not have been predicted. The European evolution is part of the definition of what Europe is. Europe is an ongoing process. Rules are important. However none will give up on the values represented by the European Union. Rules can change but not values. Therefore, countries that share common values may join.

The Problematic Future of Enlargement

Although Greeks are supportive of Turkey's entry in the EU in the hope of better bilateral relations, they are more concerned when it comes to thinking as a European. Greece is a defender of a strong Europe which can play the role of a global power. Already, after the latest, biggest enlargement, the heterogeneity of the Europe of 25 makes the transformation of the EU into a political union even more questionable and problematic. Apart from strict bilateral considerations, a number of Greeks have always taken the view that the Europe of 25 is not perhaps the optimum size of the EU. In order to promote real political and economic union the EU should perhaps have remained smaller. But now that the decision has been taken and it has been enlarged to 25, it is very difficult for the EU not to respond positively to countries who want to join such as countries of the Black Sea and the Caucasus and especially after it has given the green light to Turkey.'

If the countries of the Black Sea and the Caucasus also become full members, the EU can have an influence and active presence which could cover the whole

THE FEDERAL TRUST | 159

arc from the Caspian, and Central Asia down to the eastern Mediterranean and the Middle East. Given the geopolitical situation, the strategic role of these regions and the fact that the EU is heavily dependent for its energy on them such a European presence is very important for both them and the EU. Thus the EU should support the countries of the Black Sea and the Caucasus and help them to reform and transform themselves into the kind of societies that can become viable candidates, and have a new approach towards Russia that transcends old geographical habits and patterns.[27]

However, this EU should not degenerate into a slack and sluggish, supranational body that would be in danger of collapsing under its own weight.[28] The cost of the latest enlargement was underestimated.[29] This should not be repeated with Turkey's cost. It has been suggested that the cost of Turkish membership for the EU could be between 16.5 and 27.9 billion euro in regional subsidies and farm aid.[30] Turkish accession risks also flooding western labour markets with Turkish immigrants. For all those reasons, the safeguards were the toughest yet faced by a nation aspiring to join the EU.[31] The EU Presidency conclusions underlined that specific arrangements or permanent safeguard clauses may be considered in areas such as free movement of persons, structural policies or agriculture,[32] because Turkey is, like many of the Central and Eastern European Countries, a poor country with a large agricultural sector and deep seated problems of governance.[33]

The process of Turkish integration in to the EU should be done in a smooth and proper way, thus avoiding the risk of a social crisis, unemployment and instability that would be very difficult to deal with. If a crisis happens, this would lead to the radicalisation of Turkish society and to an anti-European feeling which would be neither in Greece's nor in the EU's interest and it would have negative effects all over the region. Thus it does not only take Turkey's goodwill for its accession to Europe. Europe should also show that it is truly committed. Is Europe ready to absorb a country as large as Turkey? Having set possible safeguards in the case of free movement of persons, it doesn't seem so.

The EU should be ready to meet the budgetary implications of Turkish accession into it and provide Turkey with all the necessary instruments to adopt the *acquis communautaire* and to ensure the irreversibility of the reform process as speculated in the Presidency Conclusions. The issue of the Copenhagen Criteria both political and economic, is very important and should apply in the case of Turkey and in the case of all candidate countries. Turkey should adopt a brand new constitution which is basic for the modernisation of the Turkish state. Moreover, changes in legislation are not enough, there should be changes in the implementation of laws. No diversion from the *acquis communautaire* has ever happened and should never happen for the sake of the unity and the future of the EU. However, now that Turkey has made a beginning it is difficult to go backwards. For Turkey, Europe should be a clear choice and it should show true commitment if it wants the process to be a success. The path to Europe should be irreversible.

Some Final Remarks

The case of Turkey's accession to the EU is a very sensitive issue. In the conclusions of the EU Presidency of 16 and 17 December 2004, it is stated that the negotiations are an open-ended process and that their outcome cannot be guaranteed beforehand.[34] However, it is in the interest of all that the result of the exercise will be positive with Turkey being fully anchored in the European structure. Turkey would also have to follow all the obligations that go with EU membership in order to promote good bilateral relations with Greece so that Greece and Turkey can extend their cooperation in the eastern Mediterranean, the Balkans and the Black Sea and promote stability and prosperity in those regions, which is also in the interest of the EU.

The fact that Greece has lifted its veto to Turkey's candidacy has already contributed to a change of climate on the other side of the Aegean. Greece prefers a secular and European-oriented Turkey. But secularism alone does not guarantee either democracy or stability in Turkey or peaceful conduct vis-a-vis its neighbours. [35] Trying to solve problems peacefully – this is what Europe is all about with the support of international law.

Now that the EU has given the green light for the beginning of negotiations with Turkey, it has to make all necessary resources available for Turkey to modernise its economy and society smoothly, thus avoiding such social frictions that would make the whole project a time bomb within the foundations of the EU. This will be the real challenge for the EU.

Bibliography

Books, Articles and Speeches:

Ronald D. Asmus: *Developing a New Euro-Atlantic Strategy for the Black Sea Region*, Istanbul Paper # 2, the German Marshall Fund of the United States.

Theodore A. Couloumbis: 'Greek-Turkish Relations in a European Setting', *Turkish Area Studies*, No.53, November 2001.

Kostandinos P. *Economides: Topics on International Law concerning Greek Foreign Policy*, N. Sakkoula, 1999.

Thomas Jansen: *Reflections on European Identity*, European Commission, Forward Studies Unit, Working Paper, 1999.

Dietrich Jung: *Turkey and Europe, Ongoing Hypocrisy?* COPRI, Working Papers 35/2001, Copenhagen Peace Research Institute.

Dimitris Keridis and Dimitrios Triandafhyllou: *Greek-Turkish Relations in the Era of Globalisation*, Brassey's 2001.

Gergana Noutcheva: 'Europeanization and Conflict Resolution', CEPS *Europa South-East Monitor*, Issue 49, October 2003.

Dimitris Papadimitriou and David Phinnemore: 'Exporting Europeanization to the Wider Europe: The Twinning Exercise and Administrative Reform in the Candidate Countries and Beyond', *South-east European and Black Sea Studies*, Vol.3, No.2, Frank Cass London, May 2003.

Keith Richardson and Robert Cox: *Salvaging the Wreckage of Europe's Constitution, Political Options for 2004*, Report, Friends of Europe.

John Roberts: 'The Turkish Gate: Energy Transit and Security Issues', CEPS, *Turkey in Europe* Monitor, Issue 11, November 2004.

Christos Rozakis: 'An Analysis of the Legal Problems in Greek-Turkish Relations 1973-1988', Yearbook 1989, Special Issue South-eastern Europe, ELIAMEP.

Pamela Sticht: *Culture europeenne ou Europe des cultures? Les enjeux actuels de la politique culturelle en Europe*, L'Harmattan, 2000.

Panayotis J. Tsakonas: 'Turkey's Post-Helsinki Turbulence: Implications for Greece and the Cyprus Issue', *Turkish Studies*, Vol.2, No.2, Autumn 2001, A Frank Cass Journal.

Panayiotis J. Tsakonas & Antonis Tournikiotis: 'Greece's Elusive Quest for Security Providers: The 'Expectations-Reality Gap', *Security Dialogue*, Vol.34, No.3, September 2003.

M. James Wilkinson: 'Moving Beyond Conflict Prevention to Reconciliation: Tackling Greek-Turkish Hostility', Carnegie Corporation of New York, June 1999.

Speech of Tayyip Erdogan, Prime Minister of Turkey at the Council on Foreign Relations, New York, 26 January 2004 in *Turkey in Europe Monitor*, Issue 2, February 2004.

Speeches of Mr. Kemal Dervis, Member of the Turkish Parliament and Mrs. Anna Diamantopoulou, Member of the Greek Parliament: 'The European Future of Turkey', The Hellenic American Union, 3 December 2004.

'Strategy for the EU and Turkey in the Pre-Accession Period', a joint project of the Center for European Policy Studies, Brussels & Economics, Foreign Policy Forum, Istanbul, Turkey in Europe Monitor, Issue 2, February 2004.

Council of the European Union: 'Presidency Conclusions', 16238/04, 16/17 December 2004.

Websites:

Yasmin Alibhai-Brown: *What perspective for Islam and Muslims in Europe? An Overview*, The European Policy Centre, 05/03/2004, http://www.euractiv.com/cgi-bin/cgint.exe/1?204&OIDN=251240&-tt=JS

Costas Melakopides: *Turkish Political Culture and the Future of Greco-Turkish Rapprochement*, Occasional Papers, OP02.06, ELIAMEP. http://www.eliamep.gr

John Sitilides: *Greek-Turkish Partnership in Balkan Business Development*, Policy Analysis, 14 November 2000. http://www.westernpolicy.org/Policy%20Analyses/nov14.asp

Nathalie Tocci and Tamara Kovziridze: 'Europeanization and Secessionist Conflicts: Concepts and Theories', chapter I, in *Europeanization and Conflict Resolution: Case Studies from the European Periphery*, JEMIE, Journal of Ethno politics and Minority Issues in Europe, Issue 1, 2004, http://www.ecmi.de/jemie/specialfocus.html

The Annan Plan: http://www.cyprus-un-plan.org

'The latest Situation of Turkey-EU Relations: Post-Helsinki Phase', January 2002, http://www.mfa.gov.tr/grupa/ad/adc/latest.htm

'The Greek-Turkish Relations in the Post-Cold War: Crisis or Détente?': Hellenic Resources Network, http://www.hri.org/forum/intpol/97-11-14/panel-a.html

The Hellenic Presidency, 'eu2003-Greece's Foreign Policy-Greece in Brief'. http://www.eu2003.gr/en/cat/42

Hellenic Republic – Ministry of Foreign Affairs: 'The question of the Imia islands, Turkish allegations on 'Grey Zones' in the Aegean Sea. http://www.mfa.gr/english/foreign_policy/europe_southeastern/turkey/turkeys_claims_imia.html

Hellenic Republic – Ministry of Foreign Affairs: 'Delimitation of the Continental Shelf'. http://www.mfa.gr/english/foreign_policy/europe_southeastern/turkey/aegean_continental_shelf.html

Hellenic Republic – Ministry of Foreign Affairs: 'The Military Status of the Islands of Eastern Aegean Sea'. http://www.mfa.gr/english/foreign_policy/europe_southeastern/turkey/turkeys_claims_greece_position

Endnotes

1 Dietrich Jung: *Turkey and Europe: Ongoing Hypocrisy?* COPRI, Working Papers 35/2001, Copenhagen Peace Research Institute, p.5.

2 Hellenic Republic, Ministry of Foreign Affairs: 'Delimitation of the Continental Shelf'. http://www.mfa.gr/english/foreign_policy/europe_southeastern/turkey/aegean_continental_shelf.html

3 Panayiotis Tsakonas & Antonis Tournikiotis: 'Greece's Elusive Quest for security, Providers: The Expectation-Reality Gap', *Security Dialogue*, Vol.34, No3, September 2003, p 303.

4 Christos Rozakis: 'An Analysis of the Legal Problems in Greek-Turkish Relations 1973-1988', in *ELIAMEP Yearbook 1989*, Special Issue South-eastern Europe, p.235.

5 Christos Rozakis: An Analysis of the Legal Problems in Greek-Turkish Relations 1973-1988, in *ELIAMEP Yearbook 1989*, p. 220.

6 Hellenic Republic – Ministry of Foreign Affairs: 'The Military Status of the Islands of the Eastern Aegean'. http://www.mfa.gr/english/foreign_policy/europe_southeastern/turkey/turkeys_claims_greece_position

7 Hellenic Republic – Ministry of Foreign Affairs: 'The question of the Imia islands, Turkish allegations on 'Grey zones' in the Aegean Sea'. http://www.mfa.gr/english/foreign_policy/europe_southeastern/turkey/turkeys_claims_imia.html

8 Hellenic Republic – Ministry of Foreign Affairs: 'The question of the Imia islands, Turkish allegations on 'Grey zones' in the Aegean Sea'. http://www.mfa.gr/english/foreign_policy/europe_southeastern/turkey/turkeys_claims_imia.html

9 Kostandinos P. Economides: Topics on International Law concerning Greek Foreign Policy, N. Sakkoula, 1999, p. 155.

10 Kostandinos P. Economides: *Topics on International Law concerning Greek Foreign Policy*, N. Sakkoula, 1999, p. 156.

11 The Hellenic Presidency, *eu2003 – Greece's Foreign Policy – Greece in Brief*, p.2. http://www.eu2003.gr/en/cat/42

12 Costas Melakopides: *Turkish Political Culture and the Future of the Greco-Turkish Rapprochement*, Occasional Papers, OP02.06, ELIAMEP, p.5. http://www.eliamep.gr

13 Speech of Tayyip Erdogan, Prime Minister of Turkey at the Council on Foreign Relations, New York, 26 January 2004 in Turkey in Europe Monitor, Issue 2, February 2004, p. 2.

14 E Kathimerini, May 24 2004, p.2.

15 E Kathimerini, April 28, p.2.

16 Council of the European Union: 'Presidency Conclusions', 16238/04, 16/17 December 2004, p.5.

17 Nathalie Tocci and Tamara Kovziridze: ''Europeanization and Secessionist Conflicts: Concepts and Theories', Chapter I, in *Europeanization and Conflict Resolution: Case Studies from the European Periphery*, Journal of Ethno politics and Minority Issues in Europe, Issue 1, 2004, p.7., http://www.ecmi.de/jemie/specialfocus.html

18 Theodore A. Couloumbis:'Greek-Turkish Relations in a European Setting', *Turkish Area Studies*, No.53, November 2001, p.5.

19 Panayotis J. Tsakonas:' Turkey's Post-Helsinki Turbulence: Implications for Greece and the Cyprus Issue', *Turkish Studies*, Vol.2, No.2, Autumn 2001, A Frank Cass Journal, p.1

20 Theodore A. Couloumbis: 'Greek-Turkish Relations in a European Setting', *Turkish Area Studies*, No.53, November 2001, p.3.

21 Dimitris Keridis: 'Domestic Developments and Foreign Policy, Greek Policy toward Turkey', in *Greek-Turkish Relations in the Era of Globalization*, Brassey's 2001, p.14.

22 John Sitilides: 'Greek-Turkish Partnership in Balkan Business Development', Policy Analysis, 14 November 2000, p.1-2. http://www.westernpolicy.org/Policy%20Analyses/nov14.asp

23 M. James Wilkinson: *Moving Beyond Conflict Prevention to Reconciliation, Tackling Greek-Turkish Hostility*, Report, Carnegie Corporation of New York, 1999, p.13

24 John Roberts: 'The Turkish Gate: Energy Transit and Security Issues' , CEPS, *Turkey in Europe Monitor*, Issue 11, November 2004, p. 7.

25 EU is hypocritical towards Turkey, say 62 per cent of Turks, 24/03/2004, http://www.euractiv.com/cgi-bin/cgint.exe/1?204&OIDN=1507428&-tt=

26 Yasmin Alibhai-Brown: *What perspective for Islam and Muslims in Europe? An Overview*, The European Policy Centre, 05/03/2004, http://www.euractiv.com/cgi-bin/cgint.exe/1?204&OIDN=251240&-tt=JS

27 Ronald D. Asmus: *Developing a New Euro-Atlantic Strategy for the Black Sea Region*, Istanbul Paper # 2, the German Marshall Fund of the United States, pp. 6-15.

28 E Kathimerini, May 21 2004, p.1.

29 Keith Richardson and Robert Cox: *Salvaging the Wreckage of Europe's Constitution, Political Options for 2004*, Report, Friends of Europe, pp. 12-13.

30 International Herald Tribune, 5 October 2004, p.3.

31 International Herald Tribune, 18/19 December 2004, p.4.

32 Council of the European Union: 'Presidency Conclusions', 1638/04, 16/17 December 2004, p.7.

33 'Strategy for the EU and Turkey in the Pre-Accession Period', a joint project of the Center for European Policy Studies, Brussels & Economics, Foreign Policy Forum, Istanbul, Turkey in Europe Monitor, Issue 2, February 2004, p.7.

34 The Council of the European Union: 'Presidency Conclusions', 16238/04, 16/17 December 2004, p.7.

35 *The Greek-Turkish Relations in the Post-Cold War: Crisis or Détente?*: Hellenic Resources Network, http://www.hri.org/forum/intpol/97-11-14/panel-a.html

Cyprus: Not Yet A Problem Solved?

Lord Hannay

Ever since Cyprus' independence constitution broke down over forty years ago the Cyprus problem has weighed like a ball and chain round the ankle of Turkey's foreign policy. At first the problem was one of protecting the Turkish Cypriot minority from harassment and worse by their Greek Cypriot compatriots. Following Turkey's military intervention in 1974, when a Greek Cypriot coup overthrew President Makarios and the threat to Turkish Cypriots intensified, that problem ceased; but it was succeeded by another, the fact that the international community, most specifically the United Nations Security Council and the European Community which it was Turkey's long-term aim to join, condemned Turkey's continued occupation by military force of a share of the island quite disproportionate to the Turkish Cypriots' population share and also refused to accept any permanent division of the island and the ethnic cleansing on both sides which had followed the military operations in 1974. The problem was only compounded when, in 1983, the Turkish Cypriots, with Turkey's support, established an independent Turkish Republic of North Cyprus. Not only did no single country apart from Turkey recognise the TRNC; but the knock-on effects on the Turkish Cypriots' trade with Europe and on their international communications on which their tourist trade depended was negative, increasing their isolation and widening the already substantial prosperity gap between them and the Greek Cypriots, leaving Turkey with an annual subsidy bill, quite apart form military costs, of some $200 million.

From the earliest stage of the dispute the United Nations was involved, both in peacekeeping along the Green Line, which divided the island in two, and in its attempts to facilitate a comprehensive political settlement which would re-unite the island. Successive UN Secretary-Generals and their Special Representatives grappled with the complexities of such a settlement, which required a territorial adjustment, a new basis for the governance of the island to replace the 1960 constitution, robust security provisions which would guarantee the security of two communities who had been at each other's throats, and property arrangements for all those on both sides who had been displaced and had become refugees. Some progress was made in two high level agreements reached in 1977 and 1979, which established a broad framework for a bi-zonal, bi-communal federation in place of the bi-communal, unitary state set up in 1960; but again and again it proved impossible to flesh out the details of such a federation. A major set of negotiations ran into the sands in 1992, as did subsequent negotiations for Confidence Building Measures which would have returned some territory to the Greek Cypriots and would have re-opened Nicosia Airport (stuck in the buffer zone) to use by both sides.

The responsibility for the failure of these negotiations was pretty evenly shared between the two parties on the island and their two motherlands, Greece and Turkey. The Greek Cypriots were only fitfully interested in a settlement which would necessarily have involved reaching compromises on sensitive issues which their politicians had many times assured them would not be compromised. Greek governments which, for much of the time were in an adversarial relationship with Turkey, were content to nurse a grievance on an issue which put Turkey at an international disadvantage and were wary of being seen to put any pressure on the Greek Cypriots. The Turkish Cypriot leader, Rauf Denktash, was an expert at intransigence. Turkish governments vacillated between the view that the Cyprus problem had been settled with their military intervention in 1974 and generally short-lived periods of wanting a negotiated settlement which never lasted long enough to overcome the rooted objections to any remotely negotiable terms of Denktash, whose influence on the Turkish domestic political scene was powerful. At no stage did the international community as a whole feel sufficient alarm at the continuation of the dispute to give to its solution a high priority.

This situation could have continued almost indefinitely had it not been for developments in the relationships between the European Union on the one hand and Cyprus and Turkey respectively on the other. The application for EU membership by the Greek Cypriots made steady progress through the 1990's and it became clear that Cyprus would be in the first wave of the next enlargement whenever that might be. The view of Turkey and the Turkish Cypriots that the application was illegal in terms of the 1960 Treaty of Guarantee was never countenanced by any member of the European Union. The prospect therefore loomed ever closer of a divided Cyprus joining the European Union well ahead of Turkey and thus being able to sit in judgement on Turkey's own application; and it was quite clear that such a Cyprus would not tolerate Turkish accession if a Cyprus settlement was still being blocked by Denktash's intransigence.

At the same time Turkey's own long-standing application for EU membership, after a temporary setback in 1997, also began at the end of 1999 to make progress and became the major objective of Turkish foreign policy. These various developments brought gradually into sharper focus the fundamental incompatibility between the achievement of Turkey's European aspirations and the maintenance of the status quo in Cyprus. Unfortunately for Turkey neither

Rauf Denktash, nor his principal adviser Mumtaz Soysal, shared these EU aspirations either for Turkey or for the Turkish Cypriots and indeed regarded them as the biggest threat to Denktash's longstanding control over Turkey's Cyprus policy. The stage was thus set for tension and policy paralysis; and that was indeed what ensued.

The UN's negotiating process for a Cyprus settlement was re-started at the end of 1999 and proceeded haltingly and desultorily for a year, when Denktash walked out; it was then resumed at the end of 2001 and came to a climax between November 2002 and March 2003, when it collapsed following Denktash's refusal to put Kofi Annan's compromise plan to a referendum of his people. Annan's subsequent report to the Security Council left no shadow of a doubt that he believed the primary responsibility for the lengthy delays, amounting effectively to a filibuster, was Denktash's and that the Greek Cypriot leader, Glafkos Clerides, had been negotiating throughout in good faith and demonstrating considerable flexibility and willingness to compromise. The unintended consequence of the filibuster was that a whole series of crucial milestones in Cyprus' EU negotiations were passed without any serious pressure being put on the Greek Cypriots to reach a settlement which would enable a re-united island to join the EU. That a solution was the settled aim of the members of the European Union was not in doubt. It was repeated by them in successive communiqués of meetings of Heads of State and Government, as was their willingness to accommodate any settlement reached in the UN-led negotiating process even if this required considerable stretching of the *acquis communautaire*. But effective pressure could not be brought to bear on the Greek Cypriots so long as it was Denktash and not they who were the main obstacle at the negotiating table. In this way any number of opportunities were missed and a price is now being paid for that.

The Annan Plan, which was first tabled in November 2002, and which subsequently went through four sets of adjustments to take account of points made by both sides, was an ambitious and ingenious effort to meet the vital interests of all concerned, including the two motherlands. It would establish a federal government with relatively few powers (many of which would in fact be exercised collectively in the EU), composed of two constituent states each exercising full autonomy in the extensive fields for which they would be responsible. There would be a phased draw down of Turkish and Greek troops; complete demilitarisation of Cypriot military forces and a mandatory arms embargo; an international (UN) military presence to underpin the settlement; and continuance in perpetuity of Turkey's (and others) guarantees and right of intervention which would apply not only to Cyprus as a whole but also to the Turkish Cypriot constituent state. There would be a territorial adjustment of approximately nine per cent of the island to the benefit of the Greek Cypriots. There would be some returns of Greek Cypriots to their property in the north, but within strict limits; and the political bi-zonality of the settlement would be protected. It was this plan, (which was not greatly changed when the negotiations were resumed in the Spring of 2004) which Denktash refused to put to a referendum ahead of Cyprus' signature of its Treaty of Accession to the EU.

The new AK Party government which took office in Ankara in November 2003 grasped from the outset that Turkey's Cyprus policy would need to be changed if its EU aspirations were to be successfully pursued. It was that view that was summed up in their policy statement that 'no solution in Cyprus is no solution'. But it took time for them to translate that policy into action and to give effect to it at the negotiating table; and during their early months in office they were heavily distracted by the gathering storm over Iraq and by the difficulties of responding to the US request to use Turkish territory in any action there. As a result Denktash continued to be given a free hand, most crucially at the meeting in The Hague in March 2003; and the result was the breakdown of the negotiations.

The situation was not however as hopeless as it at first appeared. Denktash had deeply angered a majority of Turkish Cypriots who, unlike him, believed that membership of the European Union by a re-united Cyprus was the only way to secure their future and prosperity; and they had come to realise that Denktash's fundamentally rejectionist approach was never going to achieve that for them. As a result the parliamentary elections in the north in December 2003 opened the way to the formation of a new government committed to resuming negotiations on the basis of the Annan Plan. This in turn enabled the government in Ankara to give strong support to this approach. Negotiations were then resumed under the aegis of the UN Secretary-General, first in New York and then (without Denktash) in Switzerland. Faced with prevarication and a filibuster, on this occasion by the Greek Cypriot side, Annan tabled the last of the revisions of his plan. And it was this version which was put to votes in Cyprus on 24 April, being approved in the north by nearly two thirds of the voters and rejected in the south by three quarters. It was a sadly inconclusive outcome to a very long process.

What are the consequences of this major setback to attempts to reach a settlement of the Cyprus problem, and what happens next? One thing should be clear and that is there can be no legitimacy or justification for any EU member state arguing that the situation in Cyprus represents an obstacle to a decision at the end of 2004 to open accession negotiations with Turkey. Had both Turkey and the Turkish Cypriots not so categorically and clearly accepted the Annan Plan there was always a risk, indeed a probability, that member states hesitant about Turkish membership would have used Cyprus as an excuse for delay or obstruction; even if there was no legal justification for doing so. That decision could now be based on the question of Turkey's conformity with the Copenhagen criteria and that alone. And on 17 December the European Union did indeed give the green light to Turkey's accession negotiations starting in October 2005.

Meanwhile it should be possible to start narrowing the very wide gap in economic prosperity between the north and the south of Cyprus. The European Union immediately after the referendums pledged ¤260 million towards that; and is considering how best to encourage trade and investment which will bring the Turkish Cypriots closer to the European Union. No doubt there will be technical and legal obstacles put in the way of all this, not least by the Greek

Cypriots, but, if the other member states and the Commission stand firm, it should be possible to make steady progress. After all Turkish Cypriots are citizens of the European Union whose present position in a kind of limbo is no fault of their own. It would be quite unreasonable if they were to be punished as a result of the shortsightedness of their Greek Cypriot compatriots. At the same time it is urgent for the EU Commission to put in hand all the preparatory work needed to apply the *acquis communautaire* in the north of Cyprus once the political obstacles to accession are removed. Doing that should send a good and clear signal to all concerned.

And then there is the future of the Annan Plan, which surely remains the only viable basis for a settlement. No doubt it will take time for the Greek Cypriots to realise that they voted on 24 April with their hearts and not their heads. Meanwhile it is important that they should understand that they have no support anywhere in the international community for their rejection of the plan; nor for the many spurious criticisms of it which they have now uncovered, having kept very quiet about them during the lengthy period of negotiations. On the Turkish and Turkish Cypriot side it will be important to how closely to the Plan and not to resume a pursuit of the will of the wisp of international recognition which is no more attainable now than it ever was and which has never brought the smallest tangible benefit to the Turkish Cypriots.

Will all this work out? That cannot be said to be certain. But, now that a positive decision to open accession negotiations with Turkey has been taken, the final outcome should not be in doubt, even if it may be delayed for some time. The determination shown by the international community and the European Union when Denktash stalled the negotiations in the spring of 2003 paid dividends after a pause for reflection. There is no reason why this policy should not work again.

Endnote: Turkey and Europe

Norman Stone

There is a great unwritten book on the history of Turkey: the story of the Western and Central Europeans who lived there. There is a further book within it, as to how they were used by the Turks. Turkey had in common with Russia (and also Japan) a conscious process of westernisation, which is conveniently, but not altogether accurately, dated from 1839, when the Sultan decided upon 'beneficial re-orderings' (*Tanzimat*). It was a bold business, which involved legal equality for non-Muslims at a time when Catholic emancipation was not long on the English statute-book, and Protestant or Jewish emancipation was not yet on the Austrian one. All westernising processes required a Western presence – scholars, businessmen, soldiers, *cocottes*, and adventurers with their own version of Dead Souls. Peter the Great's new Academy of Science deliberated in German, and the Russian army, to this day, uses German names for various ranks. Books, beginning with J P Mackay's *Pioneers for Profit*, have been written about the resident foreign businessmen. In the places that were consciously westernising, they had enormous importance, and the question needs to be asked: how successful was the implant? A good part of opinion in all classes received them with sullenness and a consciousness both of superiority and inferiority – why *are* these people here? Another part maybe despised its parents and exteriorised the self-hatred into slavish love of the incomer. Another part, and its weight mattered most in the countries where the implants took root, just regarded the process as a matter of common sense. In other words, how ready was the native society for the Western involvement? The case of Ottoman Turkey, and still more the Turkish Republic that succeeded it in 1923, is an interesting one.

The legend of Kemal Atatürk is well-known, and the westernisation of Turkey which he pressed for was much admired. The replacement of turbans and fezzes by hats (or in fact caps, still worn by left-wing politicians) or of patronymics by surnames or of the Arabic alphabet by the Latin one – it was something of an epic, and with it came French administration, Swiss or German or Italian law. For three years in the 1930s, the radio played only classical music: no arabesque wailing; to this day, there are more women violinists in a Turkish orchestra than you would expect, because the parents have made sure that the girls escape from the women-oppressing world of Turkey's eastern and southern neighbours. The outcome has been successful, and many of Turkey's present-day problems stem from the very success of the westernisation: medical improvement, coinciding with very conservative rural and small-town ways, has meant an enormous population rise which was controlled in the old days by infant mortality. But if we take any of the standard measurements for such things – W W Rostow's old formula for self-sustaining growth, the 'take-off', or Fukuyama's magic national-income-per-head figure for democracy-plus-market, then Turkey has turned the corner. But Kemal Atatürk did not appear from nowhere. He built on what his predecessors had been doing.

It is a long and complicated story, with documents all over the place, and involves an enormous list of characters, from scholars and long-serving ambassadors who responded sympathetically, to school teachers and commercial agents. In the nineteenth century, it became the done thing, in northern European Protestant places, to damn 'the Turk', but people who knew the country responded rather differently. There was, for instance, the colonel of a grand Scottish regiment who had been military consul in Konya – as the Ottoman Empire decayed, the great powers appointed such – and who refused, when he had to land in the Dardanelles in 1915, to carry any weapon beyond a cane: he would not kill Turks (he was himself killed in action). The French were probably foremost in local knowledge of Turkey – Flaubert was not exactly wedded to northern European liberalism – but the others were good, too. Nowadays there must be at least tens of thousands of Western European residents in Turkey, and it is probably safe to say that they are less critical of the country than their supposed representatives who arrive from abroad to lecture the Turks on their short comings. Behind these residents, there is a long history.

It begins with a symbol. The great walls of Constantinople, which had withstood many sieges since the later Roman Empire, were finally breached by the Ottoman Turks in 1453. The gun which made the decisive breach in the wall was manufactured by a Hungarian, one Urban (he had previously offered the gun to the last Byzantine emperor, but he could not afford it, and so it was sold to the Sultan and, over three months, trundled from his then capital, Adrianople, to what is now the Edirne Gate in Istanbul). Hungarians, perhaps because their language resembled Turkish (the Byzantines called the king of Hungary *archon tes Tourkias*) or more probably because of their extraordinary adaptiveness, were well to the fore in Turkey, providing the first publisher (in the early eighteenth century). Even the man who wrote the first version of todays national anthem was Hungarian, as was the main violin teacher, Licco Amar. The greatest such figure enters history as Sir Arminius Vambery, who began life as a - Jewish - Hungarian nationalist, learned Ottoman in exile, and became the foremost archaeologist of the later nineteenth century, excavating the strange

Buddhist-Chinese-Indian-Hellenistic civilisation that had been buried under the Toklamakan Desert. His original impulse had been to examine the Turkic connections of the Hungarians, and this led him to a learned discussion with a local ruler. The two reckoned, sadly, that the languages were too far apart. Perhaps the music might unite them? The ruler produced an orchestra which made its native sounds, and asked Vambery for a sample of his own country's music. Vambery sang *Don Giovanni*.

In modern times, the great immigration was German. In the 1930s, about seven hundred German academics came, refugees from Hitler, and a very mixed bag – Einstein at the head (he did not stay because he would not teach) but others, also, who were not Jewish or even left-wing: Wilhelm Roepke, the spiritual father of the German economic miracle, was just an honest man who did not like the Nazis. Some of these men are still remembered by the students of their students, and modern Turkey bears their stamp: Professor Ernst Hirsch, who went on to become Rector of the *Freie Universitaet* in Berlin, taught Jurisprudence. (He was also an exceedingly brave man. In 1936, the Law Faculty of Istanbul University was chosen to be a show case of the new higher education, and Hirsch, who had acquired perfect Turkish, was told to make the inaugural address, on the interesting question, how one country's legal system could be adopted in another country. All very well, he said, but of course it would have to be translated properly, which, unfortunately, had not been the case. He gave examples, at some length, and sat down, to much applause. The translator? The Rector. He was, however, a chivalrous man, and though he did not speak to Hirsch for a year, did not have him dismissed.) But these Central Europeans (a few were Austrian or Hungarian, including Bartok) were only the latest in a long wave, with a deep current beneath it.

In a way, the country owes its name to them, in the sense that mediaeval Italians called it *Turchia* (the first reference is the seventh-century Chinese *T'u Kiou*) whereas the native name, 'Ottoman', simply referred to the founder of the state, Osman or Othman, in the fourteenth century. 'Turk' was used, but it referred to the inhabitants of rural Anatolia, and denoted 'bumpkin' – one comparison might be with the status of Saxons in the days of Robin Hood. In 1923, when the Republic was set up, it took the name *Turkiye* from the Italian version, just as it took much else from Europe: that legendary hat, of course, but also Swiss and German law, the Latin alphabet, French administration and, up to a point, education (civil servants were trained at the Ankara School of Political Science, *Mülkiye* as it was nick named, modelled on the Paris one; its graduates had the same kind of corporate solidarity and self-conscious superiority of manner). But there is much more to this story than the simple importing of foreigners for particular purposes, which happens in any state. The question is, whether they are productively used, and why. The European or Christian involvement in the Ottoman Empire is enormous, and a very important part of its history: in effect, it started off as a European empire, adding much of Anatolia, let alone Mesopotamia or Egypt, only later (Baghdad fell to Murad IV in 1638). Yes, the importation of Europeans and their ways does not constitute European-ness.

But the fact that Turkey made so much use of the European model does mean that she had the genes in the first place, whereas a country such as Iran demonstrably did not.

Involvement of non-Muslims in the making of Turkey goes back a long way, right to the very start of the Ottoman state in the early fourteenth century, and historians have examined this. A recent statement of the problem is Heath Lowry's *Making of the Ottoman State*. It is quite a contentious matter, and the sources are very difficult. The Ottoman state began as a small emirate in north-western Anatolia, and it began taking Byzantine territory, particularly the town of Bursa, which became capital, and now contains the tombs of these early Sultans. Byzantine politics sometimes meant lengthy civil wars, with which the two great Italian city-states, Venice and Genoa, were involved; there was a long-standing problem as regards the Papacy, which wanted to Latinise the Greek Church; the Ottoman Turks were brought in to the Balkans in 1354, on Italian ships, at the behest of a Byzantine ruler. They then set up an empire that was much more Balkan than Anatolian; its capital was at Adrianople, the present-day Edirne, in Thrace. There was also intermarriage, and the early Ottoman court contained its cohort of Christians; Greek was often the court language. Much later on, when they became Caliphs, the Ottomans' official line was that their ancestors had been counter-Crusaders, fighting for the Faith, as Holy Warriors, or *Gazis*. The badge was a nomad's horsetail, or *tu*, and the open blue (*gök*) sky was a symbol ('Göktu' is a first name, today). But even the *Gazi* thesis was European in origin.

That line was taken by an Anglo-Austrian scholar, Paul Wittek, who made the running in the whole field for quite a time in the 1930s and 1940s. He was in the first instance impressed by Atatürk's reversal of the vicious post-war treaty of Sevres: Turkey was the only one of the defeated Central Powers to fight back, whereas the others had had to submit to the victors' *Diktat*. He was also a sort of Holy Roman Empire Catholic nationalist, his romantic imagination running over, in the style of Viennese academic-historical painting, with bright-eyed knights riding purposefully through the snowy Alps to do battle with the wily and treacherous Italian. But Lowry shows his scholarship to have been woeful: he misread inscriptions, used only the first few lines of epic poems, and ran affairs because of his dominating and difficult personality (some people remember him as the doctoral supervisor from hell). The supposed *Gazis* drank wine and allowed uncovered women, on their own, in court circles. More than that, Lowry shows, they had Christian allies, regarded as equals in the frontier venture, and Byzantines went over to the Ottomans in droves because they abandoned their own faction-ridden and locally oppressive state, which, anyway, was being ruined by predatory Italians. In a notorious statement, a chief Byzantine official proclaimed, 'better the Sultan's turban than the Cardinal's hat'. The Turks then went on to take over a considerable number of Byzantine laws and practices, and, as a prominent Greek historian, Stefanos Vryonis, remarks, it has become a game among Ottoman historians to spot these – feudal systems of agriculture-plus-soldiery, taxation, land-measurement etc.

Legend has it that the last Byzantine emperor, Constantine XI, went down fighting bravely as the hordes of Asia extinguished the last vestige of Roman Constantinople. His niece, Zoe, went supposedly to Moscow, to pass the inheritance onto Russia, 'the Third Rome'. Legend is wrong. She went at the Pope's behest to convert Russia to Catholicism, her two first cousins were respectively *Beylerbeyi* of the Balkans and admiral of the Ottoman fleet, and the Tsars adopted the double-headed eagle of Byzantium not because they thought of themselves as its heirs, but because they were asserting equality with the Habsburgs, who had adopted the Byzantine crest first, a generation before Constantinople even fell. They were asserting empire; Muscovy did not wish to be relegated, and adopted it as well. It is a curious fact that Ivan the Terrible's mother descended from Genghiz Khan, and his grandmother was Zoe Paleologa. In many many ways the Ottoman Empire, in the first century or so, had a better claim than ever Russia did to be a continuation of Byzantium, and a much more successful one. The '*Gazi* thesis' therefore looks like *Braveheart* stuff, stirring romantic hokum with only the most tangential relationship to reality. There have been similar Greek (or Orthodox) nationalist legends as to the end of Byzantium, 'last bulwark of Christendom' etc. But Orthodoxy survived better under the Turks than under the Latins, and when Cyprus fell in 1571, the Orthodox welcomed the Turks as liberators. The same happened in Crete a century later, though less firmly, and any decent history of either island shows how each was run quite substantially by the Orthodox Church.

The black legend of 'the Turk' itself is relatively new; it is, even, a nineteenth-century phenomenon. Earlier, matters had been different. '*Les personnages turcs, quelque modernes qu'ils soient, ont de la dignité sur notre theatre, on les regarde de bonne heure comme des anciens*', wrote Racine, in the preface to *Bajazet*. A century later, Mozart would have said much the same: the Pasha in *Entführung aus dem Serail* is no doubt a despot, but he also knows about justice and clemency. In fact, in the eighteenth century, the capacity of such despots to override little local tyrants, was much admired. In Gibbon's *Decline and Fall of the Roman Empire* one hero is Julian the Apostate who, in the fourth century, tried to stop the advance of Christianity; Gibbon saw that as a prime cause of the empire's decline. The next hero, three centuries later, is Mohammed, who reversed the advance (and there is an interesting historical argument, advanced by Peter Brown, to the effect that Islam preserved the classical world far more effectively than Christianity did: 'no Alexander, no Mohammed', said the great German Orientalist, C.H.Becker. The argument is essentially that classical civilisation passed straight to the Arabs, whereas Christianity, and then the barbarian invasions, had destroyed it in the West).

Gibbon did not like Orthodoxy: 'the subjects of the Byzantine Empire, who assume and dishonour the names both of Greek and Roman, present a dead uniformity of abject vices, which are neither softened by the weakness of humanity, nor animated by the vigour of memorable crimes', he wrote. The Turks, taking Constantinople, had put them out of their misery. Gibbon might even have said that the Turks put them to good use. Of course, any history of the Ottoman

Empire has an obvious start in 1453, when Sultan Mehmet *Fatih* took Constantinople. But the siege was really an anticlimax. The city was already a ruin, with a population not above 50,000. The famous churches, and the Great Palace, of the Eastern Roman Empire had already fallen down, or been abandoned, and the Turks had taken over most of the Balkan hinterland decades before. Constantine XI, the last emperor, was already not more than a rebellious vassal of the Sultan, despairingly appealing to the Pope, or Venice, for last-minute help. His economy, such as it was, was in the hands of Italians, and, during the siege of Constantinople, the Genoese, in their fortifications on the northern side of the Golden Horn, remained neutral. The city had really fallen long before, not to the Turks, but to the Fourth Crusade, in 1204, when it was sacked by the Venetians and their Germanic or Norman mercenaries, and it never really recovered. The Byzantines recovered possession sixty years later, but did so partly through alliance with Turks in the Anatolian hinterland. When the Turks did take over, they had been living on a common frontier for the better part of five hundred years, and Mehmet *Fatih* immediately struck a bargain: the Orthodox Church became the largest landowner in the empire, its Patriarch counted among the most highly privileged officials, and the Balkans were run mainly by Greeks. The Armenians, too, profited, and helped the Turks. Their great enemy had been the Byzantine Greeks, who had not even allowed them to have a patriarchal seat in Constantinople. Mehmet *Fatih* did allow this, and the Armenians counted thereafter as 'the most loyal Christian sect' (*millet-i sadika*). It is nonsense, unfortunately rather prevalent nonsense, to present the Armenians as age-old victims of 'the Turk'. Even as late as 1914, the leader of the Russian Armenians, Boghos Nubar, was offered a ministry in the Ottoman cabinet (he refused, on the grounds that his Turkish was not very good).

Since the Armenian question still disrupts Turkey's relations with European countries, it is worth some consideration. Horrible things happened in eastern Anatolia in 1915. The best book on the subject, however, remains Franz Werfel's *Vierzig Tage des Musa Dagh* of 1934, a brilliant novel which took a few liberties (and Werfel wrote on his manuscript, *nicht gegen Türken polemisieren* – i.e., do not use this against the Turks – because he understood how important a reforming Turkey was). There has not really been any version of the whole story to match any of the truly serious accounts of the Nazi campaign of extermination against the Jews – from Gerald Reitlinger's of 1952, to Raul Hilberg's of 1961 and Christopher Browning's of 2002 (the whole question is wellhandled in Ian Kershaw's *Hitler*, vol.2). As a French Turcologist, Etienne Copeaux, remarks, any such account would probably have to be written by an outsider able to read both Ottoman Turkish (an obsolete language) and Armenian, as well as various others, including Russian. However, the historians have not had their work made any easier by attempts to muzzle them. From time to time, various European bodies 'recognise genocide' in the context of the Armenian massacres of 1915, the latest, the Swiss parliament. In France it is some sort of crime to 'deny genocide'. But, in the Armenian case, we are not dealing with the various lightweight or twisted people who deny that Hitler wanted to exterminate Jews: we are dealing with extremely serious academics. Professor Bernard Lewis, the doyen of Middle Eastern studies, fell foul of French law when he said that there was no document proving the intentions of the Ottoman government. The judgement said that he had hurt people's feelings. There have been other cases, in which people with some claim to first-hand knowledge at Princeton or the *College de France* have been silenced or worse. The fact remains that the British, occupying Istanbul for four years after 1918, did not come across any genocide-incriminating document; the 'Naim-Andonian' collection, purported as such, was shown to be a forgery long ago, and the law officers advised that there was no case against the dozens of Turks interned in Malta; who were released. It is also true that, though eastern Anatolia was under Russian occupation for two years, no mass graves have been discovered, except post-war Turkish ones. It remains interesting that bodies such as the European parliament should rush into these difficult waters: is it that hostility to Israel leads them into an effort to devalue Israel's strongest argument? Whatever the case, they should not be in the business of telling historians what to say. The Armenian deportations were part of a horrible story of mass migrations – Anatolia took in seven million refugees as the Ottoman Empire collapsed – and there can hardly be an urban family in Turkey that does not know what its grandparents or great-grandparents had to undergo. When in 1894 the Armenian Patriarch warned the nationalists that their dreams would end in tears, they shot him. But why do we have to talk about such things nowadays, at the behest of a diaspora far removed from the concerns of Armenians in Armenia or in Turkey?

These deluded Armenian nationalists, not a majority anywhere in the Ottoman lands, no doubt calculated that they could set up an independent nation at last. The result of their efforts was paradoxical. The further east you go in Europe, the later the nation-building process, and Turkey was last in the line. In Great Britain, the first real nation, nation-building was almost a semi- or even demi-conscious process: it just happened. Elsewhere, it needed conscription and language reform, but neither was necessary because the country was already relatively unified Wessex and whatnot gave up the ghost early on, and though some Scottish clans fought Edinburgh and London, others took their side (the parallel with the Kurds in Turkey is not altogether far-fetched), and almost the whole of the Enlightenment intelligentsia, Smith and Hume in the lead, tried to purge scotticisms from the speech. No one really thought, or had to think, about formal language reform, and so a grotesque system of spelling grew up. As it happens, there *was* in the Middle Ages an effort to cut out French words, and some monk produced, for 'Remorse of Conscience' the term; 'Agenbyte of Inwit', a would-be direct translation into cod Anglo-Saxon. The English intelligentsia no doubt have many faults, many, but no one has ever accused them of lacking a sense of humour: a shout of laughter went up in the early fourteenth century, and language reform was never heard of again except from cranks. Even the Americans gave it up after a brave start with the ridiculous –ough endings. Lucky England: other countries were forced into language-reform because they had to do something about the chaos. German agglutinated its prefixes and put its verbs at the end, Greek style; French went classical Latin; Hungarian ran down its Turkic participles and borrowed German idioms without acknowledgement;

Greek wrestled to find old words for new things, giving us *katharsis* for 'laundromat' and *efemeristika* for 'journalism'. What else could they do, if peasants were to be made literate in an agreed language? In Elizabethan London, masses of people could follow Shakespeare, but the equivalent very rarely applied abroad – perhaps only in Holland. Turkish had to go through an even more advanced version of the same process as in most European countries, because, without the Latin script and the emphasis on Turkish, as distinct from Arabic or Persian words, only a tiny percentage of the population would have been able to read and write. Printing never quite took off in the Ottoman Empire because the potential readership was tiny, and the profit margins therefore were exiguous, defeating even our eighteenth-century Hungarian: the calligraphers sufficed, the more so as their artefacts were extremely aesthetic in Turkish eyes (difficult for a Westerner to appreciate; the parallel is of course with China). From 1928 Turkey underwent a deep, perhaps even savage, language-reform. It has been a difficult and uncomfortable process, and many Turks lament their inability to feel their way into the national literature; it is as if Evelyn Waugh or George Orwell had to be updated regularly. The compensation is of course universal literacy, and the arrival of Turkish writers on the international market, whereas in the entire Arabic world only 333 translations appear every year, fewer than you can see at a casual glance in any Turkish bookshop.

In fact the Turkish nation-builders learned their business from Europe. Many of them came from the Balkans, where Greece (sometimes cruelly) had shown the way. Others came from areas taken over by Russia, especially the Crimea, where the Tatars had had their own state, and, in the later nineteenth century, cooperated closely with Russian liberals to escape from the educational backwardness that had been inherited from Islam at its most obscurantist. Their leader, Ismail Gasprinsky, was Turgenev's assistant in Paris, and his followers ended up in Atatürkist Turkey, where they had a considerable role in the reform of higher education. A few others copied Pan-Slavism, in a Pan-Turkic direction, though theirs was always a marginal cause, and some of them were imprisoned.

Turkey, as the twentieth century opened, faced variants of two problems common to the less fortunate European nations. On the one hand, there was the need, stated for another Mediterranean country by d'Azeglio: 'we have made Italy, now we have to make Italians'. On the other was the power of a universalist religion. In the early twentieth century, any European country faced the problem of Political Catholicism: it inspired Max Weber's *Protestantism and Capitalism* in 1903 and the French division of church and state in 1905 (nuns expelled at bayonet-point) and the *fatti di maggio* in Milan in 1898, when a monastery was bombarded on the grounds that it was concealing anarchists, and the king said *questa volta facciamo bum*. Until 1929, the Popes remained steadfastly hostile to the liberal state, with its secular education and its tolerance of divorce. In most cases, the liberal state responded with contempt. A good generation or two were needed before the problem weakened in immediacy, but it shaped the politics of any country with a religiously mixed population. Much of the Islamic resistance to change recalls Counter-Reformation Catholicism. For instance, in the middle of the seventeenth century, the telescopes at the top of the Galata Tower were thrown over, held responsible for an earthquake, which was God's punishment for astronomers' probing of His secrets. The same applied to a mathematical school designed for artillerists, in 1739. Islam, regarding naked legs as sinful, stopped football in Istanbul until the Young Turks came to power in 1908 (there had been a Turkish team before then, called 'the Black Socks', but it needed British disguise).

'Europe in the Turkish Mirror' would make a good title. It would be invoking a real book, or rather a set of lectures given at Cambridge in 1969 by the great economic historian, Alexander Gerschenkron: *Europe in the Russian Mirror*. His point was that Russia, before the Revolution, had been progressing along European lines, but that they were German and protectionist-*dirigiste* rather than British and free-trading. He concentrated on a central question, Russian capitalism, and did point to what we all nowadays accept without any difficulty, that Russia before 1914 had been progressing vastly; Stalin and his Five Year Plans were not necessary, or at any rate only necessary in the sense that the Revolution had destroyed so much. With Turkey, the mirror would not pick out these features, but it would still show versions of familiar, different ones. A good part of Turkish history is for instance just straight forwardly Mediterranean, and a few historians have noted this, Fernand Braudel in the lead, with *Mediterranee* (he had a Turkish colleague, Lütfü Barkan, who gave him access to Ottoman sources). Some of what seems to be traditional Islamic code in Turkey is quite similar to Mediterranean practices in general – attitudes to women, to virginity and divorce, for instance. In Turkey the family is immensely strong, but so it is or was in Greece or Italy or Spain, and one very obvious reason in all four cases is the relative weakness of the law-making centralised state: the family would protect you in a world of robber barons and corrupt judges whereas nothing else could.

The decline of both Spain and Turkey is usually dated from the middle of the seventeenth century, and there have been several studies of it – the effects of American silver on the price level and the resulting inflation, in both cases. Spain and the Ottoman Empire went on as sprawling, worldwide concerns for a very long time, and their cultural impact was huge. They also suffered from an unavoidable concentration on armies and navies, at a time when their technology was slipping behind. But if you look more closely, Spain and Turkey have a significant amount in common. There is the seventeenth-century decline, the erosion of the central landmass and the consequent trouble, later on, of constructing railways, with the backwardness that this brought. You took on a debt, and built a modern railway; then it needed more money than was available; then it did not bring the traffic to pay for itself; then it became a burden on the economy, and the railways themselves became very inefficient. Turkey and Spain both overcame this problem only when the technology existed for motorways through difficult soil in wildly-changing temperatures. Then again, there are minorities – Kurds and Basques, very divided among themselves by language, and between mountain-dwellers and town-dwellers, with an extreme variation, historically, between religious reaction and left-wing terrorism. Without difficulty you could compare the Catalans with the Armenians or the Ottoman Greeks – *the* successful commercial minority. Then again, there is Islam. The Islamic heritage of Spain – after all, a near-millennium – was not a popular subject under Franco, and its foremost exponent, Amerigo Castro, had to publish abroad (in Argentina). Latterly, Spanish self-confidence has recovered, and the subject is under proper study. But beyond that, there is the peripheral relationship to Europe, and the near-*Kulturkampf* that went on, in Spain leading from the civil war of the Napoleonic period to that of the 1930s, and in Turkey after about 1890, when the 'Young Turks' challenged the establishment of Abdul Hamid II. Westernisation in Turkey had meant the setting up of schools that departed from strict religious norms and it had meant the granting of civil equality to non-Muslims. Mahmud II's adoption of Western clothing caused him to be called the *Sultan gavur*, a word more insulting than the 'infidel' which is its nearest translation. Later on, there was opposition to Kemal Atatürk's far greater programme of westernisation, and after his death Turkish politics became very tense, with coups by the army against governments apparently going too far in the direction of political Islam. The Kurdish rebellions have also to be seen in that light. The equivalent of all of this in Spain is clear enough, including the important role of the army in politics.

The other obvious area for comparison, in Turkey's case, would be Russia. Again, there is the peripheral role, as far as Europe is concerned, and again there is the conscious westernisation, though in Russia 'Mad Peter' (as the Turks called him) came roughly a century before Selim III, who attempted wholesale military reform at the end of the eighteenth century and thus started the process of copying the West on a large scale. 'Westernisers' and 'Slavophils' in nineteenth-century Russia have their equivalents in Turkey, and there was also something of a *Kulturkampf* between them – Atatürk the great symbol for the first, Mehmet the Conqueror (despite his Balkan origins) for the second. An argument can be made that Russia owes much to the Turco-Tatars (one third of the nobility was Tatar, in the time of Ivan the Terrible) and the Byzantine-Orthodox roots of the Ottoman Empire have already been discussed, above. In the time of the Russian Revolution, Ankara and Moscow collaborated, each – despite a three-month time for travel, and even post – understanding the other by an uncanny instinct. But Atatürk's revolution stopped short at any destruction of property, especially on the land, whereas Lenin's went on from war Communism to the NEP ('a vegetarian period', as Akhmatova called it) to Five Year Plans and Collectivisation. Before 1914, Russia had been far ahead of Turkey, where, if you had a table made, it would wobble unless you found an Armenian carpenter who knew something about warping wood. But by 1990, the comparisons were in Turkey's favour, in terms of life-expectancy and – with great regional variation – living standards. Somewhere between Russia and Spain: such, from a European perspective, is Turkey, and far more than in a purely geographical sense.